THE METHODS AND SKILLS
OF HISTORY

A Practical Guide

THE METHODS AND SKILLS OF HISTORY

A Practical Guide

SECOND EDITION

Conal Furay

Michael J. Salevouris

Webster University

Harlan Davidson, Inc.
Wheeling, Illinois 60090-6000

Visit us on the World Wide Web at www.harlandavidson.com.

Library of Congress Cataloging-in-Publication Data

Furay, Conal.
    The methods and skills of history : a practical guide / Conal Furay, Michael J. Salevouris. — 2d ed.
      p. cm.
      Includes bibliographical references.
      ISBN 978-0-88295-982-5 (alk. paper)
      ISBN 0-88295-982-4 (alk. paper)
      1. History—Examinations, questions, etc.   2. History—Methodology.
I. Salevouris, Michael J.   II. Title.
D21.F947   2000
907.6–dc.21   99–29895
                                          CIP

Manufactured in the United States of America
10 09 08 07 05 4 5 6 7 VP

To Julia and Caroline. Late arrivals should get their due. C. F.

For Matt and Michelle, who have made my life richer than they can know. M. S.

CONTENTS

PREFACE

This book first saw the light of day in 1979 under the title *History: A Workbook of Skill Development*. The first revision came almost a decade later, with a new title (the present one) and a new publisher, Harlan Davidson. In the last decade the book attracted a loyal group of users, making it more successful than we had any reason to expect. It is tempting to let well enough alone. "Don't fix it if it ain't broke," goes the common wisdom. But the book was long overdue for some judicious changes. The need to assess the impact of computers and the Internet on college and university libraries is, alone, enough to justify a new edition. But there is more. No work can remain fresh and challenging without the rethinking that is spurred by continual reuse as well as student comments and criticisms. Still, it would be folly to jettison too much of what made the book successful in the first place. In this new edition, therefore, we have tried to improve the book in myriad ways, while keeping the essence unchanged. Regular users will find much that is familiar, along with additions and alterations that (we hope) have enhanced rather than transformed the original edition.

Two trends in American higher education prompted us to write this book in the first place—trends that, in our view, are still very much in evidence. First, there has been a drift away from traditional forms of history in many high schools and colleges in favor of "relevant" topic courses in the social sciences. Valuable though they may be, such courses often make students aware of many contemporary problems but leave them innocent of the relevant historical background. Further, these courses do little to encourage students to develop the conceptual tools to think historically. Second, there continues to be an exodus from "liberal arts" curricula to professional and preprofessional programs of study. The assumption, explicit or not, is that courses in the liberal arts—especially those in the humanities—do little to prepare one for a career in the "real world."

Both trends are deeply disturbing, for we are convinced—and there is evidence to support the conviction—that a good liberal arts education often can provide better all-around career preparation than many narrowly focused professional or vocational programs. Further, we firmly believe that, within the context of a liberal arts education, the development of basic historical literacy is essential. Not only can history give one a perspective on the world that no other discipline can provide, but the serious study of history will help the student develop skills that can be applied directly to the world of work.

The purpose of the book is thus twofold:

1. To provide a general introduction to the nature and methods of history that will help students think historically and better appreciate the importance of historical literacy.
2. To help students develop the intellectual and communication skills applicable not only to the study of history, but also to many other academic disciplines and to a wide variety of professional pursuits.

To accomplish these goals we combine theory and practice, with slightly more emphasis on the latter. Each chapter provides an introductory overview of a topic followed by a number of exercises. The aim of the essays and exercises is not to teach sophisticated research skills to prospective graduate students, but to make the study of history more meaningful for students whether they are majoring in history, taking a history course as an elective, or simply reading history on their own. It is our hope that this book will enhance students' appreciation of history on a purely intellectual level and at the same time help them develop skills useful in other academic disciplines and in their post-college lives—the "real world," if you will.

The exercises in this book range from the relatively simple to the complex. Most of them have two sets of questions—Set A and Set B. Few instructors will want to assign both sets or even every exercise in a given set. But should the instructor feel that the repetition of an exercise might help a particular student, a second set of materials is provided. Although most of the exercises call for written responses, ideally students should have the opportunity to discuss their answers in a classroom setting. History, obviously, is not a subject in which only one answer is "correct," and the value of many of the exercises will be greatly enhanced by general debate and discussion. It might be worth noting here that we have deliberately included exercises or sections of exercises for which there are no universally acceptable "right" answers. In using this book in our own classes we find that "offbeat" questions are often more useful educationally than traditional questions, for the former require careful definition of terms and frequent reorganization of ideas on the students' part.

Another important point: Although we have ordered the chapters in a way we think makes sense (see the section below on features of this second edition), both students and instructors should feel free to use the chapters in whatever order seems most appropriate to their immediate purposes. For example, students beginning to collect information for research papers might want to skip ahead to the section on taking research notes in Chapter 6 or to Chapter 12 on how to write the history paper.

This book can also be used as a programmed text for individual students if circumstances so dictate. The programmed approach may be especially valuable for students with family and work responsibilities who find it difficult to conform to class schedules designed for the resident nonworking student. It is also quite conceivable that a teacher might wish to assign certain exercises to individual students in "content" courses so that they might strengthen their skills in a particular area—e. g., writing book reviews, reading secondary sources, etc.

We might note here that many of the quoted extracts from historical literature reveal a bias toward the more traditional narrative varieties of history. This may seem old-fashioned at a time when so many researchers have abandoned the narrative approach to history in favor of analyses with a distinctly sociological flavor. But we have our reasons. First, historical thinking implies the ability to see events as part of an organic continuum linking past ages and experiences to our own. We believe that narrative, chronological history facilitates the development of this sense of historical continuity better than many purely analytical studies. Furthermore, narrative histories still constitute the bulk of most library collections, and such histories are a logical place for students to begin. Moreover, the critical skills needed to interpret and evaluate narrative histories are equally applicable to analytical histories. Finally, we share the conviction that when history is true to its intellectual heritage it *does* tell a story. A sense of chronological development—one thing happening after another—is one of the basic characteristics that distinguishes history from other academic pursuits.

The Second Edition: Features Old and New

This second edition retains the essence of its predecessor as well as some of the exercises and their content, but it offers much more.

• Since we think history should tell a story, each chapter now opens with a vignette that we hope will add an element of human drama to the otherwise more abstract elements of the discipline.

• There are a number of entirely new exercises throughout, and new material augments some of the exercises carried over from the previous edition.

• The chapters have been reorganized in a way to progress from a theoretical discussion of the nature of history (Part I), to practical considerations involved in confronting historical accounts (Part II) and then actually "doing" history (Part III). The final section (Part IV) provides a brief overview of how history as a discipline evolved and how it relates to other academic disciplines.

• Given the heightened concerns nationwide with the importance of writing skills, we have incorporated more writing exercises as well as a series of "Writing Capsules" that focus on techniques of organization and the writing of coherent paragraphs. This is in addition to Chapter 12, Writing: The History Paper.

• This new edition features two entirely new chapters: History on Film (Chapter 8) and Oral History and Statistics (Chapter 10). Two chapters on writing in the previous edition have been amalgamated into one (Chapter 12), but with a few items relocated to other chapters. There is no longer a self-standing chapter on classification; instead content and exercises from that chapter now appear in Chapter 6 (Libraries) and Chapter 11 (Interpretation). The earlier appendix on History and the Disciplines is now a full-fledged chapter with accompanying exercises.

• Finally, Chapter 6, Libraries: Real and Virtual, has been rewritten to reflect the impact of computers and the Internet on modern libraries, and Chapter 13, The History of History, has an expanded section on developments of the twentieth century.[1]

We are deeply indebted to a number of people who assisted us along the way. Of most importance was the emotional support and sound editorial advice of our wives Jean Furay and Peggy Brockmann. We also owe our thanks to numerous colleagues at Webster University who have given unselfishly of their advice and classroom materials: to historian John Chappell for his aid in identifying landmark titles in recent American social and cultural history; to political scientist Kelly Kate Pease for allowing us to incorporate her ideas on paper writing; to literature professor Harry James Cargas, whose brief essay on writing term papers was incorporated in our previous book and elements of which appear in this one as well; to reference librarian Ellen Eliceiri for her help in preparing the chapter on

---

[1]Chapter 6 (Libraries), Chapter 8 (History on Film), and the material in Chapter 10 (Oral History and Statistics) first appeared in Michael Salevouris and Conal Furay, *Learning American History* (Wheeling, Ill.: Harlan Davidson, 1997). Certain exercises and exercise content is also shared by both books.

libraries; and to department associate Ruth Nolle for favors both great and small, all of which smoothed our path in preparing this manuscript.

Our students over the last decade have been indispensable partners in this enterprise, and this revision reflects their comments, complaints, suggestions, and answers—both brilliant and questionable—in ways that cannot be enumerated. Lucy Herz, production manager at Harlan Davidson, lent her considerable talents to revising this book's design. Our heart-felt thanks to publisher Andrew Davidson, who encouraged us to tackle the task of revision and patiently accepted our excuses for missing a series of realistic deadlines.

Finally, who can write a book such as this and fail to thank the many scholars from whose works we have sought counsel? They have been our mentors throughout. Of course, the standard closing line is appropriate: For all errors of commission and omission, we are fully responsible, though we wish we could find someone else to blame.

Conal Furay
Michael Salevouris
Webster University, 2000

PART I
HISTORICAL THINKING

CHAPTER 1   THE USES OF HISTORY

"Those who have employed the study of history, as they ought, for their instruction, for the regulation of their private manners, and the management of public affairs, must agree with me that it is the most pleasant school of wisdom."

John Dryden

"When history was no longer an instrument of the [Russian Communist] Party, the Party was doomed to failure. "

David Remnick

In mid-August 1991, Colonel Aleksandr Tretetsky of the Soviet Army wondered whether to continue his gruesome task. The word out of Moscow several hundred miles away was that the overthrow of the Gorbachev regime by a hard line Communist faction was imminent and that "treasonable" projects like the one he was overseeing were to be immediately terminated.

Some months earlier the government had assigned Tretetsky to manage the excavation of mass graves near the Katyn Forest in eastern Poland. The graves contained the remains of thousands of Polish army officers who, in the Russian version of things, had been murdered by the Nazis during their 1941 invasion of eastern Poland and Russia. Hints that the Russian secret police had really been responsible for the massacre had circulated for years, but in Russia such stories had been ruthlessly suppressed by the state. Information control was the centerpiece, perhaps the vital factor, in sustaining the long, seventy-year rule of communism in Russia. Press reports, film productions, and especially history textbooks had to clear censors in the Moscow bureaucracy. The result was that the Russian people received a cliché-ridden, doctored, party-line version of the past that systematically hid from view the criminal viciousness of earlier Soviet regimes. An entire nation, with few exceptions, believed in a vast fairy tale.

Things began to change in the mid-1980s, especially when Mikhail Gorbachev came to power. Gorbachev was a true believer in the Communist system, yet at the same time it was he who took the Soviet Union onto a new path of *glasnost* (openness) that included leanings toward honesty concerning the historical record. (Perhaps it is significant that both his grandfathers had suffered imprisonment during the Stalinist era). Gorbachev seemed to believe that the course of development of the socialist state would be advanced if it confessed to its earlier sins—a public cleansing that somehow might bring renewed public devotion to the original Marxist ideals. He therefore ordered the "blank spaces"—essentially those ugly episodes of the Communist past previously hidden by party slogans and lies—filled in. Now, as one writer put it, "the lion of history came roaring in."[1]

What followed went far beyond Gorbachev's intent. The "return of history" shook the Soviet regime to its foundations and brought the eventual collapse of the Communist state. After the August 1991 coup by the Communist Party hard-

---

[1]David Remnick, *Lenin's Tomb: The Last Days of the Soviet Empire* (New York: Vintage Books, 1994), 49.

liners against Gorbachev failed, Colonel Tretetsky was able to resume the work of detailing the massacre, in the process confirming that it had indeed been a Soviet secret police operation. But this was but a small part of a much larger movement. Throughout the Soviet Union, historians, researchers, writers, and journalists, with the historical record now open to them, provided elaborate accounts of the perversity and horror of Communist crimes. Finally, the Soviet people were informed that since the Russian Revolution in 1917 literally millions of citizens had been systematically exterminated, and that millions more had been imprisoned without trial in Siberian labor camps. In time the "return of history" completely destroyed the Communists' credibility, and with it their power to govern. David Remnick, in his dramatic account of the collapse of the Soviet Union writes:

> [D]espite Gorbachev's hesitation, the return of historical memory would be his most important decision, one that preceded all others, for without a full and ruthless assessment of the past—an admission of murder, repression, and bankruptcy—real change, much less democratic revolution, was impossible. The return of history to personal, intellectual, and political life was the start of the great reform of the twentieth century and, whether Gorbachev liked it or not, the collapse of the last empire on earth."[2]

The foregoing is but one lucid example of how history can be influential in shaping human affairs. But history has other uses as well, giving each of us an informed perspective on the world around us. The twentieth century, with its rapid and far-reaching changes, has made the past seem irrelevant and uninteresting to many. Yet a moment of historical reflection will show us that in countless areas of life organic connections with the past have not been broken. The legacies and burdens of the past, the long-term continuities, are with us still. In fact, one could argue that precisely because change has been so rapid in our time, the need for good history has actually increased. There is much truth in the aphorism "the more things change, the more they stay the same." Without historical perspective we are in danger of falling into the mistaken and perhaps arrogant notion that the problems we face and the solutions we propose are unprecedented and bear no relationship to past human problems. Just one of the contributions history can make is to serve as a useful antidote to such narrow present-mindedness.

Even the rapid change we see around us should not hide the basic reality that all we do, all we think, indeed all we are is the cumulative result of past experiences. The future is an abstraction, the "present" but a fleeting moment, all else history. The past and judgments about the past are inescapable. Daily we speak and act according to some perception of past events; and though our knowledge of the past may be incomplete or fallacious, we are thinking historically. When we choose to enroll in a particular course because we like the teacher, when we vote Democratic or Republican on the basis of our assessment of each party's record, when we decide not to go to a movie with someone who "isn't our type," we are making judgments based on our analysis of past experience. We are thinking historically.

Not only is it impossible to escape history, it would be catastrophic to try. Imagine for a moment what life would be like if you totally lost your memory. You would, in a very real sense, have no sense of belonging—no family, no friends, no home, no memories to guide your behavior, no identity. In short, you would no longer "be" you. Clearly, your sense of personal identity is not so much a function

---

[2]Remnick, *Lenin's Tomb*, 4.

of what you are at the moment, but what you *have been* your entire life. The same can be said of society as a whole. A society's identity is the product of the myriad individuals, forces, and events that constitute its past. History, the study of the past, is society's collective memory. Without that collective memory, society would be as rootless and adrift as an individual with amnesia. Of the many legitimate reasons for studying history, this seems to us to be one of the most compelling. Individually and collectively *what we are* is the product of *what we have been*. In the words of philosopher George Santayana, "A country without a memory is a country of madmen."

History and the Formation of Public Policy

Comments on the uses of history are not just rationalizations that historians come up with to make themselves feel important. History often has been used by high government officials to guide their deliberations on public policy. One good example is the Swine Flu panic of 1976.

In 1976, during the brief administration of President Gerald Ford, the Federal government launched a massive influenza immunization program. Public health officials feared a reappearance of the deadly "swine flu," a virus responsible for a worldwide epidemic in 1918. More people died of the swine flu, or "Spanish Flu" as those in 1918 called it, than had been killed in the four bloody years of World War I (1914–1918). To avoid a similar disaster, the U.S. government appropriated millions of dollars to vaccinate Americans against the disease.

The dreaded killer never arrived. There was no massive outbreak of the swine flu. As for the immunization program, government and public health officials increasingly saw it as a mistake. Because of that perception, in 1977 Joseph Califano, Jr., secretary of the Department of Health, Education, and Welfare, decided to review what had happened in order to prevent similar fiascoes in the future. "He sought," says a HEW publication, "lessons for the future useful to a man in his position."

Where did Califano turn for his lessons? To history. HEW commissioned two scholars, Richard Neustadt and Harvey Fineberg of Harvard University, to write a report on the swine flu affair. Neustadt and Fineberg, neither of them historians, decided that writing a history of the episode was the most effective way to give Secretary Califano the information and perspective he wanted. The authors wrote in the foreword of their book: "[W]e know no better way to draw most lessons than to tell the applicable portions of the story. . . . [U]nderstanding is imparted best by a selective narrative. This calls for a reconstruction of events, which we have undertaken by combining press accounts, hearings, official files, and interviews with participants. . . . " In other words, history was the most useful vehicle for identifying the "lessons" of a public policy gone wrong.

Source: Richard E. Neustadt and Harvey V. Fineberg, M.D., *The Swine Flu Affair* (Washington, D.C.: Dept. of HEW, 1978), 1–3. In 1983 Vintage republished the report with additional material by the authors under the title *The Epidemic That Never Was.* Neustadt, along with Ernest R. May, is also the author of *Thinking in Time: The Uses of History for Decision-Makers* (The Free Press, 1986).

EXERCISES

Our discussion of the uses of history emphasized the relationship between the past and the present, and the role history plays in defining our own identity. These concepts are summarized below, along with a variety of other reasons why the study of history is a rewarding venture.

A. **History provides us a sense of our own identity.** This has already been dis cussed above, but a bit of elaboration may be useful. Each of us is born into a nation, but also into a region, into a culture, into an ethnic group, into a social class, into a family. Each of them can or does influence us in a number of ways. Thus, the life experiences and values of an African American born into a poor rural family in the South are apt to differ greatly from those of a white middle-class Californian. The study of history helps us to get our bearings in such respects—in other words it allows us to achieve a social as well as a personal identity.

B. **History helps us better understand the present.** The cliché is true that to understand the present one must understand the past. History, of course, cannot provide clear answers to today's problems (past and present events never exactly parallel each other), but a knowledge of relevant historical background is essential for a balanced and in-depth understanding of many current world situations.

C. **History—good history—is a corrective for misleading analogies and "lessons" of the past.** Many who believe the proposition that history is relevant to an understanding of the present often go too far in their claims. Nothing is easier to abuse than the historical analogy or parallel. Time and again politicians, journalists, and sloppy historians can be heard declaring that "history proves" this or "history shows" that. But the historical record is so rich and varied that one can find examples that seem to support any position or opinion. History in this sense is much like the Bible. If one reads selectively, Biblical passages can be found to support a variety of strange and peculiar notions. Good history, on the other hand, can expose the *inapplicability* of many inaccurate, misleading analogies.

D. **History enables us to understand the tendencies of humankind, of social institutions, and all aspects of the human condition.** Given the vast range of its inquiry, history is the best "school" for study of the many dimensions of human behavior: heroism and degradation, altruism and avarice, martyrdom and evil excess, freedom and tyranny—all these are part of the record and part of the story that history tells.

E. **History can help one develop tolerance and open-mindedness.** Most of us have a tendency to regard our own cultural styles and values as right and proper. Studying the past is like going to a foreign country—they do things differently there. Returning from such a visit to the past, we have, perhaps, rid ourselves of some of our inherent cultural provincialism.

F. **History provides the basic background for many other disciplines.** Historical knowledge is extremely valuable in the pursuit of other disciplines— literature, art, religion, political science, sociology, and economics. Further, with regard to the last three, it is fair to argue that the social sciences "are in fact *daughter* disciplines [to history], for they arose, each of them, out of historical investigation, having long formed part of avowed historical writing."[3]

---

[3]Jacques Barzun and Henry Graff, *The Modern Researcher,* rev. ed. (New York: Harcourt, Brace and World, 1970), 218.

_D_ 6. "The ultimate reason for studying history is to become conscious of the possibilities of human existence." *(Rudolf Bultman)*

_G_ 7. "History is, in its essence, exciting; to present it as dull is, to my mind, stark and unforgivable misrepresentation. *(Catherine Drinker Bowen)*

_A_ 8. "To be ignorant of what happened before you were born is to be ever a child." *(Cicero)*

_F_ 9. "History is not only a particular branch of knowledge, but a particular mode and method of knowledge in other disciplines." *(Lord Acton)*

_D_ 10. "History enables bewildered bodies of human beings to grasp their relationship with their past, and helps them chart on general lines their immediate forward course." *(Allan Nevins)*

Set B, Exercise 2

On a separate sheet of paper, write a short, paragraph-length essay on the following topic: What is the most important reason for studying history. Before you begin, review the Writing Capsule 1 (on page 8).

CHAPTER 2   THE NATURE OF HISTORY: HISTORY AS RECONSTRUCTION

"God alone knows the future, but only an historian can alter the past."

Ambrose Bierce

"The past does not influence me; I influence it."

Willem de Kooning

About a century ago a young man left his Michigan farm and moved to Detroit, there to pursue his dream of building a "horseless carriage." He wasn't the only mechanic to have such hopes, and he wasn't even the first person to build a workable automobile, but he succeeded far beyond the others, in time becoming the "Automobile King" of the early twentieth century. His name was Henry Ford, and, in the colloquial use of the term, he was an American "original." Ford was a man of rarely equaled mechanical genius, yet a man whose contradictions are particularly striking. He created one of the largest industrial empires of this century, yet believed his accounting department should consist of a man with two burlap bags, one for receipts, the other for expenses. He was the first American industrialist to pay his workers a living wage, yet he also proved to be the fiercest opponent of unionization in the entire industrial world. In the 1920s he hired thousands of African-American workers (handicapped workers and ex-convicts as well) when no one else would do so, yet he was quick to fire any employee immediately for even the slightest deviation from his own Puritan morality.

Ford had lots of offbeat notions: he assembled his own delegation and sailed to Europe on a chartered "Peace Ship" during World War I, motivated by the quaint notion that rulers of the warring nations would surely accept terms of settlement proposed by the world's leading industrialist; he was a folk medicine enthusiast who used common kerosene as hair oil, confident that it would do wondrous things for the scalp; he was a reincarnationist, an "old soul" he called himself, who, having accumulated mechanical knowledge in several earlier lives, was now prepared to fulfill his mechanical destiny. One thing more: Henry Ford was a deadly enemy of history as taught in the schools. "History is bunk," said he in his no-nonsense way.

Yet Henry Ford, his negative remark notwithstanding, displayed a deep love of the past that has rarely been equaled. By the mid-1920s the Ford Model T was everywhere in America, the destructive agent, ironically, of all Henry Ford most valued about the past: close family ties, warm neighborhood friendships, a relaxed pace of life—in general the comfortable rural world he had known as a boy. As the sole owner of the Ford Motor Company, Ford had colossal wealth and set about to literally "bring back" the past in the form of "Greenfield Village," near Detroit. He bought entire nineteenth-century buildings from elsewhere in America and had them rebuilt down to the last authentic inch in the Village—stagecoach taverns, gristmills, log cabins, county courthouses, one-room schoolhouses, and the like. He scouted antique shops throughout the countryside and would often take a dealer's entire stock at a premium price: four-poster beds, gas lamps, cast-iron

11

stoves, and creaky rocking chairs. To add to the nostalgia he even provided a ballroom, where visitors could see and experience "real" dances like the minuet, the waltz, the polka, and the schottische, rather than such disgraceful and obscene modern dances such as the bunny hug, the fox trot, and the Charleston. In sum, Henry Ford brought history to life. He reconstructed a segment of nineteenth-century life at Greenfield Village and invited the public into it. At this point you may well ask: How could someone so obsessed with the past declare that "History is bunk"?

What Is History?

It may be said that Ford hated history and yet loved "history," which leads us to the main difficulty, that "history" has two distinct meanings. First, "history" is the sum total of everything that has actually happened in the past—every thought, every action, every event. In this sense, "history" is surely one of the broadest concepts conceived by the human intellect. "History," broadly defined, encompasses the entire scope of the human experience on this planet. And this meaning of the word—things that happened in the past—is what most people have in mind when they use the term in daily conversation. And this is the "history"—the past of his memory—that Henry Ford so loved.

There is a second meaning of the term "history," one more central to this book. If "history" is the past, it is also an *account* of the past—i. e. , books, articles, and lectures. It should be clear with just a moment's thought that the past (all of those thoughts and events that actually happened) is lost forever. Our only contact with the past is through the relatively scant records left by those who lived before us and through the accounts written by historians on the basis of those records. It is this "history"—created accounts of the past—that we read, think about, and study in school, and is, incidentally, what Henry Ford was referring to as "bunk." And it is this meaning of "history"—history as a creation of human intelligence—that we are considering now. As historians James Davidson and Mark Lytle put it, "History is not 'what happened in the past'; rather, it is the act of selecting, analyzing, and writing about the past. It is something that is done, that is constructed, rather than an inert body of data that lies scattered through the archives."[1]

The Nature of History

"History," then, is both the past and the study of the past. In order to appreciate better the vast intellectual gulf that separates the past-as-it -actually-happened (history in the first sense) from historians' accounts of that past (history in the second sense) we ask you to take a brief journey of the imagination. Try to visualize yourself walking at night amidst a rugged landscape punctuated by dramatic peaks and valleys. As you walk a companion turns on a powerful searchlight that illuminates some of the recesses and promontories that were formerly veiled in darkness. As the light moves, the previously lighted objects disappear from view and new features of the landscape appear. You want to see the entire landscape spread before your eyes, but the beam of light, narrow and imperfect, lets you see only a tiny fraction of the reality before you at any given time. When the light is turned off, you can see nothing at all. The peaks and valleys and forests are still there, and

[1]James Davidson and Mark Lytle, *After the Fact: The Art of Historical Detection* (New York: Knopf, 1982), xvii.

remain there, awaiting other beams, projected from other angles, to reveal their features.

In this allegory the peaks and valleys of the landscape represent the "past-as-it-actually-happened"—history in the first sense. The person with the searchlight is the historian who, by using the beam, reveals some of the outlines of the landscape. Essentially, the historian "lights up" some segment of the past that we cannot perceive directly, just as the person carrying the searchlight illuminated a landscape hidden in darkness. The glimpse of the landscape provided by the beam, as transient and incomplete as it is, is analogous to an account of the past written by a historian.

This analogy is imperfect in that the historian cannot even shine a weak beam of light on the real past as if it were a mountain or a valley. The past, unlike any existing geological feature, is gone forever. To the extent we can know anything about the past-as-it-actually-happened, that knowledge must be based on surviving records. Still, the analogy is useful. Just as a landscape can be real, so, too, is the past that historians study. The actual events of the past are gone forever, but they were just as "real" as all the human activities you see around you every day. Further, as inadequate as the beam of light was in illuminating the totality of the landscape, it did provide useful and accurate glimpses of reality. Similarly, historians' accounts can and do provide "useful and accurate" glimpses of the contours of the past, but those accounts constitute only a pale reflection of reality.

To reiterate the central point: Even though a relationship exists between the past-as-it-happened and the historian's account of a segment of the past, the historical account can no more show past events as they actually took place than the narrow beam of light can illuminate an entire landscape. The historian can reveal a tiny piece of the past, can present us with an individual version of a segment of the past, but no one can present the past as it actually was.

This leads us to another crucial point. All historical accounts are reconstructions that contain some degree of subjectivity. Whether written or spoken, every piece of history is an individualized view of a segment of past reality—a particular vision, a personalized version. Writing history is an act of creation, or more accurately, an act of re-creation in which the mind of the historian is the catalyst. Any piece of history that we read or hear ought to be treated as an individual creation, respectable insofar as it calls forth in the reader or hearer a clear image or understanding of some past. In fact, one might even say that any history we read is as much a product of the historian who wrote it as of the people who actually lived the events it attempts to describe!

The Process of History

The subjective, recreative, nature of written history becomes clearer if we look more closely at the process whereby the historian bridges the chasm between the past being studied and the account that is the product of that study. Actually, the historian's intellectual task is as challenging as any on earth. Unlike the scientist who can experiment directly with tangible objects, the historian is many times removed from the events under investigation. The historian, as noted before, cannot study the past directly, but must rely on surviving records.

It should be obvious that surviving records, compared to the real past they reflect, are like a few drops of water in a large bucket. For instance, most past events left no records at all! Think of the number of events in your own life for

Figure 1

EVENTS OBSERVED BY SOMEONE
(Events not observed have been lost to
history.)

EVENTS OBSERVED AND
REMEMBERED
(Events observed but not remembered
have been lost to history.)

**EVENTS OBSERVED, REMEMBERED,
AND** ***RECORDED***
(Unrecorded actions and thoughts have
been lost to history.)

EVENTS FOR WHICH WE HAVE
SURVIVING **RECORDS**
(This is the raw material of history!)

**AVAILABLE/ USABLE/BELIEVABLE
RECORDS FOR A GIVEN HISTORICAL
ACCOUNT.**

THE PAST
All Actions and thoughts
by *all* individuals
in *all* times
and places

THE "ACCOUNT"

which there is no record but your own memory. Multiply those unrecorded events
in your own life by the billions of human beings who inhabit the earth and you get
some idea of the number of events each day that go unrecorded. That is only the
beginning of the problem. In the words of historian Louis Gottschalk:

> Only a part of what was observed in the past was remembered by those who observed
> it; only a part of what was remembered was recorded; only a part of what was recorded
> has survived; only a part of what has survived has come to the historians' attention; only
> a part of what has come to their attention is credible; only a part of what is credible has
> been grasped; and only a part of what has been grasped can be expounded or narrated
> by the historian. . . . Before the past is set forth by the historian, it is likely to have
> gone through eight separate steps at each of which some of it has been lost; and there is
> no guarantee that what remains is the most important, the largest, the most valuable, the
> most representative, or the most enduring part. In other words the "object" that the
> historian studies is not only incomplete, it is markedly variable as records are lost or
> recovered. [2]

Clearly, then, the historian can never get or present the full truth about a given
past (see Fig. 1). The best the historian can provide, even under ideal conditions,

---

[2]Louis Gottschalk, *Understanding History* (New York: Knopf, 1950), 45–46.

is a partial sketch of a vanished past. "Even the best history," said historian Bruce Catton, "is not much better than a mist through which we see shapes dimly moving." Or, in the words of W. S. Holt, "History is a damn dim candle over a damn dark abyss."

If all this were not enough, the historian is also a factor in the equation. Not only is the historian fallible and capable of error, but personal biases, political beliefs, economic status, religious persuasion, and idiosyncrasies can subtly and unconsciously influence the way in which existing sources are interpreted. We all have a unique "frame of reference"—a set of interlocking values, loyalties, assumptions, interests, and principles of action—that we use to interpret daily experience. Suppose there appears in the newspaper a picture of the president of the United States playing golf at a country club on a Sunday morning, under the caption "President Relaxes. "A variety of reactions would be likely, each of them reflecting a different frame of reference:

- A political opponent: "I wonder if he's as bad on the course as he is in the Oval Office."
- A party loyalist: "Good for him. He deserves a break from the political wars he's been fighting."
- A physical fitness guru: "Why doesn't he spend his free time in a more physically demanding activity?"
- A golf course neighbor: "Oh great. This means they'll have my street blocked off again what with all those Secret Service types swarming around."
- An avid golfer: "With a swing like that he ought to take up croquet."
- A clergyman: "As a role model for all of us, he shouldn't be playing golf on a Sunday morning."

Same newspaper, same caption, same picture, and six different responses. A frame of reference is like a lens through which we view the world around us. It leads us to make certain conjectures, to classify individual items in a certain way, to ask certain kinds of questions, and to develop certain interpretations. Conservative Republicans often read and interpret the political history of the United States in a very different way than do liberal Democrats. Protestants and Catholics frequently disagree when writing about the religious upheavals known as the Reformation. And Northerners and Southerners are notorious in their differences concerning the history of the American Civil War. For example, Hodding Carter III, assistant secretary of state under President Jimmy Carter, was aware at a young age that the American history he was taught in the South differed from that taught in the North. "It was easy for me as a youngster growing up in Mississippi to know that my eighth-grade state history textbook taught me a lot which didn't jibe with what my cousins in Maine were being taught. We spoke of the War Between the States. They spoke of the Civil War. . . . But our texts might as well have been written for study on different planets when it came to the status and feelings of the black men and women of the state or nation."[3]

Small wonder that there is an element of subjectivity in historical accounts, inasmuch as we have historians with widely differing ideals, loyalties, interests, motivations, yes, even biases, each of which are shaped by different ethnic experience, religious allegiance, political leanings, and class interests.

That said, we must express a certain caution. Historians are justified in viewing an event from any perspective they wish, and from that perspective explain

---

[3]Viewpoint, *The Wall Street Journal* (Sept. 23, 1982).

how and why that event happened as it did. However, there is a danger involved in allowing a historical inquiry to be totally shaped by one's singular frame of reference. Excessive focus on one's own viewpoint closes the mind to the truth residing in alternative perspectives and, equally troublesome, to evidence that contradicts one's own view. Some call this tendency "Procrustean," the term referring to an ancient Greek brigand who strapped his victims to a bed—if their legs were too long, he cut them off till they fit; if too short, he stretched them to the proper length. So it is another way of describing a tendency to make the evidence fit the theory. The whole question of truth in history is a complicated one, a matter to which we will now turn.

The Question of Truth

At this point you might be asking, "Why study history at all if historical accounts are so far removed from the past they attempt to understand?" What happens to the search for "truth" if we acknowledge that historical accounts are by nature subjective and incomplete? How can we justify the pursuit of knowledge that appears so shallow and fleeting?

This entire book addresses this question, but for now it is sufficient to note that an element of subjectivity by no means invalidates the importance or substance of historical studies. First, it is worth reminding ourselves that the past *did happen*. Even though the records of past events are inadequate and difficult to interpret, they do constitute a tangible link between past and present. And even though historians can never completely escape their personal frames of reference, that does not preclude their writing credible and convincing accounts firmly grounded in the existing evidence. As Stephen Jay Gould, the Harvard paleontologist and historian of science, puts it: "We understand that biases, preferences, social values, and psychological attitudes all play a strong role in the process of discovery. However, we should not be driven to the opposite extreme of complete cynicism—the view that objective evidence plays no role, that perceptions of truth are entirely relative, and that scientific [or historical] conclusions are just another form of aesthetic preference."[4]

This is an important point: history is not fiction. Different historians will interpret the past differently for many different reasons. But in all cases their accounts must be based on all the available relevant evidence. A version of the past that cannot be supported by evidence is worthless and will quickly be rejected by other historians. Thus one opinion (no matter how strongly held) *is not* as good as another, and the student of history, whether beginner or seasoned professional, must learn to discriminate closely between reasoned claims supported by the available evidence and those that fail this basic test. (Don't panic right now if you don't know how to make this kind of determination; it is something that this book intends to teach you.)

Finally, history is not unique in its subjectivity, nor is it the only discipline in which conclusions are tentative and constantly open to revision. No field of study is ever static, since all research is, to some degree, conditioned by the "climate of the times" and the values and attitudes of the researchers themselves, not to mention the discovery of new evidence. Even theories in the so-called "hard sciences" are subject to the vagaries of time, place and circumstance.

---

[4]Stephen Jay Gould, *Wonderful Life: The Burgess Shale and the Nature of History* (New York: W. W. Norton, 1989), 244.

warships were lying quietly at anchor in the sun on this Sunday morning. "

_____ 2. "In the U. S. armed forces, women gained increasing influence as well. A new, light weapon—the M-16 rifle—made women's participation at the front more feasible, while the Supreme Court ordered the gender integration of the Citadel [a military school] in Charleston, South Carolina. In 1990, when President George Bush called for American troops to fight in the Gulf War, women formed part of the battlefield troop movement. "

_____ 3. "On first seeing a portrait of Falkenhayn [a World War I German general], one's immediate reaction is: 'this is a typical Prussian general.' The hair is close-cropped, the nose well-bred, the features vigorous and stern. The eyes have that Prussian turn-down at the corners. . . . But when one comes to the mouth, partly concealed under the aggressive military moustache, the whole picture changes. It is not the mouth of a determined leader, a man of action, but that of an indecisive, introversive man of thought, and the sensitive, dimpled chin confirms the implications of weakness. "

_____ 4. "Future historians, therefore, must surely look back on the three decades between August 1914 [beginning of World War I] and May 1945 [end of World War II] as the era when Europe took leave of its senses. The totalitarian horrors of communism and fascism, when added to the horrors of total war, created an unequalled sum of death, misery, and degradation"

_____ 5. "On the afternoon of June 25, 1876, with guns blazing and sandy hair shining, Lieut. Colonel George Armstrong Custer, along with some 220 of the troopers under his command, was massacred near Montana's Little Bighorn River. "

_____ 6. "And yet, given the depth of his ambition, he [Ford Motor Co. 's automotive operations chief Jacques Nasser] has a ways to go. Ford is still No. 2 behind GM [General Motors] in market share. There are billions more to cut from costs, mostly in the product development area; his vast team is scrambling to create a vehicle lineup that . . . offers more variety by way of standout designs. "

_____ 7. "Certainly, Vietnam marked a definitive exit point in American history and the 1960s, a sharp break with the past. There [at that time], the war story finally lost its ability to mobilize young people under 'freedom's banner' except in opposition to itself, a loss experienced by a generation as both a confusing 'liberation' and a wrenching betrayal. There, the war story's codes were jumbled, its roles redistributed, its certitudes dismantled, and new kinds of potential space opened up that proved, finally, less liberating than frightening. "

_____ 8. "Rock [music] itself split into several directions in the seventies. Although the Beatles broke up in 1970, the British invasion continued. British vocalists Elton John and David Bowie proved to be among the decade's most popular performers. A smaller share of the popular music audience patronized American vocalists like Joni Mitchell, who mixed folk and rock. . . . The Carpenters offered a sugary and immensely popular variation of this singing sensitivity. Very much in contrast was 'hard' or 'progressive' rock. Its elaborately orchestrated compositions, performed at full blast encouraged . . . the purchase of still more expensive record and tape players."

Sources
1. Edwin P. Hoyt, *Japan's War* (New York: McGraw-Hill, 1986), 225–26.
2. Glenda Riley, *Inventing the American Woman,* 2nd ed. (Wheeling, Ill.: Harlan Davidson, 1995), 363.
3. Alistair Horne, *The Price of Glory,* abr. ed. (New York: Penguin Books, 1964), 40.
4. Norman Davies, *Europe: A History* (Oxford: Oxford University Press, 1996), 897.
5. *Time,* May 28, 1984, 49.
6. *Fortune,* June 22, 1998, 82.
7. Tom Engelhardt, *The End of Victory Culture* (University of Massachusetts Press, 1998), 14-15.
8. James L. Baughman, *The Republic of Mass Culture* (Baltimore: The Johns Hopkins University Press, 1997), 196.

Set B, Exercise 3

This exercise gives a slightly different twist to Exercise 2, which required you to distinguish between fact and opinion. When you did that exercise it should have occurred to you how difficult it is to find any passage longer than a sentence or two that is completely and unambiguously factual. The historian's judgments, perspectives, values, and priorities are an almost inseparable part of any piece of historical writing.

   This exercise asks you to go a step further. In order for an opinion to be acceptable it should be supported by points that validate it. Each of the following excerpts presents an opinion. Some of them are validated by specific supporting points, others (as presented here) are not. Mark supported opinions with an "S" (for "Supported"), the others with an "NS" (for "Not Supported"). Hint: first focus on the lead sentence, then see how effectively it is developed. We have completed the first item for you. (For purposes of this exercise some of these excerpts have been edited.)

____S____ 1. "Television's enormous appeal forced rivals to attend to the tastes of subgroups that the older mass culture had slighted. Radio and popular music were the first to seek subgroups, often adolescent ones. The fancier of classical music usually had her station, and country fans . . . had at least one outlet. Beginning in the mid fifties, the motion picture industry emphasized blockbusters that in time appealed to a minority that constituted the regular moviegoing population. The slowest to adapt to the television challenge proved to be the publishers of newspapers and magazines. . . . By the 1970s, however, the deaths of three mass circulation magazines—*Life, Look,* and the *Saturday Evening Post*—forced publishers to rethink their place in the republic of mass culture and to devote their energies to smaller clusters of readers."

Comment: *The first sentence states the theme of the excerpt, namely that television's huge popularity forced other mass media forms to make changes. The author then details the adaptations made by radio, the movie industry, and the print media.*

_____ 2. "Sitting down to talk at McDonald's rural campus near Chicago, the new CEO (as of Aug. 1) is candid about the company's recent fumbling. If the international business is well run and highly profitable, accounting for half of corporate earnings, McDonald's USA—investors' No. 1 concern—has been a test kitchen for management mistakes: The company was pathetically slow to respond to the discounting craze in the late 1980s ('It took us three years," says Greenberg). And a series of new-product gaffes didn't help: the flaky McPizza, the ill-conceived McLean burger, and the 'adult' Arch Deluxe. Failing at innovation, McDonald's went for market share the only way it knew how—by building thousands of new restaurants, which proceeded to steal away customers and profits from existing franchises."

_____ 3. "Warfare, not just the French and Indian War, but two hundred years of periodic struggle in Britain's overseas provinces, had helped to shape American society. It would have been remarkable had the identity of the people who inhabited England's colonies not been touched by their experience with warfare, for wars were endemic, recurrent in America's early history."

_____ 4. "The source of the Roman obsession with unity and cohesion may well have lain in the pattern of Rome's early development. Whereas Greece had grown from scores of scattered cities, Rome grew from one single organism. Whilst the Greek world had expanded along the Mediterranean sea lanes, the Roman world was assembled by territorial conquest. . . . The key to the Greek world lay in its high-prowed ships; the key to Roman power lay in its marching legions."

_____ 5. "States' rights, the doctrine upon which the Confederacy had been founded, was no help in wartime. Several governors . . . showed a narrow jealousy of every exercise of Confederate power. They developed revenue programs of their own and obstructed Confederate tax collections in their states. They retained control of state troops and even prevented them from leaving the state. In Georgia, men who wished to escape Confederate service could do so by enlisting in the state militia. Governor Vance [in North Carolina] hoarded food and supplies for North Carolina troops that Lee's starving army at Richmond desperately needed."

_____ 6. "The evolution of the cabaret forms the critical element in the growth of public nightlife in the years from 1890 through 1930. According to a New York Department of Licenses Report of 1927, a cabaret 'shall mean any room, place or space in the city in which any musical entertainment, singing, dancing or other similar amusement is permitted in connection with the restaurant business or the business of directly or indirectly selling the public food or drink.' Prior to the 1910s, cabarets were little known or were considered backroom joints or dives."

_____ 7. _Spellbound_ (1945). "This 1945 Hollywood view of psychiatry, directed by Alfred Hitchcock, is alternately interesting and silly, but it is a curious and valuable historical document, showing what psychiatry had come to mean in the popular American mind. Salvador Dali designed the dream sequence."

_____ 8. "Climate . . . is the chief among those physical agents which define within what limits and in what ways man can seek his livelihood. It is so, because all plants can grow only within certain climatic limits. Some, like the olive, can survive summer drought; wheat requires a certain growing period free from frosts, which, by a careful breeding of plants, man has reduced to a minimum of about ninety days; rice and citrus fruits require much moisture as well as heat; and even grass, the food for stock, cannot survive extreme cold or summer drought. ”

_____ 9. “Contrary to popular mythology, the ancestors of blacks who came to the New World were neither primitive nor savage. They were certainly not "natural slaves. ” The great majority of those transported to America on slave ships came from the coastal regions of West Africa. With few exceptions, blacks brought to port for sale to European slavers came from less than 300 miles into the interior. ”

_____ 10. “Although the German army of 1914 was a fearsome power, compared with that of 1870 [when they had beaten the French easily], it was a bludgeon to a rapier. It had had no dummy run against the Austrians at Sadowa. . . . [Further], in Germany the 'caste' system had tended to frustrate the rise of brilliant officers of humbler origins, such as Ludendorff. The idiotic sycophancy that surrounded the Kaiser, whereby at war-games the side commanded by His Majesty always had to win . . . also had its effect. Moreover, the army that moved on France, a million and a half strong . . . was far too big and unwieldy for a man of Moltke's calibre to command effectively. ”

Sources

1. James L. Baughman, *The Republic of Mass Culture* (Baltimore: The Johns Hopkins University Press, 1997), 219-20.
2. *Fortune,* June 22, 1998, 34–36.
3. John Ferling, *Struggle for a Continent* (Wheeling, Ill.: Harlan Davidson, 1993), 207.
4. Davies, *Europe,* 149.
5. Virginia Bernard, David Burner, Elizabeth Fox-Genovese, *Firsthand America,* Vol. 1 (St. James, N.Y.: Brandywine Press, 1992), 439.
6. Lewis A. Erenberg, *Steppin' Out* (Chicago: The University of Chicago Press, 1981), xi-xii.
7. Norman F. Cantor, *The American Century* (New York: HarperPerennial, 1998), 519.
8. W. Gordon East, *The Geography Behind History* (New York: W. W. Norton & Co. , Inc. , 1965), 44.
9. Patrick Gerster and Nicholas Cords, *Myth in American History* (Encino, Cal.: Glencoe Press, 1977), 15.
10. Horne, *The Price of Glory,* 22-23.

CHAPTER 3 CONTINUITY AND CHANGE

"A society in stable equilibrium is—by definition—one that has no history and wants no historians."

Henry Adams

"All things flow, but they need not necessarily rush down a cataract."

G. J. Renier

In June of 1939 Admiral Isoroku Yamamoto was made commander-in-chief of the Combined Fleet of the Empire of Japan. An original thinker and instinctive gambler, Yamamoto was Japan's most distinguished military man, and he knew how vulnerable America was in the western Pacific. He recognized that Japanese power could readily overrun the Philippines, Indo-China, Malaya, the Dutch East Indies, and many island chains to the south and the east. But Yamamoto was also a keen student of history, both of his own country and of the United States. He told his countrymen that easy early victories might prove too costly in the long run, because they would arouse America's "fierce fighting spirit," shown in so many Civil War battles and in the naval actions of the Spanish-American War. He did not want to see that force, nor the force of American industrial strength, unleashed against Japan. Again and again he urged caution upon his nation's rulers.[1]

By late 1940, however, the Japanese war party had become dominant, and soon Yamamoto was directed to prepare for war, though he told the Japanese premier "If I am told to fight regardless of the consequences, I shall run wild for the first six months or a year, but I have utterly no confidence for the second or third year."[2] It was the reluctant Yamamoto who conceived the bold Pearl Harbor attack plan (based on his historical awareness of the successful surprise attack against Port Arthur in the Russo-Japanese War of 1904), organized it, and brought it to completion on December 7, 1941. Yet so strongly did his sense of history enter into his thinking that while toasts to his great victory still lingered in the air, he remarked that he feared that all they had done was awaken a slumbering giant and fill him with a terrible resolve.

Though he did not survive the war, Yamamoto's vision of what would happen in the Pacific proved prophetic as the Japanese navy began its long slow retreat in June of 1942. Yamamoto was a prophet not because he could look directly into the future, but because he saw that forces active in the past would reassert themselves. He knew that, as they had in the past, the raw industrial power of the United States along with American organizational skills would be decisive in the long run. In a word, Yamamoto had a sense of history.

Yamamoto's well-developed foresight is a good example of something very important about education. Most of us are aware, if only vaguely, how much more there is to education than factual information about a variety of subjects. We learn grammatical rules, geometric axioms, principles of government, how to operate a computer, and other segmented bits of knowledge. These things are worthwhile,

---

[1]Edwin P. Hoyt, *Japan's War: The Great Pacific Conflict* (New York: McGraw-Hill, 1986), 187–93.
[2]Nathan Miller, *War At Sea* (New York: Oxford University Press, 1995), 195.

27

even occupationally crucial in some cases, but there is something much more important about education. A computer can be programmed to "learn" all of the above and more, but it is a poor imitation of the educated human mind. This "something more" is a special quality of the mind that develops through years of study—a cultivation, a breadth, an enlargement. This is not the exclusive product of any academic discipline, for it can be learned while pursuing many fields of study. But we believe, perhaps immodestly, that the study of history is especially conducive to developing it. In fact, many historians would argue that the development of this quality of mind, which in these chapters we are calling "historical thinking," is far more important than any sterile memorization of facts. It is an outgrowth of serious reflection upon the past and is its longest lasting benefit.

Though historians may vary in their emphasis on each of the several components of historical thinking, they generally agree that the following are essential:

- Awareness of the themes of continuity and change in human affairs, as well as the interplay of long-term and short-term causes.
- Sensitivity to multiple causation.
- Sensitivity to context, how other times and places differ from our own.

The first of these components of historical thinking—the interplay of continuity and change—will be discussed in this chapter; the others will be discussed in chapters 4 and 5.

Change

Someone once said, "The mountain has no history." Neither does the polar ice cap, nor do oceans. Why? Because they never seem to change, at least not to our eyes. Geologists would disagree with this observation, but it serves to bring out a major point: There can be a "history" only when there is change. In essence, history is the story of change.

Change is an ever-present part of life, especially for those who live in modern industrialized states. We routinely change our clothes, change courses, change schools, change jobs, change apartments, none of which are of any great significance. But we use the same term to describe developments that are of potentially enormous importance, such as major policy swings after an election, the sudden outbreak of a war, a coup, or a revolution, a decisive shift in public attitude, the advent of a new technology, the effects of a natural disaster. Ideally we would have three or four different words to distinguish between minor and major changes. In this case, however, the English language, ordinarily so rich in vocabulary, fails us.

History is concerned with *significant* change. Sometimes this involves an entirely different state of existence for society, such as that brought on by wars, revolutions, and plagues. At other times, a society remains the same structurally but important social, political, and attitudinal changes have occurred. And then there are the changes that are even more gradual, such as population shifts, that can greatly affect the balance of political power or the economic advance of nations and peoples.

Continuity

When we open a history book, often we find we have entered a world where change is so constant that it is almost overwhelming. Events parade by us in bewildering succession, each representing a change from that which preceded it.

We get a sense of perpetual motion and can begin to lose our perspective. (Today the subject is the Ancient Greeks, but we discuss the Renaissance tomorrow!) We know things don't happen that way in our personal lives, and gradually we retreat from that historical world that seems so unreal.

As preoccupied with change as our society is, if we were asked personally whether change or continuity was more dominant in our lives, most of us would probably say "continuity." We would then speak of the monotony of the things we do, including eating, working, sleeping, talking to friends, watching television, making monthly payments—all adding up to continuity. Life, as experienced on the day-to-day level, is inevitably routine and frequently boring, so we hunger for some variety, anything fresh, such as a major news event, some exciting gossip, or even a crisis on our favorite soap opera. Yet, almost paradoxically, we also happily return to familiar patterns.

This leads us to qualify an earlier statement. To regard history as a story of change is a half-truth, or at best, a three-quarters truth. There are some important words to remember concerning human society: inertia, preservation, apathy, stability, tradition. All such terms in one way or another refer to a social guardianship of the status quo. Most changes take place in the overall context of continuance of many of the old ways of doing things, and are often no more than patchwork alterations of the existing system. Further, social, political, and economic inertia create limits to the extent of change. A few months after his inauguration in 1961, John F. Kennedy remarked to an associate that he had found that despite his impressive constitutional powers there was very little a president could do to bring about substantive change. To cite another example, it is worthwhile to remember that the Confederate States of America were created for the *preservation* of the traditional southern way of life in the face of encroaching change. The most effective historians remain conscious of the essentially conservative nature of human society and weave their stories with threads of both change and continuity. "Indeed, given human and cultural patterns, it would be most surprising if major changes in public mentality occurred at anything more rapid than a glacial tempo."[3]

Continuity and Change: Striking the Balance

Historians are well aware of the resistance to change represented by the fixed ways of society, even though in telling their story they may not discuss these continuities directly. Their approach is more often to explore emergent factors, which in their combined influence become strong enough to produce change despite resistance. Their discussion might include such themes as *newly prominent* ideas, dissatisfied interest groups, charismatic leadership, compelling motivations, institutional weaknesses, significant recent events—with appropriate detail concerning each. To counterbalance a preoccupation with the new, historians will then consider existing elements of the status quo, such as historic political party alignments, traditional institutions, attitudes and values, or long-existent economic patterns. There is always something old in anything new. In the next chapter on multiple causality in history we will further explore the various possibilities mentioned above.

---

[3]Conal Furay, *The Grass-Roots Mind in America: The American Sense of Absolutes* (New York: New Viewpoints, 1977), 136.

The Stages of Historical Consciousness

Even at this stage it should be clear that thinking historically is not as easy as it might at first appear. Below we list the four stages one passes through on the road to a more sophisticated appreciation of history and mastery of historical thinking. You are probably farther along that road than you think. At what stage are you?

Stage I: History as Fact

> To me (says the typical Stage I student) history is a bunch of facts—dates, names, events—that I have to memorize for the test. The books and lectures are full of facts, but I really don't see how they all fit together. I take history because I have to, and it bores me. Once I get my requirements out of the way, I plan to avoid history like the plague.

Too many people in our society never get beyond this view of history. It is not always their fault: All too often history teachers teach the subject as if memorization of facts were the essence of historical study. Of course such people are bored by history. They lack any sense of the causal relationships that give meaning to the study of the past, and they certainly don't have the faintest understanding of the role interpretation plays in history writing.

Stage II: History as Causal Sequence

> I now see (says the student at Stage II) that history is more than facts. History provides a story of sequential developments over time, you know: Event A leads to event B which leads to event C, and so forth. The stories are often interesting (my teacher tells some great anecdotes!) and it is satisfying to know why things happened as they did. More important, I am now beginning to see where I fit into the picture. I understand my own origins a bit better, and I know where those values they are forcing me to study came from. The only thing that bothers me is that my textbook and my instructor sometimes contradict each other. It's a shame that historians can't get their act together and come to some sort of agreement on the true causes of events. Maybe in time they will.

Generally, a large number of people reach this stage. Stage II "consciousness" is still quite basic, but it is far beyond the very simplistic outlook of Stage I. People at Stage II can be fascinated by history and can understand cause and effect relationships. But they still do not realize the complexity of such relationships and cannot accept the possibility of alternative interpretations. When they come across contradictions, they assume that one version is, of necessity, false and the other true. Furthermore, the notion that both versions could be false yet could contain a part of the truth never occurs to them. Put another way, what they seek from a history book is *the* truth, not *a* truth. Such people also have difficulty in perceiving the difference between fact and opinion.

Stage III: History as Complexity

> I'm confused, says the Stage III student. History is a subject in which there is so much to learn, I no longer know where to begin. There are too many variations in the accounts you read, even accounts of the same time and place! Some books (or lecturers)

CHAPTER 4 IT'S NEVER THAT SIMPLE: MULTIPLE-CAUSALITY IN HISTORY

"It is better to know some of the questions than all of the answers."
James Thurber

"What men believe to be true of themselves and of their times is often as great a force in moving history forward as are the more sober facts of the case."
Lewis Spitz

One of the leaders of the Russian Revolution of 1917, Leon Trotsky, said that war is the locomotive of history, taking society a long way from where it had been. It was a perceptive remark, especially since the war that spawned the Russian Revolution, World War I (1914-1918), was destined to change the face of Western society, putting a permanent stamp on the entire twentieth century. The Great War—as contemporaries knew it—was a destroyer of empires and led, among other things, to World War II (1939-1945), which in turn led to the Cold War (ca. 1946-1991). "By entering into military conflict in 1914," laments one historian, "the European states unleashed the mayhem from which were born not one but two revolutionary movements—one of which [Nazism] was crushed in 1945, the other [Soviet Communism—one of Trotsky's legacies] left to crumble in the dramatic events of 1989-91."[1]

How can we explain the decades-long shadow that the First World War cast over the twentieth century? There are many contributing factors, but one of them certainly is a grave mistake that was made in the war's immediate aftermath. The victors of World War I decided to blame the entire war and its attendant destruction on Germany, the defeated enemy. The causes of the First World War were tangled and complex, and many nations participated in the conflict, yet the victors chose to highlight a single cause. It was a decision that was not only intellectually indefensible, but was to have unimagined, and horrific, consequences.

The war began in 1914, and its story, on the Western Front, was one of a long grueling stalemate. In the spring of 1918, after Germany's last desperate drive failed, the Allies (essentially France, Britain, and the United States) seized the initiative, and by mid-August the Germans knew they were beaten and began to look for peace. Their backs against the wall, they accepted the generous peace terms offered them by U.S. President Woodrow Wilson, and an armistice ended the fighting on November 11.

The peace conference to create the official, final, settlement convened at Versailles outside Paris in early 1919, and the deliberations continued for five months. The treaty that emerged bore little relationship to the peace terms promised by President Wilson. It was a harsh, punishing document that took away much German territory, sharply reduced its industrial capacity, virtually destroyed the Ger-

---

[1]Norman Davies, *Europe: A History* (Oxford: Oxford University Press, 1996), 900.

man military, and required Germany to pay huge war reparations. Worse, by the terms of the infamous Clause 231, the treaty required Germany to accept entire responsibility for having caused the war.

This "War Guilt" provision caused a firestorm in Germany. "May God palsy the German hand that signs the Versailles Treaty," cried one patriot. But under duress the document was signed, and the clause became an enduring symbol to Germans of all that was wrong with the treaty. It was an emotional sore spot that never failed to arouse resentment, which a clever politician named Adolf Hitler effectively exploited in his rise to power in the late 1920s and 1930s.

Without having to read a page of history the German people instinctively knew that wars don't happen in a one-factor vacuum. The world is more complicated than that. And historians of the origins of World War I have agreed with this instinctive wisdom. Even the most anti-German of historians would acknowledge that no single cause—the Treaty of Versailles notwithstanding—can ever be a satisfactory explanation of even seemingly simple events. And World War I was hardly simple. Historians have spread countless gallons of ink writing about the origins of World War I. And, whatever their disagreements, they agree on one thing. There was not one cause, but many, including intense nationalism, an interlocking alliance system, imperial rivalries, internal political pressures in several countries, a sensation-seeking press in all countries, a weapons buildup on all sides, and more—much more. In other words, the key to understanding the onset of World War I is multiple causality.

The Importance of Questions

Viewing history through the lens of multiple causality is a basic ingredient of historical mindedness. We have said before that the essence of history is explaining how and why some given event happened as it did. In practice this requires the historian to take a situational view, meaning a thorough inquiry into the conditions and circumstances surrounding an event under study. If taken literally this is clearly an impossible task, since the circumstances and conditions that determine the direction of human affairs are almost numberless. In the real world, however, the task is somewhat simplified, if not made simple.

The skill is called "analysis," which means nothing more than breaking the whole into its parts to find out how it works. Applied to a historical event this means you begin by looking at separate "pieces" of the event in isolation as a step toward understanding the event in its totality. How do you do this? *You ask questions— appropriate questions—that will lead you through an event step by step.* James Thurber remarked that knowing questions is more important than knowing answers. He was right. In many endeavors and walks of life the ability to ask the right question at the right time often separates success from failure, the great scholar (or journalist, manager, or physician) from the not so great.

Teachers want students to know the events of the past, of course, but more than that they want them to develop the habit of asking—in a systematic way— certain broad questions in order to *understand* those events. In other words you need to develop a strong sense of how things tend to happen. In the long run this mental habit of seeing events with wider vision is one of the crucial intellectual skills to be gained through the study of history.

What sorts of things does a historian seek to know in order to understand the how and why of a historical event? A list of specific questions that historians might ask would be endless, but certain broad categories of questions are more or less standard. When attempting to understand a specific segment of the past, historians usually like to ask, at minimum: How did ideas, both emergent and traditional, affect the situation? What was the role played by politically active organized groups? By important individuals? By economic and technological factors? How influential were long-standing legal, customary, and diplomatic practices or situations? Before we examine these questions, a couple of important qualifications are in order.

First, these questions are "starter" questions. They are aimed at making sure that you "touch all the bases," that you follow a systematic search pattern. You will find some of the questions irrelevant when you apply them to a particular historical situation. Others will yield results, often in the form of promising conjectures that must be checked against the evidence—a process that leads to more pointed and precisely phrased questions. In any event, the lists of questions below are meant to be suggestive, not definitive.

Second, while it is true that historians must ask the standard questions while studying a given historical event, it is also true that they usually, as a matter of personal inclination, wind up emphasizing only one or two of the standard questions when presenting the story. Survey textbook writers sometimes try to cover all the bases, usually to the numbing frustration of their readers. Most historians choose just one or two main themes, which results in the many varieties of history (economic, political, intellectual, etc.) that exist.

Ideas in History

The adage that "men do not possess ideas, rather they are possessed by them" has considerable truth, especially if "ideas" are taken to include ideals, attitudes, and values. Often ideas are below the surface, not mentioned in a direct way, but present nevertheless as assumptions. In his public addresses, for example, President John F. Kennedy never specifically cited Keynesian economic ideas, but he used them to revitalize the economy in 1962. The American electorate's unspoken but instinctive distaste for radicalism was a decisive factor in Senator George McGovern's crushing loss in the presidential election of 1972.

At least as often ideas are "out front" in the movement of events. When English power in North America was at its height, in the seventeenth and eighteenth centuries, England's statesmen publicly espoused and followed the principles of mercantilism. The American radicals in 1776 just as candidly borrowed the main ideas of Englishman John Locke in their Declaration of Independence. Other examples include the impact of *Uncle Tom's Cabin* (written by Harriet Beecher Stowe), which changed Northerners' perceptions of slavery in the pre–Civil War period; Alfred T. Mahan's ideas on the role of seapower in history, which prompted an enormous naval buildup in late-nineteenth-century Germany; the anti-Semitism of the German people, which Hitler so successfully manipulated in the 1930s; and the ardent feminism that emerged from the publication of Betty Friedan's *The Feminine Mystique* in 1963. In any case the historian must remember to look for both emergent ideas of compelling power and traditional ideas with their enduring hold on people's loyalties.

In dealing with the role of ideas, whether political, economic, theological, scientific, or social, there are various questions one might ask in assessing their impact:
• Had any particular idea become newly fashionable?
• Had certain familiar and almost axiomatic truths begun to be questioned?

- What prestigious old ideas continued to hold the loyalty of major individuals and groups involved in the situation?
- Is there any evidence of manipulation of opinion by appeals to traditional ideas?
- Does it appear that some individuals and groups were in a sense imprisoned" by certain ideas?
- Did any individual's conception of the situation or of his or her role in it have importance?
- Was there a distinctive "public mood" that appears to have aided any groups or individuals?
- Did the "intellectuals" have a marked influence at any particular point?

Again, these questions are merely suggestive of the angles of inquiry that may be pursued. Also, it should be obvious that few of them permit spontaneous answers. Rather, they point in the direction of further reading and research.

Finally, in recent years a significant development in historical studies revolves around the concept of "mentalities." Traditional history writing (or telling) has always given due attention to ideas, whether considered as "principles" (such as "separation of church and state," or "literacy as a voting requirement") or seen as "ideologies" (such as Puritanism, communism, Social Darwinism, or isolationism). But some modern scholars widen the range of inquiry to include such mental processes among common folk as emotional inclinations, typical life ambitions, instinctual tendencies, value systems, common anxieties, unspoken assumptions, and popular attitudes. Such inquiries go beyond the details of political or economic events to explore the various ways the common people of a given era perceived, experienced, and reacted to the world. Thus, the history of mentalities is a type of social history that considers occupational outlooks, family associations, religious tendencies, but also popular culture preferences.

Economic and Technological Factors

There is a popular axiom that to understand seemingly puzzling events one simply needs to "follow the money." Good advice indeed, especially for historians. "Economics" refers to the processes by which a society and its members make a living. That immediately involves us in such matters as market demand, trade patterns, accessibility to raw materials, the interests of economic classes and subgroups, productivity, and   employment levels. While this is not the place for a minicourse in economics, the following sorts of questions can be quite helpful in sorting out the relevant factors of a historical situation.

- Were the markets for the nation's or region's major products and services improving or declining?
- Were existing trade patterns within and without the nation or region being disrupted by new developments?
- Did entrenched economic interests feel endangered by new government policies? By competitive pressures? By other economic groups?
- Were serious clashes occurring among different economic classes within the population?
- Did any economic group have especially strong political muscle, giving it an advantage over other interests?
- Was the nation or region in a discernible stage of the economic cycle (depression, recovery, boom, recession)?

All of the foregoing are large-scale questions that, while useful in framing the overall picture, are not sufficiently focused to define the more localized economic forces and motivations in a historical situation. One must ask "small-scale" questions as well, perhaps something like:

• What were the economic stakes involved in a particular strike that occurred, i.e., for the workers—fringe benefits and wage levels—and, for the employer—the profit margins and competitive situation in the market?

• To what extent did an office-seeker's financial resources affect the outcome of an election?

• Were any key figures in any way motivated by greed, perhaps leading them to cut corners on a building project or to manipulate the contractor awarding process?

We will have more to say later in this chapter about such small-scale questions. You'll note that some of the above questions, particularly several of the large-scale questions, do require a certain amount of economic literacy but not at a level much beyond that obtained by reading newspapers and weekly news magazines.

Related to economic factors are technological developments that influence a society's production processes and its lifestyle. Such developments can bring sharp changes in a society's direction, as happened in America in 1793. Before that date slavery was commonly regarded in the South as a crumbling system. Southerners lacked a profitable cash crop to support its expenses. Then, while visiting at a South Carolina plantation, young Eli Whitney put together a simple but ingenious device called a "cotton gin." It made what was then called "green-seed cotton" a viable crop—this at exactly the time when English mills were voraciously consuming every fiber of cotton that could be produced. Thus, for the South, cotton became, in the words of *New York Times* writer Anne O'Hare McCormick, "map-maker, trouble-maker, history-maker."[2]

Rarely are technological developments in the foreground of historical situations. Rather, they become integrated with a society's economy, creating new products that displace others, enhancing one region's economic potential at the expense of another's, and shifting balances in international trade. Still, though technology is in a sense submerged, it is an area that calls for occasional scrutiny because of its impact on the economy and popular culture.

Organized Groups

There are few historical situations that can be understood without careful consideration of the role that group interests played in shaping the course of events. We use "interests" here in a broad sense and include in it all of the following: organized political parties, such as Republican, Democratic, Populist, Tory, Socialist, Communist; factions within parties, such as liberal, centrist, conservative; interest groups of all kinds, such as religious, economic, environmental, political, and educational; lobbying organizations; little cabals like "kitchen cabinets" or "the gang in the back room"; government bureaucracies; legislative bodies; commissions; and many, many others.

The variety of organizations and groups listed above suggests a frightening complexity to human affairs. Fortunately, in most historical situations only a few

---

[2]Quoted in J. G. Randall, *The Civil War and Reconstruction* (Boston: D. C. Heath and Co., 1937), 8.

such groups play a significant role at a given time. The key to the whole business is for us to keep ever in mind David Potter's dictum that historians deal with human beings less as individuals than as groups—religious groups, cultural groups, ideological groups, interest groups, occupational groups, or social groups.[3] What this means in practice is that the historian must remain acutely conscious of groups, and in research and reading see them as the focal points both of change and resistance to change. Put another way, human affairs should be viewed as an arena in which groups with differing interests band together or oppose one another to achieve their goals.

Some questions worth considering when addressing any historical situation are:

- What organized groups played an important role in the situation you are investigating?
- How well organized and how disciplined were each of the various groups that were involved in the situation? How committed was each group on the issues involved in this situation?
- Where did any given group stand in the "pecking order" of political, economic, and social prestige?
- How much political clout did each group have? How much access to the power centers? What methods did they utilize to achieve their ends?

Given the tenor of the foregoing questions, namely that various groups with conflicting interests compete with each other to achieve their goals, it is important to consider the arena in which the battles are joined: politics. Ultimately it is through the governmental apparatus that any group imposes its will upon society. In a democracy, at least, this involves organization of a clientele, swaying of public opinion, manipulation of the legislative process, and other forms of political activity. The story of a society can scarcely be told without recurrent reference to the ongoing competition for control of power levers. This is not to disparage the emphasis in recent years upon social history, but only to reiterate that power struggle in the political arena is and will remain an essential ingredient of a people's history.

Individuals in History

This is not the place to engage in the debate over whether "the individual makes the times" or "the times make the individual"—the "superperson or any person" argument. It will suffice to say that since human beings do act, their personalities, characters, and motives are of inevitable importance in influencing events. Henry VIII (ruled 1509–1547), for example, was a spendthrift, and his extravagant ways made England a difficult place in which to live, thus preparing the way for "the great historic going forth of the English people" to America and elsewhere. Woodrow Wilson (U.S. president, 1913–1921) was a man of such lofty moral principles that he found it impossible to compromise with more mundane souls over the issue of his "morally right" League of Nations. Did he thus help set the stage for World War II? The courage and eloquence of Rev. Martin Luther King, Jr., profoundly shaped the civil rights movement of the 1950s and 1960s. The point of these examples is to show that individuals—with their quirks, principles, virtues, and vices—do affect the course of events.

---

[3]David M. Potter, "The Historian's Use of Nationalism and Vice Versa," *American Historical Review,* 67 (July 1962), 924.

Concerning the man or woman who was at or near the center of a historical situation, these are some of the questions you might want to ask:

- What aspects of his or her personality were dominant?
- To what degree did social background influence his or her point of view?
- Did temperamental factors enter into his or her choice of action?
- How was the individual reflected in his or her policies?
- What qualities of leadership did the individual conspicuously display or lack?
- To what degree was he or she willing to compromise?
- What were his or her relations with other major figures, and how much did their support (or lack of support) influence matters?

We cannot list all possible questions here, but we can indicate the kinds of questions you might ask concerning individual actors in the historical drama.

Long-standing Legal, Customary, and Diplomatic Conditions

In a sense this category overlaps each of those preceding it, but it deserves to be treated independently. To understand fully any historical event we must not only look at the influence of groups, ideas, and individuals, we must consider the basic "rules of the game" that serve as a permanent backdrop to all human dramas. More concretely, the historian must understand the established ways of the society in question, including common beliefs and attitudes, fixed elements of the social structure, long-existing economic arrangements, and relatively permanent institutions and governmental patterns. Without knowledge of such basic continuities, any concept of change is meaningless. (See Chapter 3.)

This is an admittedly foggy category, but it refers to all those habitual and relatively consistent patterns of behavior that most of us take for granted in our day-to-day lives. These patterned responses, sometimes based on formal law and sometimes on custom or social convention, do affect the course of events and must be taken into account by the historian. The laws, institutions, traditions, diplomatic ties, and social customs of a people live beyond the events of the moment or even the lives of individuals. These things do change, of course, but (periods of revolution excepted) not quickly. Most historical situations are, to a greater or lesser degree, influenced by the weight of legal and behavioral tradition. As William Faulkner said in *Absalom, Absalom!* "the past is never dead, it's not even past." Two examples might make this clearer.

The historian who is trying to write the history of a given presidential election, say Clinton vs. Dole in 1996, will certainly ask several of the questions we have discussed: What was the role played by key individuals and groups and how did economic and ideological factors influence the event? To answer those questions our imaginary historian will also have to know, at minimum, something about the laws that govern the nominating process, the key issues of the election, and the traditional voting behavior of various ethnic, religious, regional, and professional groups. The sensitive historian will also have to know something about the intangible and unwritten "rules" that set limits as to how candidates can and cannot behave. For example, there is no law that says a male candidate must wear a suit and tie while campaigning, but they all do—at least most of the time. (When was the last time you saw a presidential candidate giving a speech wearing Levi's and a sweater?)

Sometimes habitual behavior patterns become so entrenched that they frustrate the best attempts of individuals and groups to initiate change. Such behavioral inertia is a characteristic of many large bureaucracies. For instance, beginning in the early 1920s Soviet leaders had serious problems in directing the large-scale collectivization of Russian industry and agriculture. Soviet leader V. I. Lenin complained five years after the Revolution that though he had in place a "vast army of governmental employees," he lacked any real control over them, and that "down below . . . the bureaucrats function in such a way as to counteract our measures."[4] More than thirty years later, Soviet leader Nikita Khrushchev similarly lamented bureaucratic obstructionism:"It is very difficult indeed to carry through specialization and cooperation in production where there are so many ministries and departments, because the departmental interests of the numerous ministries and central boards raise obstacles in the way."[5]

Contingency in History

Engaging in historical inquiry is like peeling an onion. It must be done from the outside, with each layer separately removed, each of the "starter" questions separately asked. As we get closer to the onion's center we sometimes get to layers we can't at first name—in history these are known as "special" or "chance" factors. Since those special factors are so close to the heart of the onion (the historical occurrence), they must be carefully studied, even though, strictly speaking, they may not be classifiable under one of the major headings given in this chapter.

One of the difficulties in explaining historical events is that each of them is more or less unique. In the background of each event are the conditions or factors we have been discussing (the "Questions"), which are present in varying proportions in each case, some strong, some weak, some not at all. Yet, while these factors have a major importance, in many historical situations specific unforeseen events and accidents (the meaning of "contingency") decisively affect the situation. Such odd, unexpected, chance developments also must be given due attention.

As examples, consider the following:

- The assassination of the Austro-Hungarian crown prince at Sarajevo in 1914 provoked his government into a harsh line against Serbia, thus setting into motion a chain of countermeasures that soon brought the onset of World War I.

- The news that Democratic candidate Grover Cleveland had fathered an illegitimate child changed the tone of the presidential election of 1884.

- On D-Day, June 6, 1944, when Allied forces assaulted the Normandy beaches, Germany's most skillful field commander, General Erwin Rommel, was back in Germany visiting his family. His absence from the scene of operations almost surely contributed to the Allied success in establishing a beachhead on that vital day.

- The Iranian hostage crisis and the intense media coverage of futile U.S. attempts to recover the hostages contributed in a major way to Jimmy Carter's defeat in the presidential election of 1980.

Other particular and unpredictable events can change the course of history: the delivery of an effective speech; a sudden illness; a badly handled press confer-

---

[4]Merle Fainsod, "The Pervasiveness of Soviet Controls," in Michael Dalby and Michael Werthman, *Bureaucracy in Historical Perspective* (Glenview, Ill.: Scott Foresman, and Co., 1971), 121.
[5]E. Strauss, "Varieties of Bureaucratic Control," in Dalby and Werthman, *Bureaucracy,* 86.

fore, on nondiplomats to carry out his policies. William Jennings Bryan was his secretary of state, and that doughty reformer knew practically nothing of foreign affairs and certainly little of Mexico. Then Wilson chose another nondiplomat, John Lind, a former governor of Minnesota, to do nothing less than persuade Huerta to stand aside, allow free elections, and declare that he was not a candidate for the presidency. This proposal was, of course, indignantly rejected.

¶4 So far as historians are aware, most of the Mexican people despised Huerta, but they too reacted angrily at Wilson's efforts to change their government. Whatever their problems, they wished to settle them among themselves, without the indignity of intervention by a moralistic, preaching Norteamericano (the term uniformly preferred in Latin America for citizens of the United States . . .). Whatever the "Colossus of the North" does in Latin America is necessarily regarded with distrust, just as Scots distrust their larger neighbor, England, and Danes react against everything German.

Questions

Indicate in the spaces provided in what way any of the following were involved in the situation. In each instance note the appropriate paragraph number(s). If you feel a given element was not present, write "none."

1. Ideas:

New Ideas: _____

_____

Entrenched Ideas: _____

_____

2. Economic Factors:

Economic Goals Sought: _____

_____

Established Trade Patterns: _____

_____

Concerns of Entrenched Economic Interests: _____

_____

3. Organized Groups:

Groups Actively Pursuing Interests: _____

_____

Activity by Established Bureaucracy: _____

_____

4. Individuals:

Individuals Playing Major Role: _____

_____

Evidence of Individual's Distinctive Conception of Role: _____

_____

Evidence of Personality Traits Influencing Situation: _____

_____

5. "Rules of the Game" (i.e., long-standing legal, customary, diplomatic practices and situations):

_____

_____

Set B, Exercise 2: The Historian's Frame of Reference

In the final segment of this chapter (and in Chapter 2) we discussed how a frame of reference can shape a historian's explanation of an event. Remember, frame of reference influences the questions historians ask as well as the elements of a historical situation they choose to emphasize in their writings.

Each of the passages below tries to explain the governmental corruption during President Ulysses S. Grant's administrations of 1869–1877. And each explanation emphasizes the importance of one (possibly two) of the following variables at the expense of the others: ideas, economic or business factors, Grant's individual personality traits, the "rules of the game" (in this case primarily political "rules"). Read each passage, then in the spaces provided classify the author's frame of reference according to whether the passage emphasizes (1) ideological factors, (2) economic/business factors, (3) elements of the political system (rules of the game), or (4) individual traits as most responsible for the corruption under Grant. Briefly explain your choice(s). In some cases more than one orientation might be present.

1. No President before 1869 had been so unqualified for office as was Ulysses S. Grant—a man who had no experience in politics, no capacity for absorbing such experience, no sensitivity for statescraft, and little judgment about men. Grant had impeccable personal integrity. He had as a soldier displayed the qualities of leadership and fortitude that won him deserved glory. He had, as his enemies in battle had learned, incomparable courage. But as a public servant Grant was a fool and a failure. He appointed an undistinguished Cabinet, of which several members were

knaves who duped him shamelessly. He found most matters of public policy utterly bewildering. He did not himself generate the gross and greedy spirit of the time, but a stronger and wiser man would have yielded less readily than Grant to its rapacious temper. Truly pathetic in his inadequacies, he was also singularly obtuse about his choice of friends. He accepted expensive gifts from favor hunters; he received personal loans from Jay Cooke, whose Northern Pacific Railroad was seeking federal subsidies; he welcomed the company of Jim Fisk, a conscienceless gambler in stocks.

Orientation:_____

Basis: _____

2. One of the many ironies in the reconstruction story is that some of the radical Republicans took the first steps toward destroying the political alliances on which the Republican political position in the South depended. During the first Grant administration a new set of leaders won a dominant position in the presidential circle. These were men who were most responsive to the economic pressures created by the cyclonic growth of American capitalism after the Civil War. They helped to make Congress, the state legislatures, and state political machines the willing collaborators of railroad, oil, textile, and steel interests that wanted government favors. The older crusading radicals found this new Republican leadership appalling, particularly as evidence of corruption began to come to light. "Like all parties that have an undisturbed power for along time," wrote Senator James Grimes of Iowa, "(the Republican Party) has become corrupt, and I believe it is today the most corrupt and debauched political party that has ever existed."

Orientation:_____

Basis: _____

3. But even the most determined presidential effort could not have immediately tamed the spoils system. The sheer numbers, combined with the cost of maintaining party machinery, led to the development of a system which obliged party workers to pay fees for appointments, or incumbent officeholders were taxed an annual assessment on their salaries. Officeholders, well aware that their tenure was impermanent, unsurprisingly took it for granted that they were to milk the post for all it was worth. The result was inescapably a pervasive corruption. Efforts to control the system, as more than one president swiftly discovered, ran afoul of the congressional presumption that spoils were its peculiar prerogative-a presumption which if defied was promptly sustained by congressional refusals to support executive proposals.

Orientation:_____

Basis: _____

4. Profiteering, dishonesty, and political corruption neither began nor ended with Ulysses S. Grant; scandal had been disturbingly constant in American political life. But during the Grant era no one seemed to mind. For a time Americans shrugged

their shoulders at corruption, apparently figuring that the self-made politician compromised himself no more than the self-made industrialist, who made a fortune and became a folk hero. Even when the politician and the industrialist joined forces, the popular reaction seemed more often envy than disgust.

Orientation:_____

Basis: _____

5. Men like Blaine and Conkling remained the party's most influential national spokesmen throughout the period. They largely shaped national legislation during the era. Since they were Republicans, they believed in an effective and energetic national economic policy. In general, the purpose of this policy was to encourage industrial expansion. For this they were often criticized by Democratic politicians who retained their party's traditional faith. This Democratic faith rested on the belief that government should not meddle actively in the economic lives of Americans.

But the Republican Party, founded in an era when the national government had to expand its powers to preserve the Union, saw nothing wrong with continuing this trend at the war's end. To encourage economic development, party leaders aided business in every possible way. In accomplishing this purpose, they forged an informal alliance between the national government and the great majority of businessmen-bankers, industrialists, and merchants in foreign trade. While this alliance did further economic growth, it had other less fortunate consequences as well. It gave the era a reputation for corruption unparalleled in American history until then.

Orientation:_____

Basis: _____

6. During Grant's two terms as President, the word "politician" became synonymous with double-talking and self-serving. The corruption in Washington, and elsewhere in the country, was the result of a lowering in the moral tone of the nation during and after the Civil War. Immense fortunes in industry had been made during the war. Wealth was worshipped, and material display became a passion. Few politicians could resist the bribes for favors which businessmen dispensed freely. Grant was not responsible for this general moral laxity, but by his infatuation with business success and his negligence in office he allowed it to flourish. The early idealism of the Republican Party was smothered in this atmosphere of materialism. In fact, both major parties became agencies for obtaining and dispensing the spoils of office.

Orientation:_____

Basis: _____

Sources

1. John M. Blum, Bruce Catton, et al., *The National Experience* (New York: Harcourt Brace Jovanovich, 1977), 369.

2. Edwin C. Rozwenc, *The Making of American Society,* Vol. II (Boston: Allyn and Bacon, 1973), 596.

3. J. P. Shenton and Alan M. Meckler, *U.S. History Since 1865* (Homewood, Ill.: Learning Systems Co., 1975), 16.

4. Henry F. Bedford and Trevor Colbourn, *The Americans: A Brief History*, 2nd ed. (New York: Harcourt Brace Jovanovich, 1976), 288.

5. Allen Weinstein and R. Jackson Wilson, *Freedom and Crisis* (New York: Random House, 1974), 532.

6. Rebecca Gruver, *An American History* (Reading, Mass.: Addison-Wesley, 1978), 600.

CHAPTER 5 THINKING IN TIME: CONTEXT

"Men resemble their times more than they do their fathers."

Arab Proverb

"The past is a foreign country; they do things differently there."

L. P. Hartley

Historians are firm believers in the cliché that truth is stranger than fiction. What could be stranger, for instance, than the episode recounted by Robert Darnton in his intriguing essay, "Workers Revolt: The Great Cat Massacre of the Rue Saint-Severin."[1] The essay deals with a rather grisly episode in the Paris of the late 1730s— the attempt one day of a number of printer's apprentices to kill every cat they could get their hands on. After killing the favorite cat of their master's (employer's) wife, the workers "drove the other cats across the rooftops, bludgeoning every one within reach and trapping those who tried to escape in strategically placed sacks. They dumped sackloads of half-dead cats in the courtyard. Then the entire workshop gathered round and staged a mock trial. . . . After pronouncing the animals guilty and administering last rites, they strung them up on an improvised gallows."

Does this episode strike you as grisly and barbaric? Most people today would think so. But there is something decidedly peculiar about the whole thing: The workers who participated in the slaughter thought it was all a hilarious joke. The apprentices, says Darnton, were overcome with laughter and joy as they gathered and dispatched the local cats, and, in the days that followed, they riotously reenacted the comic events of the massacre over and over again. The fact that we have trouble appreciating the humor of the slaughter of animals often considered cuddly pets is an indication that we don't know enough about the era and culture we are studying. As Darnton notes: "Our own inability to get the joke, is an indication of the distance that separates us from the workers of preindustrial Europe."[2]

Darnton has presented an interesting puzzle. Why did those eighteenth-century workers think killing and torturing cats was so hilariously funny? We can find the answer, as Darnton shows, by examining the historical *context* in which the event took place. To get the "joke" of the cat massacre we have to enter the thought-world of eighteenth-century popular culture. On one level the frolicsome massacre of cats, as it turns out, represented the venting of worker hostility against an overbearing and unpopular employer. For a number of nights the workers had yowled like cats in order to irritate the master who had been mistreating them. In desperation the master ordered the apprentices to get rid of the offensive "cats." The workers did so with great glee,

---

[1] See Robert Darnton, *The Great Cat Massacre and Other Episodes in French Cultural History* (New York: Basic Books, 1984).
[2] Darnton, *Cat Massacre,* 76–78.

63

and in the process killed the house pet of their employer's wife. The master and his wife were outraged, but helpless, in that they themselves had given the order to eliminate the cats.

This helps a little, but it is not enough. The core of Darnton's analysis is his discussion of popular amusements in eighteenth-century Europe and the role cats played in the popular mind. First, the torture of animals of all kinds, but especially cats, was a popular form of entertainment in that era. More important, cats had long been popularly associated with witchcraft, sexuality, and fertility. By first imitating cat cries and then executing the mistress's cat, the apprentices, according to Darnton, were both accusing their master's wife of witchcraft and "assaulting" her in a sexually symbolic way, thus ridiculing the master as having been cuckolded (our phrase would be "cheated on"). To workers who had grown up in a culture that tortured animals for amusement, who had long suffered insults and mistreatment from an unpopular master, the "great cat massacre" was both funny and deeply satisfying.

This bare outline hardly does justice to the sophistication and intricacy of Professor Darnton's analysis. But the essential point should be clear. To "understand" even this relatively minor incident in the history of premodern France, the historian must uncover the rich texture of beliefs, customs, and values within which the event took place. The historian must, in a word, pay very close attention to context.

Context and Historical Understanding

The importance of context in history is based on the simple premise that the past is different than the present, and to interpret the past using the values and beliefs of the present will distort and misrepresent that past.[3] A distinguishing mark of the good historian is the ability to avoid judging past ages by the standards of the present, and to see former societies (to the greatest extent possible) as those societies saw themselves.

It is extremely difficult, even for the most fair-minded of observers, to understand and evaluate the habits, thoughts, and values of people who lived long ago and far away. An analogy would be the difficulty faced by anyone today venturing into a foreign culture. Even in the late twentieth century, travelers abroad confront a bewildering array of customs, practices, laws, and values that seem "strange" and even "illogical" to them as outsiders. For instance, the reverence toward cows that one finds in India bewilders visitors for whom beef is a major source of nourishment. A siesta during the searingly hot hours of midday is mere common sense to residents of many tropical countries, but to some Americans such behavior smacks of laziness. Western visitors to the Middle East or parts of Asia may unwittingly insult the locals by crossing their legs and pointing the sole of their shoe at someone. And so it goes. The successful traveler is the individual who is open-minded enough to try to understand these cultural differences and adapt to them.

Likewise with the historian embarking on an intellectual journey into the past. In the words of British novelist L. P. Hartley, "The past is a foreign country; they do things differently there."[4] Just as the conscientious traveler today must learn the local cus-

---

[3]The notion that the past is radically different from the present is a surprisingly modern notion. Throughout much of history people thought of past events as though they were part of present reality. Witness the countless Renaissance paintings of Biblical themes in which the figures are dressed in the height of fifteenth century Florentine style!

[4]Quoted in David Lowenthal, *The Past is a Foreign Country* (Cambridge: Cambridge University Press, 1985), xvi.

toms, values, laws, and language to feel at ease in a foreign country, historians must become fully acquainted with the institutions, cultural habits, and beliefs of the society they are studying. Only then can they appreciate the significance and complexity of historical events. As Robert Darnton put it, "other people are other. They do not think the way we do. And if we want to understand their way of thinking, we should set out with the idea of capturing otherness."[5]

To think historically, then, you must constantly remind yourself that the past is different from the present and that historical events must not be evaluated in isolation from the total cultural and intellectual environment of the time in which they took place. To do so is to risk massive oversimplification or, worse, to misunderstand the events completely. A popular story about the Battle of Bunker Hill (June 17, 1775), for instance, holds that the commander of the American troops shouted something like: "Don't fire until you see the whites of their [the British troops'] eyes!" Whether this piece of popular patriotism is true or false, it illustrates the dangers of taking things out of their proper context. On the surface the order seems to reinforce a rather idealized vision of the colonial rebels as supermen—determined, stalwart, and brave in the face of an attack by disciplined British regular troops. However, a more intimate knowledge of the conventions and technology of eighteenth-century warfare reveals a more mundane explanation for the famous order. Actually, the muskets of the time were so inaccurate that a soldier had no hope of hitting an enemy infantryman unless he was close enought that one could see the "whites of his eyes." Military necessity, not superior military valor, best explains the famous and stirring order. The British commander probably said something similar to his men.

The example above should dramatize the importance of knowing as much as possible about the historical period you are studying in order to interpret the past in a fair-minded manner. The investigator's knowledge, as Jacques Barzun and Henry Graff see it, "must include an understanding of how men in other eras lived and behaved, what they believed, and how they managed their institutions."[6] You should, consequently, always try to "think" your way into an alien situation and empathize with those who live (or lived) there. To the best of your ability you should attempt to see the world through the eyes of those you are trying to study. You need not abandon your own values in favor of those of a different place or time. (No need, for instance, to see a massacre of helpless cats as a grand joke.) But you should be able to distance yourself from your own values sufficiently to be able to *understand* why the printer's apprentices thought killing the local cats was so funny. The exercise of such *imaginative sympathy* is a prerequisite of sound historical thinking.

All of this is easier said than done. Very often the tendency to judge the past according to one's own values and standards is inherent in the very nature of historical studies. It is often impossible for the historian to see events exactly as contemporaries saw them for the simple reason that the historian knows "how things came out," whereas the participants did not. Historians narrate and interpret the past with the enormous advantage of hindsight, and it is much easier to be an armchair quarterback than to play the game itself. Hindsight makes it very tempting for the historian to make grand generalizations about the incompetence, naiveté, and shortsightedness of those in the past who could not, as we do, know their future. Allan Nevins, in *The Gateway to History*, points out the fallacy involved with this sort of history. Historical hindsight, Nevins warns, makes past problems seem much more simple (and more easily solv-

---

[5]Darnton, *Cat Massacre,* 4.

[6]Jacques Barzun and Henry Graff, *The Modern Researcher,* rev. ed. (New York: Harcourt, Brace and World, 1970), 116.

able) than they actually were, and "the leaders that dealt with them . . . smaller men."[7] Hindsight, in short, makes it very difficult for even the best-intentioned investigators to approach the trials and triumphs of past ages with true imaginative sympathy.

The difficulty of judging the past by its standards rather than your own is increased when you are trying to understand behaviors repugnant to contemporary moral codes (e.g., "the great cat massacre"). It is difficult to get beyond moral outrage, yet true understanding demands that you do so. The same problem besets historians who write biographies of villains, scoundrels, or the merely unsavory. David Harris Willson confronted this problem when working on a biography of King James I of England (ruled 1603–1625). This biography, still one of the best treatments of this rather flawed and obnoxious king, is a model of impartiality. Willson succeeded in writing a fair and sympathetic treatment of James,[8] in spite of the fact that he never really liked the English king, no matter how hard he tried to do so.

Context and Moral Judgments in History

Above we referred to King James I of England as a "rather obnoxious king." In its most basic sense "obnoxious" means "very unpleasant" or "objectionable." What right do we have to be so moralistic and judgmental? Does not such a label violate the central lesson of this chapter—i.e., thou shalt not judge the past by the standards of the present? Is this not a violation of a basic tenet of historical mindedness? Perhaps.

But if after carefully reading and evaluating the relevant original sources of James's reign we conclude that many of James's seventeenth-century contemporaries thought him "obnoxious" (even if they used different words to express it), then we are justified in "calling 'em as we see 'em." That is, the evidence would have justified the use of the term. On the other hand, if we deem James "obnoxious" because *we* find his behavior morally objectionable, that is a different situation altogether. In the latter case we could be accused of interpreting events "out of context." But even in this case the verdict of practicing historians would not be unanimous. There is marked disagreement among professional historians as to the legitimacy of passing moral judgments on past events and individuals.

Any discussion of the importance of thinking contextually about the past ventures into troubled waters when the issue of moral values surfaces. Many practices that today we consider morally reprehensible have been viewed quite differently in the past. Slavery and serfdom, for example, although almost universally condemned today, were historically considered part of the natural order of things. Slavery was a prominent feature of ancient Greek and Roman life; in the European Middle Ages (and much later in Russia and Eastern Europe) serfs lived lives not far removed from those of slaves; and, as everyone knows, slavery was an integral part of the culture of the American South for over two hundred years. In cases such as this, what position should the conscientious historian take? Should these past cultures be condemned as "immoral" because they countenanced slavery? Should the historian become a moral "relativist" and judge those societies in terms of his or her own standards of right and wrong? Or should the historian avoid making moral judgments altogether?

Herbert Butterfield, a British historian, believed that moral judgments should be irrelevant to historical understanding. If readers did not recognize the immorality or

---

[7] Allan Nevins, *The Gateway to History* (Chicago: Quadrangle Books, 1963), 257.
[8] D. H. Willson, *King James VI & I* (New York: Oxford University Press, 1967).

morality of past deeds, he argued, the historian's moralistic pronouncements would certainly not change their mind. Further, moral judgments would do nothing to help researcher or reader understand the past in any meaningful way. Says Butterfield:"Moral judgments on human beings are by their nature irrelevant to the enquiry and alien to the intellectual realm of scientific history.... These moral judgments must be recognised to be an actual hindrance to enquiry and reconstruction...."[9]

Butterfield and those like him are sometimes called "amoralists. "That is, they believe that moral judgments do not serve any useful purpose in a historical narrative. Ranked opposite are those who believe historians have a *duty* to inject moral pronouncements into their work. Their case also has merit. This groups believes that certain moral and ethical norms are universal and transcend time and space. It is appropriate, then, to point the finger at evil and condemn it wherever one finds it. As Goldwin Smith wrote, "A sound historical morality will sanction strong measures in evil times; selfish ambition, treachery, murder, perjury, it will never sanction in the worst of times, for these are the things that make times evil—Justice has been justice, mercy has been mercy, honour has been honour, good faith has been good faith, truthfulness has been truthfulness from the beginning."[10] We sacrifice too much, in other words, if we rank "understanding" above defending solid moral values.

There are others who occupy a middle ground. This group believes it is legitimate and important for historians to provide moral critiques of the past, but they also believe (along with Butterfield) that the historian should not play the role of the judge, condemning the guilty and absolving the innocent. This position is held by American historian John Higham, who believes that what he calls "moral history" can be an important spur to historical understanding. Moral history can help us appreciate the nature and importance of moral imperatives in different times and places. It can help us understand how certain values—honor, courage, and other concepts of "character"—changed over time. It can also help us "ponder the moral responsibility of the agents of decision [leaders]," by helping us understand the real alternatives available to leaders at key moments in history. In Higham's words, "The historian is not called to establish a hierarchy of values, but rather to explore a spectrum of human potentialities and achievements."[11] Higham's position, then, is somewhat "relativistic." The historian can and should venture into the realm of moral judgments, but those judgments must take into account the broad context of the time and place being studied.

And the debate goes on. Wherever your sympathies lie on this issue, it is necessary to keep in mind that there is a problem here for which there is no easy solution. It is the historian's job to understand and interpret the past, and this is most difficult if basic moral values are in conflict. Perhaps the best advice is this: Be aware of the dilemma, so that in your own studies and researches you can act out of conscious choice rather than ignorance.

---

[9]Quoted in Hans Meyerhoff (ed.), *The Philosophy of History in Our Time* (New York: Doubleday, 1959), 230.
[10]Meyerhoff, *Philosophy of History,* 225.
[11]John Higham, *Writing American History* (Bloomington: Indiana University Press, 1970), 150-56.

Context and Success in Business

We have been considering the importance of context in historical inquiry. It should be clear that the principles we have outlined are not important only for the "ivory tower" world of the university classroom. Contextual awareness is equally vital in a wide variety of professional activities. Journalists who ignore the lessons of context do so at their own risk. It is difficult to report and assess the significance of world events if those events are studied independently of cultural and historical context. Likewise government officials would be well-advised to consider the "big picture" whenever considering specific policies and proposals. Doctors know it is not enough merely to ask their patients for a list of their symptoms. It is often vital to know as much as possible about the totality (i. e., context) of a person's life in order to prescribe the best treatment.

Finally, a failure to appreciate the importance of context can cost money, as numerous corporations have discovered. Businesses have made embarrassing and costly marketing errors simply because they were unaware of critical cultural differences in foreign markets. To cite some examples:

- Very few people in Southeast Asia responded to Pepsodent's promise to make their teeth whiter. Why? In that area of the world, where many people chew betel nuts, discolored teeth are a status symbol.
- General Foods had trouble marketing Jell-O in England. It turns out that British shoppers buy gelatin in cakes, not in powdered form.
- One firm tried advertising refrigerators in the Moslem Middle East by using pictures of the refrigerator full of appetizing food, including a very prominent ham. Of course, Moslems do not eat pork.
- Advertising disasters have also resulted from ignorance of the significance of certain colors in various countries. In Japan, for instance, white is the color of death. In Africa green is the color of disease.

As the above examples testify, it is not only the historian who has to cultivate some of the key attributes of historical mindedness. Abandon the concept of context only at your own peril.

(The examples of business marketing errors were drawn from: "Business Blunders: Some Funny, but, All Costly," *St Louis Post-Dispatch*, November 13, 1980.)

EXERCISES

Set A, Exercise 1: Cromwell in Ireland

The following excerpts are intended to help you appreciate the importance of trying to understand past events within the proper historical context. The passages (drawn from secondary sources) are all concerned with a notorious episode in the life of Oliver Cromwell (1599–1658), the English revolutionary leader who led the anti-royalist Parliamentary forces during the English Civil War (1642–1649). By 1649 Parliament had won the civil war, had executed the king, Charles I, and Cromwell had become the effective ruler of England. In the same year Cromwell led an army to Ireland to snuff out an anti-English rebellion that had been raging since 1641. It is Cromwell's behavior in Ireland that is the primary concern of the passages that follow. When in Ireland, Cromwell's soldiers massacred the inhabitants of two towns, Wexford and Drogheda.

Keep in mind that in the 1640s the great split in Western Christianity, the Protestant Reformation, was not that far in the past, and violent hatred between Catholics and Protestants continued to fuel many international disputes. England, of course, was a Protestant country at this time, but Ireland remained steadfastly Catholic. To complicate matters, the Protestants in Britain were split between the state-sanctioned Anglican Church and the Puritans who wanted even more radical religious reforms. The one thing both Protestant groups could agree on was their distrust of and distaste for Catholics.

The following passages attempt to examine the event by putting it in a broader historical context. The aim is not to justify a military atrocity, but to help you *understand* the event in all its dimensions. After reading the initial passage, read the subsequent passages carefully in order to ascertain what *new* pieces of information each presents. Note how a wider appreciation of the situation in 1649, the mind-set of Cromwell, the worldview of the seventeenth century, and the relevant historical background all help us to understand better the complex dynamics of a seemingly straightforward occurrence. Then answer the questions that follow.

The Event:

Cromwell stayed in Ireland for a little over nine months-from August 1649 to May 1650. His siege of Drogheda lasted ten days (September 2–11), and its successful conclusion was followed by four days of general massacre directed by Cromwell himself, during which period some four thousand people were murdered. When, on October 1, Wexford too was stormed, the same vengeance was exacted, and two thousand people more—men, women, and children, priests, nuns, and laymen—were put to death.... Having given this grim warning, Cromwell refrained from further atrocities in Ireland.... Nevertheless, on account of Drogheda and Wexford, Cromwell left behind him in Ireland a name for cruelty such as the passage of three hundred years has scarcely erased from memory.

Supplementary Information:

A. What then is the explanation of Cromwell's cruel and compulsive behavior in Ireland? From childhood he had been raised in an atmosphere of paranoiac hatred for Catholicism. When he was only six, a group of desperate English Catholics had tried to blow kings, Lords, and Commons sky-high; after the Gunpowder Plot of 1605, a fear and loathing of Catholicism that was to last for many years swept England and formed the background of Cromwell's childhood education.... Finally, in Cromwell's adult years came the reports of the unspeakable atrocities committed by Irish Catholics in 1641—reports that, as we have seen, were grossly overstated but that seemed to establish irrefutably the unchanging nature of the evil that was Catholicism.

B. The rules of war of the time, with regard to sieges, were clear. If a commander refused to accede to a summons to surrender, and the town was subsequently won by storm, then he put at risk the lives not only of all his men, but of all those who could be held to be combatants. The significant moment was when the walls were breached by the opposing side: thereafter quarter could not be demanded. . . . Nor was the civilian population of the town necessarily protected from the rash consequences of the commander's refusal to surrender. . . . Grotius in *De Jure Belli ac Pacis,* a work first printed in 1625, that attempted to prescribe some limits to the vengefulness of war as a result of the appalling slaughters of the Thirty Years' War [1618-1648], still postulated that it was lawful to kill prisoners of war, and furthermore, that "the slaughter of women and children is allowed to have impunity, as comprehended in the right of war and 137th Psalm."

C. Cromwell's Irish policy was not personal but national. When he crossed to Ireland in 1649 the Irish revolt against English rule . . . had dragged on for eight years. So long as it continued, Ireland offered a backdoor to foreign intervention against the regicide republic [Cromwell's Parliamentary party had beheaded King Charles I in January 1649], now isolated in monarchical Europe. . . . The government of the English republic decided that Ireland must be subdued quickly. Hence the massacres of Drogheda and Wexford, for which Cromwell is remembered in Ireland to this day.

D. In England [Cromwell] was prepared in fact to tolerate Catholics as well as Episcopalians [Protestants to be sure, but not "progressive" enough for Cromwell and his Puritan allies]: Roman Catholic historians agree that their coreligionists were better off during the Protectorate [the period of Cromwell's rule] than they had ever been under James or Charles I. But in Ireland it was different. . . . Again we must refer, by way of explanation though not justification, to the political associations of Irish Catholicism. . . . It was a political religion in a sense in which Catholicism in England had ceased to be political.

E. It is necessary to set this story in perspective because it has so often been used to picture Cromwell as a monster of cruelty, differing from other generals and statesmen in English history, and secondly because it is frequently assigned as a main reason for the poisoning of Anglo-Irish relations in modern times. In fact, Cromwell's Irish policy—wrongheaded as it may have been—was identical with that of Queen Elizabeth I, King James I, Strafford, and Pym. All of them sponsored the colonization of Ireland by Protestant settlers. To the Puritans [the more radical English Protestants] Ireland was a nearer alternative to Massachusetts or Virginia and the natives as capable of absorption or extrusion as the Indians.

Sources
"The Event" & Passage A. , Giovanni Costigan, *A History of Modern Ireland* (New York: Pegasus, 1970), 76-77, 79.
B. Antonia Fraser, *Cromwell* (New York: Knopf, 1973), 335-36.
C. Christopher Hill, "Political Animal," *New York Review of Books,* June 9, 1977, 40.
D. Christopher Hill, *God's Englishman* (New York: Harper & Row, 1972), 121-22.
E. Maurice Ashley, *The Greatness of Oliver Cromwell* (New York: Collier Books, 1966), 233-34.

Questions
1. For each passage (A through E) note the specific additional pieces of information that enable you to put the massacres of Wexford and Drogheda into a broader historical context:

Passage A: _____

Passage B: _____

Passage C: _____

Passage D: _____

Passage E: _____

2. The quoted passages help put Cromwell's expedition into historical perspective by supplying: (1) information on Cromwell the individual (personal values and beliefs); (2) commentary on the *immediate* political situation (i. e., 1649); (3) insights into the broad cultural, religious, and moral values of seventeenth-century society (the "worldview"); and (4) relevant historical background information (developments in England and Ireland *before* 1649) that had an impact on events.

Indicate by letter (A–E) the specific passage or passages above that contain important information related to each of the general categories just listed. Multiple answers are possible, and you may use each letter more than once.

a. Cromwell the individual: _____

b. Immediate political situation: _____

c. Societal values/worldview: _____

d. Historical background (pre–1649 in England): _____

Discussion Topics:

1. Generally, the quoted passages allow you to make a more balanced appraisal of Cromwell's Irish campaign because they suggest what a modern-day court of law would call "mitigating circumstances." The purpose is not to condemn or exonerate Cromwell's behavior, but to allow you to view Cromwell's actions *as his fellow countrymen in the seventeenth century might have viewed them*. In what ways do you think the seventeenth-century assessment would differ from a twentieth-century judgment? Why?

2. Which passage or passages added most to your understanding of the events in question? Which added least to your understanding? Why?

Set A, Exercise 2: Writing History

Assume you are writing a paper that attempts to explain why Cromwell and his troops acted as they did in Ireland. The most important part of that paper will be the introduction. Read Writing Capsule 3 (below) and, using the passages above (including our brief description of the event) as your source materials, write a brief *introductory* paragraph to such a paper. In your introduction do two things: (1) provide the background information that you see as essential for a clear understanding of the events in question; and, (2) clearly state your major point, or thesis, indicating important supporting points. For instance, if your thesis is "Three factors in particular influenced Cromwell's actions in Ireland," be sure to list briefly what those factors were. It will be profitable to compare your paragraph with those of your colleagues in class.

Writing Capsule 3
Essays: The Introduction

Just as a paragraph requires a clear and informative topic sentence, a history essay or paper needs a good introduction. The introduction, usually a paragraph or two, provides a gradual lead-in to the paper itself. And make no mistake, writing a good introduction is not easy. You have to condense complex ideas and information into a few clear summary sentences. On one hand, a good introduction indicates the problem your paper is addressing, and the historical context of the events you are exploring. You cannot assume your reader is familiar with the period or event you are writing about so you must, briefly, summarize the necessary information.

In the introduction you should also unequivocally state the conclusion(s) you have, and that your paper will, come to, i.e., your thesis. Your thesis, the basic interpretive generalization you intend to prove, is the cornerstone of any effective history paper, so you have to make sure it is clearly expressed.

Often a thesis is so broad that it needs a bit of elaboration before you proceed any further. If you claim, for example, that "Elvis Presley had a profound and lasting impact on American popular culture," you should summarize briefly the major reasons you think this is so. Later in the paper you will have to support these points with evidence; in the introduction it is sufficient to identify your points for the reader.

(For more on introductions see Chapter 12, "Writing the History Paper," page 207.)

Set B, Exercise 1: Appeasement, 1933–38

Few diplomatic policies have been as universally condemned as that called "appeasement" in the 1930s. So dramatic was the failure of appeasement that the policy became, in the words of one historian, "the most influential negative lesson for a whole generation of Western leaders" who came afterwards.

Appeasement refers to the attempts of the British and French, especially the British, to dampen the aggressive ambitions of Adolf Hitler's Nazi regime in Germany in the 1930s. Britain and France had been allies against Germany in World War I (1914–18) and, in the Treaty of Versailles, imposed upon the defeated Germans a set of military, economic, and territorial restrictions and penalties. The victors wanted to make sure that the Germans would not be able to seek revenge in the future. Adolf Hitler (1889–1945) became Chancellor of Germany in 1933 and immediately sought to overthrow the restrictions of the Versailles Treaty. He embarked on a campaign of rearmament and territorial expansion, which, within a short time, made Germany the most powerful country in Europe. Eventually Hitler's aggressive actions (the remilitarization of the German Rhineland in violation of the Treaty of Versailles, the annexation of Austria, the dismemberment and ultimate invasion of Czechoslovakia, and, finally, the invasion of Poland) led to the outbreak of World War II (1939–45).

From 1933 until 1938 the British argued that the best way to avoid war with a rearmed and aggressive Germany was to satisfy Hitler's territorial demands and ignore his violations of the Versailles Treaty. This was appeasement. The primary British proponent of appeasement was Neville Chamberlain, Prime Minister from 1937 to 1940. Chamberlain was the prime mover behind the September 1938 Munich Conference, which allowed Hitler to annex parts of Czechoslovakia without opposition. Munich was the most extreme example of the British determination to appease Hitler; and it was dubbed by one critic as "one of the most disastrous episodes" in British history. Most historians have echoed that sentiment. For, rather than ensuring peace, appeasement led to war. J. W. Wheeler-Bennett writes: "It is a tragic irony of history that this very will for peace was among the most important contributory factors to the Second World War, for it is clear that early and bloodless victories convinced Hitler that Britain and France would never oppose him by force...."[12]

All of this is very obvious to us now. Appeasement was a failure and the appeasers were shortsighted and naive. "The total upshot of their efforts," said one contemporary, "was to aid Nazi Germany to achieve a position of brutal ascendancy, a threat to everybody else's security or even existence, which only a war could end."[13] But are shortsightedness and naiveté enough of an explanation? No. Here, as elsewhere, the broader context is critical for an understanding of the attitudes and policies of the appeasers. The passages below (drawn from secondary sources) should help you understand the total environment in which the appeasers worked. Read each one carefully, and, in the spaces provided at the end of the exercise, note the *new pieces of information* each passage provides to help you understand why British policy makers and the British public were so committed to appeasement.

Supplementary Information:

A. Appeasement rested on a number of assumptions. Perhaps its basic foundation was the conviction among the survivors of the First World War [1914–18] that Europe could not survive another such bloodletting. Every French town had its *monument aux morts* [war memorial] with its long list of the dead; no British village was without its war memorial. Even tiny villages displayed prodigious lists of casualties. Mutilated war veterans were conspicuous reminders, as was the arrival of the "hollow years" in the 1930s. Added to this were science fiction conceptions of the next war, with its aerial bombardments and poison gas. Millions of deaths were predicted....

B. In the end, Chamberlain's critics were proven to be right, and the appeasement policy helped to bring on the war that the prime minister was seeking to avoid. This was not, however, due solely to his gullibility. Hitler's gifts of persuasion were considerable, and Chamberlain was not the only European statesman who was deluded by his ability to mask his true intentions until he felt strong enough to be able to disregard potential opposition.

C. One moral argument told strongly in Germany's favour: the argument which had been pressed, particularly by the Left, ever since the end of the first World War. The Treaty of Versailles had been presented as unjust, punitive and unworkable. Germany was entitled to equality in armaments and everything else. The Germans of Austria, Czechoslovakia, and Poland were entitled, like other nationalities, to self-determination, even if this meant an increase in German power. More broadly,

---

[12]*Munich: A Prologue to Tragedy* (New York: Viking Press, 1965), 6.
[13]A. L. Rowse, *Appeasement* (New York: W. W. Norton, 1963), 118.

Germany was entitled to a place in Europe and in the world commensurate with her greatness in population, economic resources, and civilisation.

D. Why then did Britain, the second beneficiary of the treaties [the Treaty of Versailles and others] look upon them as provisional or even objectionable, in part at least, while the French at the same time clung to them with an almost desperate devotion? The explanation lies partly in Britain's traditions and the happy experiences which she has had in her relations with the Dominions [e.g., Canada, Australia] and other parts of her Empire in applying a flexible policy. She has moved on from one temporary agreement to another, regarding each one only as a step in a continuous and inevitable historical evolution.

E. Since the inauguration of the League of Nations in 1920 Britain had taken very seriously the obligations incurred under the Covenant [of the League], more particularly those involving the reduction of armaments, and this tendency had been further encouraged with the increase of economic burdens. In an honest but fatal endeavour to achieve universal disarmament, successive Governments had reduced the armaments of Britain to a point at which many believed them to be no longer compatible with the demands of national defence, in the vain hope that others would be moved to emulate such an example of unilateral rectitude.... At this moment it was believed by all parties that the risk of financial disaster was far greater than the menace from any rival power.

F. [Economist] J. M. Keynes said the Treaty [of Versailles] was filled with clauses "which might impoverish Germany now or obstruct her development in future." Many Englishmen read, and accepted, his criticisms. Ashamed of what they had done, they looked for scapegoats, and for amendment. The scapegoat was France; the amendment was appeasement. The harshness of the Treaty was ascribed to French folly.... France was blamed for having encouraged Britain in an excess of punishment. Justice could only be done by helping Germany to take her rightful place in Europe as a Great Power....

If Germany was to be won for friendship, France's friendship must be discarded. Dislike of France ran deep in English life.... While Germany gained a new master and a new discipline in 1933, France remained slovenly, excitable, under the influence of left-wing politicians.... French weakness was a great crime. It was a weakness the communists could exploit; a weakness which offered a chance of power to the agents of Moscow. A deal with France would be a deal with danger. But the Germans were wiser and stronger, and anti-communism was a leading point in Hitler's program.

G. In one sense it [appeasement] was Chamberlain's own policy, and a very personal one: but it rested on illusions which were very widely shared. Chamberlain's hatred of war was passionate, his fear of its consequences shrewd. He believed ... that much could be accomplished by personal diplomacy in conference; that there "must be something in common" between different peoples since "we are all members of the human race;" that there was a human side to the dictators, which could be appealed to, especially in tête-à-tête [face-to-face] discussions.

H. Originally "appeasement" did not mean surrendering to a bully's demands nor did it mean that nations must surrender their vital national interests in order to avoid war. Instead "appeasement" meant a reduction of international tensions between states through the removal of the causes of friction. It also meant concessions to disgruntled nations in the hope that the concessions would alleviate their grievances and lessen their tendency to take aggressive action. It was hoped that after the aggrieved nations had been pacified through appeasement, an era of confidence, peace, and prosperity would emerge.

Sources
A. Robert O. Paxton, *Europe in the 20th Century,* 2nd ed. (San Diego: Harcourt, Brace Jovanovich, 1985), 428.
B. Gordon A. Craig and Alexander L. George, *Force and Statecraft,* 3rd ed. (New York: Oxford University Press, 1995), 82.
C. A. J. P. Taylor, *English History, 1914-1945* (Oxford: Clarendon Press, 1965), 417.
D. Arnold Wolfers, *Britain and France Between Two Wars* (New York: W. W. Norton, 1966), 214-15.
E. J. W. Wheeler-Bennett, *Munich: A Prologue to Tragedy* (New York: Viking Press, 1965), 230-31.
F. Martin Gilbert and Richard Gott, *The Appeasers* (Boston: Houghton Mifflin, 1963), 3, 8-9.
G. C. L. Mowat, *Britain Between the Wars, 1918-1940* (London: Methuen, 1968), 590-91.
H. Keith Eubank, *The Origins of World War II,* 2nd ed. (Wheeling Ill.: Harlan Davidson, 1990), 69.

Questions
1. For each passage (A through H) note the specific additional pieces of information that enable you to put the British appeasement policy into a broader historical context.

Passage A: _____

Passage B: _____

Passage C: _____

Passage D: _____

Passage E: _____

Passage F: _____

Passage G: _____

Passage H: _____

2. The quoted passages help put the British appeasement policy into historical perspective by supplying: (1) information on the role played by specific *individuals*; (2) commentary on *immediate* political and economic realities (i.e., during the 1930s); (3) insights into the influence of Britain's *long-term* historical experiences; and (4) information about how contemporary Britons *perceived* reality and *interpreted* their world. Indicate by letter (A-H) the specific passage or passages that contain important information related to each of the general categories just listed. Multiple answers are possible, and you may use each letter more than once.

a. Specific individuals: _____

b. Immediate political/economic situation: _____

c. Britain's historical experiences: _____

d. Perceptions of reality: _____

Discussion Topics:

1. Which passage or passages added most to your understanding of the 1930s appeasement policy? Why?

2. Which passage or passages added least to your understanding of appeasement? Why?

Set B, Exercise 2: Writing History

Assume that you are writing a paper that attempts to explain why British policymakers pursued the appeasement policy in the 1930s. The most important part of that paper will be the introduction. Read Writing Capsule 3 (on page 72), then, using the passages above as your source materials, write a brief *introductory* paragraph to such a paper. In your introduction do two things: (1) Provide the background information you consider essential for a clear understanding of the events in question; and, (2) clearly state your thesis, indicating important supporting points. For instance, if your thesis is "A number of factors help us understand the passion with which the British government pursued the appeasement policy," be sure to list briefly those factors. It will be profitable to compare your paragraph with those of your colleagues in class.

PART II
CONFRONTING
THE HISTORICAL ACCOUNT

CHAPTER 6 LIBRARIES: REAL AND VIRTUAL

"Knowledge is of two kinds. We know a subject ourselves, or we know where we can find information upon it."

Dr. Samuel Johnson (1709–1784)

"My library was dukedom large enough."

William Shakespeare
(Prospero in The Tempest*)*

Revolutions change the course of history, and revolutionary leaders have long fascinated historians. Charismatic figures make good copy, whether they are popular orators (Sam Adams, Georges Jacques Danton, Rosa Luxemburg), politicians (George Washington, Nelson Mandela), conspirators (Maximillian Robespierre, V. I. Lenin), strategists and military leaders (Oliver Cromwell, Mao Zedong), or populist heroes (François Toussaint L'Ouverture, Che Guevara). Yet one of the most influential revolutionaries of the last two centuries was not primarily a man of action. He defended no barricades, led no troops, and never held political office. He "totally lacked," in the words of one of his biographers, "the qualities of a great popular leader or agitator." Instead he was something of a bookworm, a man of ideas who spent "the greater part of his working life . . . in comparative obscurity in London, at his writing-table and in the reading-room" of Britain's national library.[1] His name was Karl Marx.

Libraries don't seem to us the sort of places where world-shaking events take place, but to the extent that ideas move individuals to act, we have to give libraries their due as among the most important institutions in a civilized society. Certainly Karl Marx (1818–1883) proves the point. Marx was a journalist and political organizer whose radical activities and revolutionary writings (e.g., *The Communist Manifesto*) prompted his expulsion from Germany and then France in 1849. He spent the rest of his life in London, where he spent countless hours reading in the British Museum and writing many of the articles and books (e.g., *Das Kapital*) that became the founding texts of the international socialist and communist movements.

As an individual Marx was unkempt, irascible, and remote. A Prussian government spy wrote that Marx led a gypsy existence. "Washing, grooming and changing his linen are things he does rarely, and he is often drunk." But, though his work habits were irregular, he often worked day and night with tireless endurance.[2] The result was an immense body of work that was destined to change the world. His ideas were revolutionary in two senses: they inspired radical and revolutionary political movements in every corner of the globe, and they had a lasting impact on the way philosophy, economics, the social sciences, and history (for more on Marx's vast influence see Chapter 13) have been studied and understood ever

---

[1] Isaiah Berlin, *Karl Marx: His Life and Environment* (New York: Oxford University Press, 1963), 1.
[2] David McLellan, *Karl Marx: His Life and Thought* (New York: Harper Colophon, 1973), 280.

since. In the words of Sir Isaiah Berlin, "No thinker in the nineteenth century has had so direct, deliberate and powerful an influence upon mankind as Karl Marx."[3] Perhaps it's true that there is no weapon more powerful than a library card.

Now, more than a hundred years after Marx's death, the library is still the most important educational resource on a college campus. Not only does the library house the books, journals, documents, films, videos, and audiocassettes that serve as the lifeblood of learning, it can also serve as your entry ramp to cyberspace—the so-called electronic information superhighway. Finally, don't overlook the library as a pleasant (and increasingly colorful) place to browse, study, think, and even socialize.

The only way to learn how to use a library properly is to use one. This is true even for seasoned scholars who may be quite ignorant of sections of libraries (or library services) they rarely use. Jaroslav Pelikan, an eminent historian of Christian doctrine, once dumbfounded a Yale University library employee by asking where the periodicals room was. Pelikan explained that he knew, "where the incunabula" [rare books] were, but since he never used recent magazines in his research, he had no idea where to find the periodicals room. Like Pelikan, you will learn how to locate library resources and use library services as the need arises. Be assured, the mastering of the skills of accessing library resources will be well worth your time in the long run. The faster you are able to collect your sources, the less time any research project will take.

There are four basic things you must know to begin: (1) the layout of your library, (2) how books are classified, (3) how to initiate a search for the information you need, and (4) how to use the reference section (as well as whom to ask for help).

Layout of the Library

First, play the role of a tourist in your own library. Ask for any available informational guides or pamphlets; then wander around and note the location of the following:
1. The main circulation desk and the reference desk
2. The catalog (electronic or card)
3. Computer terminals providing access to electronic indexes and services
4. The reference area (printed encyclopedias, indexes, dictionaries, map atlases, etc.)
5. The periodicals room or area.
6. The book stacks—especially those relevant to your immediate needs
7. The reserve room or reserve shelves
8. The audiovisual (A–V) area

The Classification System

As overwhelming as a library may seem at first glance, the thing to remember is that there is a place for everything, and those who understand the organizational scheme will be able to make the library work for them.

The Library of Congress system is by far the most common system of classification in college and university libraries. Introduced around the turn of the twentieth century by the Library of Congress in Washington, D.C., this system uses twenty-one letters of the alphabet to designate general categories:

---

[3]Berlin, *Karl Marx*, 1.

A.   General works
B.   Philosophy/Religion
C.   Auxiliary Sciences of History

D.   UNIVERSAL HISTORY
E–F. AMERICAN HISTORY

G.   Geography/Anthropology
H.   Social Sciences
J.   Political Science
K.   Law
L.   Education
M. Music
N.   Fine Arts
P.   Language and Literature
Q.   Science
R.   Medicine
S.   Agriculture
T.   Technology
U.   Military Science
V.   Naval Science
Z.   Bibliography/Library Science

Subcategories can be created by adding a second letter to the general designation. For instance:

D   History (general)
DA Great Britain
DB Austria, Liechtenstein, Hungary, Czechoslovakia
DC France
Etc.

You don't have to memorize the entire system, but it is a good idea to know the designation(s) for your own field of study. Also don't ignore the benefits and pleasures of simply browsing through the stacks. Browsing makes the system more comprehensible, and, for those who enjoy the atmosphere of a good bookstore, it can be a satisfying and intellectually rewarding experience.

Initiating the Search

Understanding your library's classification system will help you locate the relevant book collections, but to find specific works on specific topics you will have to turn to the catalog—the most important research tool in the library. For generations libraries used card catalogs, but in recent years electronic catalogs have made the traditional card catalog increasingly obsolete. It is no longer the card drawer but the computer terminal that will be your first stop when attacking a classroom assignment or research project.

The catalog gives you access to listings of all the materials held by your library. With a computerized catalog you simply type an author's name, a title, a subject, or a keyword, and the computer will show what is in the collection. When you see a promising title, a simple command will display an array of information on that source: among other things, the classification number, whether it is in the reference or general collection, the number of pages, whether the book is illustrated, the date of publication, and, related subject areas. You might also be able to find out if it is already checked out or on order.

Looking up a specific title or the works of a given author is relatively easy, but finding *all* the relevant books on a given subject or topic is not always so simple. The electronic catalogs allow you to enter key words based on your subject, and you can combine key words in order to narrow the limits of your search. For instance, if you type in the word "war" you will get far more "hits" or matches than if you type in "Civil War." Using "United States Civil War" as the entry will narrow the list still further.

As convenient as all of this is, it can lead to a fatal overconfidence. If you have struck gold with a well-chosen subject or keyword entry, don't assume your search is complete. Try to think of additional subject headings that might yield results. To continue with our example of the U.S. Civil War, when we typed in the name of "Abraham Lincoln," dozens more entries appeared, many of which were not included in the Civil War lists. Often the catalog itself will tell you to "see also" this or that subject. Further, the information display on a specific book will include alternate subject headings that you might want to try. Browsing through relevant sections of the book stacks can also help you turn up sources you didn't discover during the catalog search.

The Reference Section

The catalog is only the first step in your search for information. Next you should try to find journal and periodical articles on your subject, and perhaps relevant books that are not currently in your library's collection. To do this you have to consult various indexes and bibliographies (i.e., lists of books and articles on a particular subject) found in your library's reference section.

As Montaigne noted, without much exaggeration, "There are more books upon books than upon all other subjects." Unfortunately, books that list other books are not especially exciting reading. They are, however, quite necessary if you are going to do a thorough job of research. Keep in mind, though, that these indexes, bibliographies, and abstracts do not contain the actual historical information you are seeking; they are intended to help you find the books and articles that do contain that information.

Many of the most useful indexes are now available either online (i. e. , via direct electronic link to a centralized database) or on CD-ROM (Compact Disk with Read Only Memory). Unlike the CDs you buy at the local music store, CD-Roms contain massive amounts of information that can be read by computers. Most libraries provide computer terminals on which you can tap into a number of these major indexes (see the list of resources on pages 85–88) by performing the same subject and keyword searches discussed earlier. In this way you will be able to find not only new materials in your own library, but important books and articles that your library might not have. The latter you may wish to order through interlibrary loan or obtain by visiting another library.

At the end of this chapter there is a short list of indexes, bibliographies, and abstracts useful to the history student. Some titles that merit special mention are the periodical indexes that do for journal and magazine articles what the catalog does for books. The most important are the *Readers' Guide to Periodical Litera-*

ture and the publication known variously as the *International Index* (to 1965), the *Social Sciences and Humanities Index* (to 1974), and now, separately, the *Social Sciences Index* and the *Humanities Index*. Although recent volumes of these indexes are also available electronically, the printed volumes of these publications will still be of use to history students who often need reference materials from the more distant past.

The *Readers' Guide, Social Sciences Index,* and *Humanities Index* list articles alphabetically by author and under one or more subject heading. The *Readers' Guide* will help you find articles published in popular magazines (e. g. , *Time, Newsweek,* etc.), and the *Social Sciences Index* and *Humanities Index* will list articles that appear in the more scholarly journals. A brief look at the key in the front of these volumes will help you understand the sometimes-confusing abbreviations they use to save space.

In addition to these guides to books and articles, the reference section also has countless volumes that do contain a wealth of actual historical information. Included in this group are dictionaries, encyclopedias, biographical dictionaries, atlases, and statistical compilations. Somewhere in your reference collection there is a book that contains the answer to just about any informational question you might have. In the category of dictionaries, for instance, there are historical dictionaries, pronunciation dictionaries, slang dictionaries, and rhyming dictionaries. There are dictionaries of forgotten words, new words, common words, foreign words, technical words, crossword-puzzle words, uncouth words, and even words used by criminals.

Finally, and perhaps most important, when you are doing library research your best friends could be the reference librarians. They are not there to do your research for you, but their advice can be invaluable. If you need help, just ask for it!

Surfing Cyberspace: The Internet

As the preceding sections make clear, computer literacy is an essential survival skill in our increasingly technological society. But, like the apple in the Garden of Eden, computer literacy brings with it a certain loss of innocence. Since computer networks now give researchers access to more information than mere mortals can ever use, never again will you be able to say, "I couldn't find any information on that subject." As one newspaper columnist wrote recently, "What I found confirmed my worst fears; there is more information out there than I could possibly process."[4]

Still, computer networks can make your life as a student much easier. You may even be able to access your library's catalog using the computer in your dorm room, assembling a preliminary bibliography without ever physically entering the library. But this only scratches the surface of possibilities. There are now literally thousands of computer networks around the world (and the number is growing daily) that you can access using the Internet.

The Internet presents history students with a world of research opportunities never before available. It can help you search the catalogs of libraries all over the world, plug into historical bulletin boards and discussion groups, read journal articles and newsletters, examine an array of original documents and photographs, and survey the full text of court cases or the stories appearing in contemporary

---

[4]Christine Bertelson, "On-Line Journey Leaves Traveler Seeking Real Talk," *St. Louis Post-Dispatch*, October 18, 1994: B1.

Using the Internet: The World Wide Web[5]

The Internet presents to history students a world of research opportunities never before available—and pitfalls to match. On the plus side, the information to which you have access is no longer limited by physical location. You can live in the deserts of Utah or the wilds of the Northwest Territory and access information in libraries, universities, and museums around the world. On the other hand, just about anyone with a computer can publish on the Internet, so the quality of much of the information out there is suspect. Still, the Internet is here to stay, and you will have to know how to use it—and how to evaluate the information you glean from it.

It is not our intention to write an in-depth primer on Internet use. There are plenty of them out there, and they often run to hundreds of pages. Also, the world of cyberspace is changing so rapidly that anything written today ay well be outdated tomorrow. However, there are a few introductory points that might be helpful.

For our purposes, it is sufficient to note that your passport to the information contained in the worldwide network of computer connections is called the World Wide Web (WWW), which allows computer users to browse through the almost infinite variety of information available on the Internet. To cruise the Web you also need a software program (a browser) that allows your computer to read the information you discover. There are two ways to use the system once you are connected.

1. You can perform keyword searches that will result in a number of "hits" i.e., a list of Web addresses or URLs (Universal Resource Locators) with some mention of your subject). When you click your mouse on one of those selections you will be linked to a "home page" [the entry door] of someone who has put information—or links to other information—on the Web. Any word or phrase highlighted in a different color (usually blue or red) represents an avenue to further information on that subject. A click of the mouse will get you in.

2. If you know the actual address of the link you want to access, you can click the "Open" icon in the menu bar at the top of the page and type the address into the box that is provided. Click "Open" or press "Return" to complete the process.

newspapers and magazines. You will still have to use traditional books and periodicals in your research, but the Internet will allow you to tap into vast resources that previous generations of students could not have conceived.

Choosing the Best Sources

Once you have found relevant information on your subject, you might ask yourself, "How do I select a usable and representative sample of sources from the vast

---

[5]Much of the information in this section is based on Andrew McMichael, Michael O'Malley, and Roy Rosenzweig, "Historians and the Web: A Guide," *Perspectives* (January, 1996), 16.

mountain of information available?" Remember, if you have been conscientious in your search, you will have more information than you need and it will be necessary to choose the most appropriate materials. There are no hard and fast rules, but the following tips might prove helpful.

1. Don't let the perfect be the enemy of the good. It is better to have enough sources and get your assignment in on time than to try to read all the sources and never begin writing.
2. Making the proper selection usually requires a good deal of preliminary research and reading. You have to get to know a topic before you can discern the books and articles historians judge to be the most important on your subject.
3. In selecting books and articles (remembering there are exceptions to all that follows), choose the most up-to-date research over outdated works and choose works with substantive source references and bibliographies. Also, check book reviews to identify the most respected works in the field.
4. You must take special care to make sure that information taken off the Internet is trustworthy. Many new pages are being added to the World Wide Web every day, and anyone can place information on the Internet. Since no one filters this material or checks it for accuracy, it is your responsibility to make sure that any Internet resources you use for research are credible and academically sound. Your library will be able to provide you with guidelines for critically evaluating Internet resources.
5. As you become aware of scholarly controversies involving your topic, try to do justice to the differing interpretations by using sources written from more than one point of view in your research.

Some Places to Begin

The following section contains a sample list of reference books and will best serve you when you actually begin a research project. Sources available on-line or on CD-ROM are indicated as such in brackets. Many more resources will be available in electronic versions in the near future.

Indexes and Bibliographies: Finding Your Source Materials

This is a selective list of some of the best places to begin your search for the sources you will use on your research project.

America: History and Life [CD-ROM]. Citations and abstracts (summaries) of periodical articles on the United States and Canada from prehistoric times to the present.

The American Historical Association's Guide to Historical Literature, 3rd ed. An excellent place to begin. The 3rd edition was published in 1995.

Book Review Digest. Contains brief excerpts of book reviews of important books. Important in helping you decide which books are the best on your subject, and indispensable in helping you decide which complete book reviews to read.

Harvard Guide to American History, Volumes 1 & 2. A bibliographical guide to the literature on American history. The opening chapter provides an excellent introduction to research methods and materials. There are many other specialized bibliographies for other regions of the world. Ask your reference librarian to help you find an appropriate subject bibliography for these areas.

Historical Abstracts [On-line]. Provides brief summaries of scholarly articles that have appeared in the world's periodical literature. Good for finding articles relevant to your research and also getting a preview of the content.

The New York Times Index. [On-line; CD-ROM] Excellent source for the beginner. This is a thorough index of the articles that have appeared in *The New York Times* since 1851. It is important to follow the directions under each subject heading in order to find the full citation.

A Reader's Guide to Contemporary History (Bernard Krikler and Walter Laqueur, eds.).

Reader's Guide to Periodical Literature. [On-line; CD-ROM] An excellent source; discussed above on pages 82–83. Note, however, that this index covers popular, nontechnical magazines (e. g., *Time, Newsweek,* etc.) representing all the important fields of study.

Social Sciences Index [On-line; CD-ROM] and the *Humanities Index* [On-line; CD-ROM] (originally the *International Index* and, then, the *Social Sciences and Humanities Index*). Discussed above, pages 82–83. Excellent guides for the student of history and politics since these indexes concentrate on more scholarly, specialized periodicals.

The Social Sciences: A Cross-Disciplinary Guide to Selected Sources (Nancy L. Herron, ed.). Discusses reference materials for history as well as political science, law, and the other social sciences.

Dictionaries and Encyclopedias: Finding General Information

The few titles listed below will help you get an initial overview of any topic you are researching. These sources are useful for getting started and for filling in the odd fact here and there, they are much too general, however, to serve as the core sources for your research. For those with personal computers, there are CD-ROM versions of certain dictionaries and encyclopedias.

In addition to the standard encyclopedias—*Britannica* [CD-ROM], *Americana* [CD-ROM], *Colliers*—the following reference works are often excellent resources for the student of history.

Dictionary of American Biography A multivolume collection of scholarly articles on prominent Americans who died before 1945. The articles have bibliographies that can serve as a guide to further research.

Dictionary of American History An eight-volume work with brief, signed, articles on aspects of American history. Each entry has a brief bibliography.

Dictionary of National Biography This is the British equivalent of the *Dictionary of American Biography.* The lack of any national designation often confuses

Comment: *This note is OK as far as it goes. It records all the essentials, but it is more a literal transcription than a summary. Such a note requires very little work on the part of the researcher. Remember, a good note should be a summary written in your own words. Now take a look at another note based on the same passage.*

II. Sample Note # 2:

Wood, Creation

Meaning of Am. Revol.

To Americans Revol. meant creation of a new world. A republic meant elimination of king and use of elections, but Wood argues it also meant a moral transformation of soc. itself. Quotes Paine: "We are now really another people. "

pp. 47–48

Comment: *This note is much better. It is shorter (by more than a third) and it translates the key ideas into the words of the researcher. In this sort of note some true intellectual work has been done, in that the passage had to be fully understood in order to be effectively summarized in different language. When it comes time to write a paper there will be no temptation to use the author's words (other than the quoted extract from Tom Paine) since the note already reflects the style and words of the student.*

Notice the use of abbreviations, a legitimate and time-saving practice. Also, the source and page number have been recorded along with a heading that indicates the general topic of the note.

For each of the passages below write a research note that summarizes the key ideas in your own words:

1. "Undoubtedly this narration of Black Hawk's early life omits much that would help [us] understand his later attitudes and actions, but several clear indications of his personality and world view do emerge. He thought of himself as a traditional Sauk. He personified tribal rivalries throughout much of his life. Thus, because the Osages had been long-time enemies of the tribe they became his enemies. He practiced the ceremonies, dances, and mourning customs with determination, often going far beyond minimal expectations, as in mourning his father for five years instead of the usual six months. He grew to manhood during an era when the Sauks and their tribal neighbors still enjoyed a good degree of isolation and freedom from the demands of the European powers then trying to divide the continent among themselves. " (Roger L. Nichols, *Black Hawk and the Warrior's Path* [Wheeling, Ill: Harlan Davidson, 1992], 18–19.)

_____

_____

_____

_____

2. "Elizabeth [I of England (1558–1603)] had no intention of surrendering her powers, or acquiescing in men's views of women. She had a great longing, she said, 'to do some act that would make her fame spread abroad in her lifetime, and, after, occasion memorial for ever'. 'She seems to me,' wrote Feria, 'incomparably more feared than her sister [Queen Mary], and gives her orders and has her way as absolutely as her father [Henry VIII] did.' She kept matters of state very largely in her own hands, and generally consulted her councilors individually, on the principle of 'divide and rule. '" (J. E. Neale, *Queen Elizabeth I* [Garden City, N.Y.: Doubleday Anchor, 1957], 67-68)

_____

_____

_____

_____

_____

_____

3. "In Colonial America, alcohol was vital to the myriad social and cultural expectations which colonists had brought with them from England and the Western world. It was universally honored as a medicine for almost every physiological malfunction, whether temporary or permanent, real or imagined. But even more, it was aqua vitae, the water of life, and 'the good creature of God'—in St. Paul's and then Increase Mather's cheerful phrases—a mystical integration of blessing and necessity. And so it had been for as long as men had recorded their fears or their satisfactions. 'Give strong drink unto him that is ready to perish,' reads the Book of Proverbs, 'and wine unto those that be of heavy hearts. Let him drink, and forget his poverty, and remember his misery no more.'" (Norman Clark, *Deliver Us from Evil: An Interpretation of American Prohibition* [New York: W. W. Norton & Co., 1976], 14.)

_____

_____

_____

_____

_____

_____

_____

4. "Early Renaissance works of art which today we admire for their sheer representational virtuosity were part of a vigorously developing worldwide market in luxury commodities. They were at once sources of aesthetic delight and properties in commercial transactions between purchasers, seeking ostentatiously to advertise their power and wealth, and skilled craftsmen with the expertise to guarantee that the object so acquired would make an impact.

Take those Annunciations [religious paintings], for example.... These sacred works are fragments of the altarpieces which dominated the interiors of fifteenth-century chapels and churches. Those who commissioned them demonstrated thereby to the congregation at large their prominent position in the community, and the awe and respect to which they were entitled by birth or office. "(Lisa Jardine, _Worldly Goods: A New History of the Renaissance_ [New York: Doubleday, 1996], 19.)

Set A, Exercise 4: Classification

Once you have some information, you then need to *manage* it by creating a system of classification. The ability to perceive and create categories for your information is critical to sound historical thinking and absolutely essential for writing well-organized essays and papers. Writing about events in chronological order is, of course, a staple of historical narration. But often you will need to organize your materials into topical categories that will allow you to write about a given segment of the past more effectively. Topical organization involves dividing your materials according to thematic similarity—e. g., politics, war, religion, ideas, etc. (See pages 191–193 in Chapter 11 for a more extensive discussion of classification.)

In this exercise you should attempt to classify book titles by listing them under one of the following four topical categories. (If you think a title fits in more than one category, list it as such and be prepared to defend your answer. But remember, you should be trying to find the best category for a given title.)

1. **Political:** Relating to government, elections, relations between governmentaL branches, diplomacy, the process of legislation, etc.

2. **Economic:** Relating to the production, distribution, and sale of goods and services. Also finance, economic ideas, labor-management relations, business practices, and the like.

3. **Social:** Relating to popular customs, leisure activities, behavior patterns, social values, life styles, gender relationships, etc.

4. **Ideological/Intellectual:** Relating to the major ideas that influence society, to public opinion, to major systems of belief, and the like.

Titles:
The WPA and Federal Relief Policy (D. S. Howard)
Crestwood Heights: The Culture of Suburban Life (J. R. Seeley, et al.)
America's Capacity to Produce (E. G. Nourse, et al.)
Propaganda Technique in the World War (H. Lasswell)
The History of Photography (B. Newhall)
American Minds (S. Persons)
Prohibition: The Era of Excess (A. Sinclair)
The New Radicalism in America (C. Lasch)
The United States and the Spanish Civil War (F. J. Taylor)
Railroads: Rates and Regulations (W. Z. Ripley)
The California Progressives (G. Mowry)
The Modern Corporation and Private Property (A. A. Berle, Jr., and G. C. Means)
1600 Pennsylvania Avenue (W. Johnson)
Labor on the March (E. Levinson)
The Liberal Imagination (L. Trilling)
The Supreme Court From Taft to Burger (A. T. Mason)
Women at Work: The Transformation of Work and Community in Lowell Massachusetts, 1826–1860 (T. Dublin)

Classification: (Please use two or three key words from the above titles)

Political:	Economic:	Social:	Ideological/ Intellectual:
_____	_____	_____	_____
_____	_____	_____	_____
_____	_____	_____	_____
_____	_____	_____	_____
_____	_____	_____	_____

Set B, Exercise 1: The Search for Sources

The catalog is the logical place to begin a search for research materials. But, to get the full benefit of a catalog search, you should check a variety of possible subject headings. For instance, a person researching the topic of the Salem witchcraft trials should not only look for books under the heading "Salem," but under subject headings such as "witchcraft," "U.S.—History—Colonial Period," "magic," "sorcery," and "occult sciences," as well.

For each of the topics below, list four or more catalog subject headings in which relevant materials are listed. Don't guess! Go to the catalog and check out the categories yourself. Note: Knowing the names of some of the important figures involved in each event/episode helps you expand the number of possible categories. For an example, see Set A, page 88.

1. Topic: The Japanese Attack on Pearl Harbor, December 7, 1941

Possible Catalog Subject Headings:

_____   _____

_____   _____

_____   _____

2. Topic: The Russian Revolution, 1917

Possible Catalog Subject Headings:

_____   _____

_____   _____

_____   _____

3. Topic: The History of African Americans in the South in the 1920s and 1930s

Possible Catalog Subject Headings:

_____   _____

_____   _____

_____   _____

4. Topic: Chivalry in the Middle Ages

Chivalry was the code of values and behavior (at least in theory) of the feudal aristocracy—the knights and members of the nobility—during the late Middle Ages (ca. 1100–1500) in Western Europe.

Possible Catalog Subject Headings:

_____   _____

_____   _____

_____   _____

5. The Feminist Movement in the United States during the 1960s and 1970s

Possible Catalog Subject Headings:

_____   _____

_____   _____

_____   _____

Set B, Exercise 2: Using the Reference Collection

Using the reference collection, answer the following questions and list the source you used for each answer. Do not use general encyclopedias (e.g, *Britannica*) or any single source for more than one answer. You may use specialized encyclopedias (e.g., *Encyclopedia of American History*). *Make sure at least half your answers are found in print sources.* The object of this exercise is to acquaint you with as wide a variety of reference works as possible. For each answer, list the source and indicate whether it was a printed volume or an electronic database.

You might want to review the list of possible references on pp. 85–88. In addition to the specific sources listed on those pages, the following categories of reference works might be helpful:

Atlases (maps plus much more useful geographic and demographic information)
Dictionaries of Famous Quotations
Almanacs and Yearbooks (information on the year just past plus many statistics)
Dictionaries of Dates

Questions

Remember: Include source title, volume number (if relevant) and page-number citation.

1. Locate a magazine or journal article written in or after 1991 (list author, title, date, name of periodical) about the Japanese attack on Pearl Harbor or about the fiftieth anniversary of that event.

Article:_____

Source: _____

2. List three reference works (no general encyclopedias) in which you can find a biographical sketch of W. E. B. Du Bois, the turn-of-the-century African-American

leader. Include the volume numbers (where relevant) and page numbers of the essays.

Source: _____

Source: _____

Source: _____

3. List three reference works, at least two of which are different from those above (again, no general encyclopedias), in which you can find a biographical sketch of Eleanor Roosevelt. Include the volume numbers (where relevant) and page numbers of the essays.

Source: _____

Source: _____

Source: _____

4. Locate an article on Chinese revolutionary leader Mao Zedong, written before 1975 and appearing in a historical journal. Cite the title of the article, the author, the journal, and the date. Note: an earlier anglicized spelling of Mao's name was "Mao Tse-Tung."

Article: _____

Source: _____

5. When did Nigeria become an independent nation?

_____

Source: _____

6. Who wrote: "A good book is the precious lifeblood of a master spirit"?

_____

Source: _____

7. When (month, day, year) was F. Scott Fitzgerald born?

_____

Source: _____

8. What is the highest mountain in Colorado?

_____

Source: _____

9. When was Margaret Thatcher prime minister of the United Kingdom?

_____

Source: _____

10. Locate and provide a citation for a book review of Jared Diamond, *Guns, Germs, and Steel: The Fates of Human Societies,* 1997. Simply provide the citation for the magazine or journal in which the review appeared, including the author of the review and the date.

Citation: _____

Source: _____

Set B, Exercise 3: Note Taking

This exercise is designed to give you some experience in taking good notes. As you do the following segments, keep in mind that a good note summarizes the important points and should be written in your own words. Don't copy the original text or lecture verbatim. Before beginning, you may want to read the comments accompanying Set A, Exercise 3.

For each of the passages below, write a research note that summarizes the key ideas in your own words. Before beginning examine the example of note taking in Set A on pages 92–93.

1. "At least two major features distinguished the Texas-Mexican generation living in the period circa 1880–1910 from the preceding one: the size and origin of the population and a more participatory role for Tejanos. In the first case, the Mexican-American community increased.... In 1880, according to Roberto M. Villarreal, the total Texas-Mexican population (including those of foreign birth) numbered 71,000. This increased to 105,821 in 1900, and then to 279,317 in 1910. In 1880, the percentage of native-born Texas-Mexicans was 39 percent of the total population, but ten years later this standing had been elevated to 51 percent and the pattern continued thereafter. In 1900, 57 percent of the Texas-Mexican population claimed the United States as their country of birth, and in 1910, 55 percent did so." (Arnoldo De León, *Mexican Americans in Texas: A Brief History* [Wheeling, Ill.: Harlan Davidson, 1992], 53.)

_____

_____

_____

_____

_____

_____

_____

2. "Women of color coped [with the Depression] by using a strategy of downward mobility—that is, they took whatever jobs they could get. Rural black women often left their homes, migrating in larger numbers than black men to urban areas in search of employment. Urban black women also became small-scale entrepreneurs, peddling such goods as home-baked bread or home-raised vegetables on the streets or door to door. Urban black women also responded to economic hard times by gathering into so-called slave markets on street corners each morning, where they offered their labor to the highest bidder on an hourly basis, often for as little as ten cents an hour. In New York City, an observer noted that hundreds of 'forlorn and half-starved girls were lucky to find a few hours' work one or two days each week.'" (Glenda Riley, _Inventing the American Woman: An Inclusive History,_ 2nd ed., Vol. 2 [Wheeling, Ill.: Harlan Davidson, 1995], 255.)

_____

_____

_____

_____

_____

_____

3. "Among professional military men in [President Harry] Truman's inner circle, the influence of General George Catlett Marshall, first as Chief of Staff of the Army, later as Secretary of State, and still later as Secretary of Defense, was supreme. Truman regarded him as the greatest military strategist of our time, the most capable and stalwart director of our foreign policies. He looked uncritically to Marshall for guidance and decision, seldom questioning his opinions, and still more seldom acted contrary to his recommendations. Truman never attributed fault or failure to him. Conjointly, Marshall's prestige in Congress and the country was helpful to the 'upstart' President. Marshall's self assurance gave him confidence." (Herbert Feis, _From Trust to Terror_ [New York: W.W. Norton & Co., 1970], 19.)

_____

_____

_____

_____

_____

_____

_____

4. "The clergy in France [in the late 1700s, just before the French Revolution] then numbered rather less than 100,000, yet they owned over one-tenth of the land, that is to say about 20,000 square miles. Despite these rich and rolling acres, most of the clergy were poor, for there existed in the Church a hierarchy quite as distinctly stratified as in the other orders of society. The bishops were all nobles, and canonries were often considered the perquisites of well-to-do bourgeois [middle class] families. Moreover, in many towns there were far more canons than there were hard-working parish priests. In Angers, for example, where Church buildings and gardens took up half the area of the town, there were seventy canons but less than twenty priests." (Christopher Hibbert, *The Days of the French Revolution* [New York: Morrow Quill, 1980], 30.)

_____

_____

_____

_____

_____

_____

_____

Set B, Exercise 4: Classification

Once you *have* some information, you then need to *manage* it by creating a system of classification. The ability to perceive and create categories for your information is critical to sound historical thinking and absolutely essential for writing well-organized essays and papers. Writing about events in chronological order is, of course, a staple of historical narration. But often you will need to organize your materials into *topical* categories that will allow you to write about a given segment of the past more effectively. Topical organization involves dividing your materials according to thematic similarity—e.g., politics, war, religion, ideas, etc. (See pages 191–193 in Chapter 11 for a more extensive discussion of classification.)

In this exercise you should attempt to classify book titles by listing them under one of the following four topical categories. (If you think a title fits in more than one category, list it as such and be prepared to defend your answer. But remember, you should be trying to find the best category for a given title.)

1. **Political:** Relating to government, elections, relations between governmental branches, diplomacy, the process of legislation, etc.

2. **Economic:** Relating to the production, distribution, and sale of goods and services. Also finance, economic ideas, labor-management relations, business practices, and the like.

3. **Social:** Relating to popular customs, leisure activities, behavior patterns, social values, life styles, gender relationships, etc.

3. **Ideological/Intellectual:** Relating to the major ideas that influence society, to public opinion, to major systems of belief, and the like.

Titles:
Varieties of Reform Thought (D. Levine)
Climax of Populism: The Election of 1896 (R. F. Durden)
Promised City: New York's Jews 1870–1914 (M. Rischin)
The Peculiar Institution: Slavery in the Ante-Bellum South (Kenneth M. Stampp)
The Presidential Election of 1880 (G. H. Knoles)
From the Depths: The Discovery of Poverty (R. H. Bremner)
Pullman Strike (A. Lindsey)
Race Relations in Virginia, 1870–1902 (C. E. Wynes)
Social Thought in America: The Revolt Against Formalism (M. White)
Boston's Immigrants (O. Handlin)
Families Against the City: Middle Class Homes of Industrial Chicago, 1872–1890 (R. Sennett)
Irish-American Nationalism, 1870–1890 (T. N. Brown)
Catalogues and Counters: History of Sears, Roebuck and Company (B. Emmet & J. E. Jeuck)
Relief and Social Security (L. Meriam)
Lincoln at Gettysburg: The Words That Remade America (Garry Wills)
Sport in Industrial America, 1850–1920 (Steven A. Riess)

Classification: (Please use two or three key words from the above titles)

Political:	Economic:	Social:	Ideological/ Intellectual:
_____	_____	_____	_____
_____	_____	_____	_____
_____	_____	_____	_____
_____	_____	_____	_____
_____	_____	_____	_____
_____	_____	_____	_____
_____	_____	_____	_____

CHAPTER 7 READING HISTORY

"Books are not made to be believed, but to be subjected to inquiry."
William of Baskerville in Umberto Eco's The Name of the Rose

Historians are frequently asked to rate and rank American presidents. The presidents most frequently listed in the "top ten" include George Washington, Thomas Jefferson, Abraham Lincoln, and the two Roosevelts, Teddy and Franklin. Another perennial member of this elite circle is the man from Independence, Missouri, Harry S. Truman (1884–1972; president 1945–1953).

Harry Truman would have seemed an unlikely candidate to be a great president to those who mourned the death of Franklin Roosevelt in 1945. Truman, Roosevelt's vice-president, was a short, bespectacled Midwesterner who spoke in a high, unimpressive voice, liberally salting his speech with "hells," "damns" and other colorful expletives. Politically Truman was a relative unknown, and his ties to the corrupt Kansas City political machine of Thomas Pendergast did little to inspire national confidence. With his rural Missouri roots and limited formal education he seemed quite a contrast to the patrician, Harvard-educated Roosevelt who had guided the country through the Depression and World War II.

Truman's early years as president were difficult. His popularity in the polls dropped steadily in 1946 and 1947, and he was the object of many a nasty remark: "To err is Truman," "I'm just mild about Harry," "What would Truman do if he were alive." Yet, in the end, Truman's honesty, basic common sense and ability to make tough decisions with conviction won him the election of 1948 and a perennial place on many great-president lists.

One of the things that misled Truman's contemporary critics was the widespread belief that Truman was relatively unsophisticated and unschooled. That impression was wrong. Though Truman had only a high school education, he was a passionate reader, intoxicated from an early age with a desire to learn. He grew up in a house filled with books, and as a young boy he read the Bible twice, had "pored over" *Plutarch's Lives,* and read an entire set of the works of Shakespeare. He spent many hours in the town library, vowing, along with his friend Charlie Ross, to read every one of the two thousand volumes (which they said they did). "I don't know anybody in the world that ever read as much or as constantly as he did," said his cousin, Ethel Noland.[1] Young Harry read everything he could get his hands on, but his greatest love was history. Truman's recent biographer, David McCullough writes:

> History became a passion, as [Truman] worked his way through a shelf of standard
> works on ancient Egypt, Greece, and Rome. "He had a real feeling for history," Ethel
> [Noland] said, "that it wasn't something in a book, that it was part of life—a section of

---

[1] David McCullough, *Truman* (New York: Simon and Schuster, 1992), 44, 58. Though Truman had no formal education beyond high school, that was a good deal more than most of his Independence, Missouri, contemporaries, most of whom did not even go to high school.

105

life or a former time, that it was of interest because it had to do with people. " He himself later said it was "true facts" that he wanted. "Reading history, to me, was far more than a romantic adventure. It was solid instruction and wise teaching which I somehow felt that I wanted and needed."[2]

What Harry Truman discovered, and today's student needs to know, is that history is a reading subject. Our culture increasingly worships at the altar of visual images, but history remains a study firmly based on the written word. To learn history you have to read history—and a lot of it. Such being the case, it seems obvious that there are tangible rewards for those who become more effective readers. It is not the purpose of this chapter to turn you into a speed-reader with a photographic memory—a virtual impossibility in any case. We will, however, explore some techniques that will allow you to get the most out of the reading you do.

Historical accounts are, of course, reservoirs of factual information, but they also attempt to explain and interpret the past. And those interpretations and explanations often differ markedly from account to account. As we have seen, there is no single, unanimously accepted version of any significant portion of the past. Instead there are many versions that often conflict with one another. As Dutch historian Pieter Geyl said, history is "an argument without end."

Certainly no student of history can ignore important pieces of information, for facts are the bricks out of which historical interpretations are built. But facts do not speak for themselves, and often the known facts will bear the weight of more than one interpretation. This is the primary reason historians keep rewriting the history of a single event or period. They are not writing simply to present facts that have already been recorded in other books. They are writing to explore alternative explanations (interpretations), firmly based on the evidence, of why and how things happened the way they did, and perhaps to introduce new evidence not included in previous studies.

Another reason for rewriting history is that as our perspectives and interests change over time, so too do the questions we ask about the past. It was no accident that the explosion of interest in African-American history and women's history paralleled the increased activism of both groups in the 1960s and 1970s. Nor should it be surprising that Americans became increasingly interested in the history of Southeast Asia during the Vietnam War, or in the history of the Balkans during the Yugoslav wars of the 1990s.

The study of history, therefore, involves not only learning the events of the past, but learning (from written histories) what others before you have said about those events. However, a word of warning is in order. Even though all good history is interpretation, not all interpretation is good history. The fact that there is a subjective quality inherent in all historical interpretations should not be taken to mean that "one opinion is as good as another." As Francis Parkman, the eminent nineteenth-century American historian noted, "Facts may be detailed with the most minute exactness, and yet the narrative, taken as a whole, may be unmeaning or untrue."[3] Thus, while there is room for much honest disagreement among historians, in certain cases we must recognize that some interpretations fit the facts

---

[2]McCullough, *Truman,* 58
[3]Francis Parkman, *Pioneers of France in the New World* (1865), introduction.

better than others, and interpretations based on shoddy scholarship or faulty reasoning should be exposed and rejected.

How to Read Historical Literature

Reading history cannot be done passively; it requires an alert mind critically engaged with the text. Unfortunately, no one has yet invented a labor-saving device to make the process effortless. You can save time and energy, though, if you know what to look for when reading history or other types of nonfiction.

Begin by remembering that when you read an article or book your main goal should be to understand the author's major interpretations and conclusions. You will come across much new information, and you should pay attention to the most salient of the new facts. But it is more important to master the author's *interpretation* of how the facts relate to one another. We all know that discreet facts are easy to forget. Once a noted expert on fish who became a college president vowed to memorize the name of every student on campus. He soon abandoned the effort, complaining, "I found that every time I learned the name of a student, I forgot the name of a fish. " Many of us share the college president's forgetfulness for facts. However, we are much better able (and it is much more important) to remember neatly summarized generalizations and conclusions.

The Thesis

When reading a book or article you should first try to discover the author's primary *thesis,* or major explanatory interpretations or conclusions. The factual information is, of course, important, but that information will be more easily assimilated if you understand the author's broader purpose in writing the account. It is an author's interpretation (thesis) that makes a book or article distinctive, and this thesis is the glue that ties together the disparate facts that can otherwise overwhelm the reader. In the late 1920s, for example, both Sidney Fay and Bernadotte Schmitt wrote lengthy studies of the origins of World War I (1914–1918).[4] Both authors used essentially the *same* documentary evidence, but each interpreted that evidence in a different way. Schmitt assigned to Germany most of the responsibility for starting the war, whereas Fay minimized German war guilt by distributing blame more widely among a number of countries. Thus, the *topics* of the books were almost identical (the origins of World War I), but their *theses* (interpretations) were radically different.

Usually the thesis of a book can be discovered quickly.[5] If it's not immediately obvious, either the book is poorly constructed (not uncommon) or you missed something. Many times the author states the thesis explicitly ("My argument/thesis is . . . "); on other occasions you must do the work yourself. Most authors summarize their central arguments in a preface, introduction, or first chapter, and recapitulate the main points again at the end of a book or article. These are the sections of a book you should read first. In the case of an article, read the first few paragraphs and the last few in order to isolate the thesis. Don't be afraid to read

---

[4]Sidney B. Fay, *The Origins of the World War,* 2 vols. (New York: Macmillan, 1928); Bernadotte E. Schmitt, *The Coming of the War, 1914,* 2 vols. (New York: Scribners, 1930).

[5]We are indebted for the discussion of thesis-finding and selective-reading techniques to Norman E. Cantor and Richard I. Schneider, *How to Study History* (Wheeling, Ill.: Harlan Davidson, 1967), especially Chapter Five.

the last chapter or section before those in the middle; a history book is not a murder mystery in which the reader needs to be kept in suspense until the end.

It is important to identify the thesis early so that as you read the rest of the book you need not read every detail with equal diligence. The facts in the book should support and illustrate the thesis, and if you have identified that thesis from the beginning, you will find it much easier to read the rest of the book. As you become more and more familiar with a given topic, you will find it easier to master additional books on that topic. With the essential facts already at your command, you will be able to concentrate on the book's interpretation and how that interpretation differs from others you have read. You will be thinking creatively, not just absorbing masses of information.

Finally, although the thesis is the most important single element in a book, you should by no means ignore the rest. As you read you should take note of the important generalizations made in each chapter or subsection of the book. You should also make a mental or written note of what factual material is covered in order to have a clear idea of what the book does and does not contain. That way, if you need a specific piece of information in the future you will know where to find it.

Topic vs. Thesis

Don't confuse the topic of a book with the thesis. The topic refers to the specific subject matter the book covers. The topic is the *what* the author is writing about. The thesis refers to the distinctive *argument* the author is making about the topic—i. e., the interpretation. Many authors have written on the causes of the American Civil War (that is, they have written on the same topic), but they have presented different theses about the cause or mix of causes that led to the conflict. To some the war was fought over slavery; to others it was a war that grew out of the economic differences between the South and the North; and still others have said the war was caused by a conflict over the issue of states' rights.

Remember:

Topic refers to the subject matter. When you say: "This book is about the origins of the Civil War," you are describing the topic of the book.

Thesis refers to the author's central argument about the topic under discussion: e. g., "The author argues that the Civil War was fought primarily over the issue of slavery." (No sentence can be a thesis statement unless it can be prefaced with the words: "The author argues that . . . ." or "I argue that . . . .").

Selective Reading

Reading a book is like mining for precious gems—the valuable stones must be separated from the surrounding rocks. A useful technique for "mining" historical accounts is *selective reading*. After you have read carefully to establish the thesis, the rest of the book can be digested rapidly. A well-constructed book will contain regular patterns that you can use as shortcuts. For instance, an author's major points are usually summarized at the beginning or end (or both) of each chapter. Similarly, central ideas in individual paragraphs are often contained in a topic sentence, usually, but not always, the first sentence in the paragraph. Once you have established where a particular author tends to locate the key ideas, it is easy to concentrate on those and skim over much of the supportive or illustrative factual material. Be aware, however, that this technique is most valuable for books on topics about which you already know something. We do not recommend this technique when you are reading a book on an unfamiliar subject. Further, we are not talking here about speed-reading (a questionable and highly overrated technique) but about selective reading. These techniques will help you discriminate between the sections of a book that should be read with relative care and those that can be read less intensively.

Authors' Choices and Hidden Agendas

"What I like in a good author," wrote American essayist and critic Logan Pearsall Smith, "is not what he says, but what he whispers."[6] Indeed, the "whispers" in a work of history—what we can read "between the lines"—are frequently as important as the author's explicit statements. In every history book the author makes countless value judgments and decisions which, though not always explicitly identified, make that particular book different from all others. It is important, therefore, to try to identify the author's underlying assumptions and values. There is no absolutely foolproof way to do so. To some extent each book and each author is unique, and the historian-detective must use any and all clues to penetrate below the surface. At a bare minimum it might help to ask the following questions of every book you read:

- **Does the book reflect an identifiable bias or point of view, and how might the author's bias have influenced the book's subject matter or conclusions?** Books reflect—often unintentionally—the political, national, religious, or ideological values of their authors. For instance, in many cases books on the religious upheavals of the Reformation during the sixteenth century clearly reveal the religious convictions of the authors. Similarly, British accounts of the American Revolution often differ quite markedly from American accounts. Critical readers should look for clues to an author's values and biases in order to weigh more intelligently the arguments made in the books. A word of caution is appropriate here. The intrusion of bias does not automatically discredit an author's thesis. The test of a historical interpretation is how well it conforms to and explains all the evidence.
- **How does the author approach the subject?** Put another way, which of the varieties or subcategories of history does the book represent? Most authors choose to emphasize some aspects of past experience more than others: e.g., economic relationships (economic history); politics (political/institutional history); individuals (biography); the role of groups (social history); ideas (intellectual history); war (military history); diplomacy (diplomatic history); everyday life (again, social history). The approach an author takes when writing about a subject reflects a conscious choice—perhaps to examine the subject from an economic as opposed to a political perspective—and you should always be aware of that choice.

---

[6]Logan Pearsall Smith, *Afterthoughts* (1931).

- **How does the author organize the book?** The author also decides whether to organize an account *chronologically* (events discussed in order of occurrence) or *topically* (events discussed in thematic units). Actually, authors often combine the two, alternating the chronological narration of events with periodic analyses of specific issues or topics. Taken as a whole, though, most books will conform predominantly to one organizational scheme or the other. A look at the table of contents may help you determine whether a book is organized topically or chronologically. Usually, however, you will have to dip into the work itself to get a firm sense of how the author has organized the material.

- **What are the author's sources and how well are they used?** Here you are concerned with the author's research apparatus. Are there extensive source references (footnotes, endnotes, or in-text citations)? Few? None? Is the bibliography large? Small? Missing altogether? This sort of information can give you a clue as to the seriousness and perhaps the credibility of the book, although it would be a mistake automatically to equate extensive source citations with quality. Also, a lack of such research apparatus does not necessarily mean that the book is worthless. It could have been the author's intention to write an introductory study (like this one) intended for a general audience. You should also note what sources the author used. Are the sources appropriate to the subject matter? For instance, a history of American slavery using only material written by southern plantation owners would be highly suspect, as would a history of the labor movement based only on the observations of factory owners. Further, did the author use extensive primary (original) sources or was the book written on the basis of secondary literature? The answer to this question can help you discover whether the author was attempting to break new ground by examining original sources or attempting to synthesize the research findings of a number of other historians. (Primary sources—letters, diaries, government documents, newspapers, photographs, etc.—are the records created by those who lived through the events being investigated. Secondary sources are the books and articles written by historians, very often based on primary sources. See pp. 144–145 for a fuller discussion of the distinction between primary and secondary sources.)

- **Who is the author?** To answer all of the above questions it helps to know something about the author both personally and professionally. Is the author a scholar? Journalist? Politician? What is the author's political persuasion? Religion? Nationality? Gender? Sexual orientation? If a scholar, is the person a historian? Political scientist? Economist? Sociologist? Psychologist? What kind of reputation does the author have in academic circles? Many times such information (or some of it) can be found on jacket covers or in a brief biographical sketch in the book itself. (The reference librarian will also be able to guide you to pertinent biographical dictionaries.) If you know of some other books the author has written it might be helpful to read some reviews of those works.

- **When was the book first published?** This piece of information can provide many clues to the quality and orientation of a book. A history of World War II (1939–45) written in 1946 might be less objective and less substantive than one written in 1996, although you should not assume that automatically. Certainly, though, the 1996 author would have had the opportunity to incorporate evidence unavailable to the author writing immediately after the war.

lengthy piece of writing unless you have really understood the thesis and major arguments of the author. Further, it provides a useful reminder that our first obligation when reading an author's work is to understand the author's ideas in a fair and open-minded way before we go to the next step of *critiquing* those ideas, which is the task of the book review discussed above.

Set B, Exercise 1: Thesis-Finding

Above, a distinction was made between the content of a book (the *topic*) and the interpretation or *thesis* of a book. The thesis will usually identify those forces, individuals, and relationships that the author considers most important for ex-plaining the events in question.

Below are a number of brief book summaries written by the authors them-selves, by editors, or reviewers.[9] Some of the summaries emphasize the material the book covers (the topic or content); others talk more about the author's argu-ments (the thesis); still others discuss both content and thesis.

Identify those abstracts that primarily summarize the content of the book by placing a "C" in the appropriate space. Identify those that emphasize the author's interpretation or thesis by writing a "T." For passages that describe both content and thesis write a "CT. " For all passages labeled "T" or "CT," underline the sentence or sentences that best represent the author's central thesis. Before doing this exer-cise you might want to review the discussion of topic and thesis on pages 107–108. For an example see Set A, Exercise 1, Number 1 on page 113.

_____ 1. *War in European History.* By Michael Howard. London, Oxford, and New York: Oxford University Press, 1976.

> This is a study of warfare as it has developed in Western Europe from the Dark Ages until the present day. In it I show not only how the techniques of warfare changed, but how they affected or were affected by social, economic, and technological develop-ments in the societies that employed them. I trace the growth and decay of the feudal organization of Western Europe for war; the rise of mercenary troops and their develop-ment into professions as the framework of the state became strong enough to keep them permanently employed; the connection between war and the development of European trade overseas; and the impact of the French Revolution on the military system of the ancien régime. I go on to show how the development of industrial technology and the social tensions within industrial states culminated in the two world wars, and end by summarizing the military situation of a continent kept at peace by a balance of nuclear terror.

_____ 2. *Lincoln at Gettysburg: The Words That Remade America.* By Garry Wills. New York: Simon and Schuster, 1992.

> The power of words has rarely been given a more compelling demonstration than in the Gettysburg Address. Lincoln was asked to memorialize the gruesome battle. Instead, he

---

[9]Numbers 1, 4, and 6 are taken from *The Journal of Modern History,* Vol. 51, (1979). The rest are taken from book covers and publicity brochures.

gave the whole nation "a new birth of freedom" in the space of a mere 272 words. His entire life and previous training, and his deep political experience went into this, his revolutionary masterpiece.

By examining both the address and Lincoln in their historical moment and cultural frame, Wills breathes new life into words we thought we knew, and reveals much about a president so mythologized but often misunderstood. Wills shows how Lincoln came to change the world and to effect an intellectual revolution, how his words had to and did complete the work of the guns, and how Lincoln wove a spell that has not yet been broken.

_____ 3. *The Coming Plague: Newly Emerging Diseases in a World Out of Balance.* By Laurie Garrett. New York: Penguin Books, 1995.

Unpurified drinking water. Improper use of antibiotics. Local warfare. Massive refugee migration. Changing social and environmental conditions around the world have fostered the spread of new and potentially devastating viruses and diseases—HIV, Lassa, Ebola, and others. Laurie Garrett takes you on a fifty-year journey through the world's battles with microbes and examines the worldwide conditions that have culminated in recurrent outbreaks of newly discovered diseases, epidemics of diseases migrating to new areas, and mutated old diseases that are no longer curable. She argues that it is not too late to take action to prevent the further onslaught of viruses and microbes, and offers possible solutions for a healthier future.

_____ 4. *Britain's Imperial Century, 1815-1914: A Study of Empire and Expansion.* By Ronald Hyam. New York: Harper & Row; Barnes & Noble Import Division, 1976.

This study integrates the formal British empire and areas of informal influence such as China, Japan, and Latin America. The Victorian drives toward expansion—economic, strategic, diplomatic, and cultural—are considered, with Palmerston cast in a key role. Part 1 establishes an overall chronological framework for the whole century of . . . activity and analyzes the way the empire was run. Part 2 consists of seven regional chapters. Territorial acquisition is regarded as the result of an interlocking between two different levels of motive: a metropolitan level, concerned with high politics and prestige, and a local one, more concerned with selfish interests. At both levels the export of surplus sexual energy (often sublimated) is seen to be more important than the export of surplus capital; the private lives of empire builders are investigated. Other topics explored include relations with the United States, Asian and African resistance, sport, freemasonry, and the racial attitudes and educational theories of the British political elite. The book is based on close references to monographic material old and new, and for the period 1880-1914 (seen as "the search for stability") draws also on my own research.

_____ 5. *The Rise of the Nazis.* By Conan Fischer. Manchester: Manchester University Press, 1995.

Conan Fischer examines the history of the Nazis in Germany. Beginning with an overview of the historical context within which Nazism grew, Fischer considers the foreign relations, politics and society of Weimar [1919-33] as well as the role of the elites in the rise of Nazism. He analyzes the anatomy of Nazism itself. What lent its ideology coherence and credibility? What distinguished the Nazis' program from their competitors' and how did they project it so effectively? How was Hitler able to put together and fund an organization so quickly and effectively that it could launch a sustained assault on Weimar? Who suppported the Nazis and what were their motives? Where, precisely, does Nazism belong in the history of Europe? In concise, readable chapters, the book offers an essential rethinking of these complex issues.

_____ 6. *The Origins of the Marshall Plan.* By John Gimbel. Stanford, Calif. : Stanford University Press, 1976.

Based on American and German primary sources, this study argues that the Marshall Plan is traceable to certain decisions on German recovery that George C. Marshall and Ernest Bevin made in April 1947, during the Moscow Council of Foreign Ministers. The larger European recovery program, called forth by Marshall on June 5, 1947, was an effort to gain political acceptance for those decisions in Europe and America. Current theories about the open door, multilateralism, and containment of Russia notwithstanding, the Marshall Plan was a series of pragmatic political and bureaucratic compromises to solve the economic problems of the German occupation. In the end, Americans provided economic aid—either directly or through Germany—to many of the nations that had expected to use German reparations and cheap German exports for their postwar recovery programs. As after the First World War, the United States helped Germany to settle its reparation obligations.

Set B, Exercise 2: Analysis of an Article

See Set A, Exercise 2.

Set B, Exercise 3: Writing the Précis

Read Writing Capsule 4 (in Set A, Exercise 3), and, on a separate sheet of paper, write a brief précis (no longer than one page, typed or word-processed, double spaced) of Edmund S. Morgan's, "The Puritans and Sex."

Edmund S. Morgan, "The Puritans and Sex"
The New England Quarterly XV (December 1942), 591–607. Reprinted by permission.

¶1 Henry Adams once observed that Americans have "ostentatiously ignored" sex. He could think of only two American writers who touched upon the subject with any degree of boldness—Walt Whitman and Bret Harte. Since the time when Adams made this penetrating observation, American writers have been making up for lost time in a way that would make Bret Harte, if not Whitman, blush. And yet there is still more truth than falsehood in Adams's statement. Americans, by comparison with Europeans or Asiatics, are squeamish when confronted with the facts of life. My purpose is not to account for this squeamishness, but simply to point out that the Puritans, those bogeymen of the modern intellectual, are not responsible for it.

¶2 At the outset, consider the Puritan's attitude toward marriage and the role of sex in marriage. The popular assumption might be that the Puritans frowned on marriage and tried to hush up the physical aspect of it as much as possible, but listen to what they themselves had to say. Samuel Willard, minister of the Old South Church in the latter part of the seventeenth century and author of the most complete textbook of Puritan divinity, more than once expressed his horror at "that Popish conceit of the Excellency of Virginity."[1] Another minister, John Cotton, wrote that

> Women are Creatures without which there is no comfortable Living for man: it is true of them what is wont to be said of Governments, That bad ones are better than none: They are a sort of Blasphemers then who dispise and decry them, and call them a necessary Evil, for they are a necessary Good.[2]

These sentiments did not arise from an interpretation of marriage as a spiritual partnership, in which sexual intercourse was a minor or incidental matter. Cotton gave his opinion of "Platonic love" when he recalled the case of

> one who immediately upon marriage, without ever approaching the Nuptial Bed, indented with the Bride, that by mutual consent they might both live such a life, and according did sequestring themselves according to the custom of those times, from the rest of mankind, and afterwards from one another too, in their retired Cells, giving themselves up to a Contemplative life; and this is recorded as an instance of no little or ordinary Vertue; but I must be pardoned in it, if I can account it no other than an effort of blind zeal, for they are the dictates of a blind mind they follow therein, and not of that Holy Spirit, which saith *It is not good that man should be alone.*[3]

¶3 Here is as healthy an attitude as one could hope to find anywhere. Cotton certainly cannot be accused of ignoring human nature. Nor was he an isolated example among the Puritans. Another minister stated plainly that "the Use of the Marriage Bed" is "founded in mans Nature," and that consequently any withdrawal from sexual intercourse upon the part of husband or wife "Denies all relief in Wedlock vnto Human necessity: and sends it for supply vnto Beastiality when God gives not the gift of Continency."[4] In other words, sexual intercourse was a human necessity and marriage the only proper supply for it. These were the views of the New England clergy, the acknowledged leaders of the community, the most Puritanical of the Puritans. As proof that their congregations concurred with them, one may cite the case in which the members of the First Church of Boston expelled James Mattock because, among other offenses, "he denied Coniugall fellowship vnto his wife for the space of 2 years together vpon pretense of taking Revenge upon himself for his abusing of her before marryage."[5] So strongly did the Puritans insist upon the sexual character of marriage that one New Englander considered himself slandered when it was reported, "that he Brock his deceased wife's hart with Greife, that he wold be absent from her 3 weeks together when he was at home, and wold never come nere her, and such Like."[6]

¶4 There was just one limitation which the Puritans placed upon sexual relations in marriage; sex must not interfere with religion. Man's chief end was to glorify God, and all earthly delights must promote that end, not hinder it. Love for a wife was carried too far when it led a man to neglect his God:

> . . . sometimes a man hath a good affection to Religion, but the love of his wife carries him away, a man may bee so transported to his wife, that hee dare not bee forward in Religion, lest hee displease his wife, and so the wife, lest

shee displease her husband, and this is an inordinate love, when it exceeds measure.[7]

Sexual pleasures, in this respect, were treated like other kinds of pleasure. On a day of fast, when all comforts were supposed to be foregone in behalf of religious contemplation, not only were tasty food and drink to be abandoned but sexual intercourse, too. On other occasions, when food, drink, and recreation were allowable, sexual intercourse was allowable too, though of course only between persons who were married to each other. The Puritans were not ascetics; they never wished to prevent the enjoyment of earthly delights. They merely demanded that the pleasures of the flesh be subordinated to the greater glory of God: husband and wife must not become "so transported with affection, that they look at no higher end than marriage it self." "Let such as have wives," said the ministers, "look at them not for their own ends, but to be fitted for Gods service, and bring them nearer to God."[8]

¶5 Toward sexual intercourse outside marriage the Puritans were as frankly hostile as they were favorable to it in marriage. They passed laws to punish adultery with death, and fornication with whipping. Yet they had no misconceptions as to the capacity of human beings to obey such laws. Although the laws were commands of God, it was only natural—since the fall of Adam—for human beings to break them. Breaches must be punished lest the community suffer the wrath of God, but no offense, sexual or otherwise, could be occasion for surprise or for hushed tones of voice. How calmly the inhabitants of seventeenth-century New England could Contemplate rape or attempted rape is evident in the following testimony offered before the Middlesex County Court of Massachusetts:

> The examination of Edward Wire taken the 7th of october and alsoe Zachery Johnson, who sayeth that Edward Wires mayd beingsent into the towne about busenes meeting with a man that dogd hir from about Joseph Kettles house to goody marches. She came into William Johnsones and desired Zachery Johnson to goe home with her for that the man dogd hir. accordingly he went with her and being then as far as Samuell Phips his house the man over tooke them. which man cared himselfe by the name of peter grant would have led the mayd but she oposed itt three times: and coming to Edward Wires house the said grant would have kist hir but she refused itt: wire being at prayer grant dragd the mayd between the said wiers and Nathanill frothinghams house. hee then flung the mayd downe in the streete and got atop hir; Johnson seeing it hee caled vppon the fellow to be sivill and not abuse the mayd then Edward wire came forth and ran to the said grant and took hold of him asking him what he did to his mayd, the said grant asked whether she was his wife for he did nothing to his wife: the said grant swearing he would be the death of the said wire. when he came of the mayd; he swore he would bring ten men to pul down his house and soe ran away and they followed him as far as good[y] phipses house where they mett with John Terry and George Chin with clubs in there hands and soe they went away together. Zachy Johnson going to Constable Heamans, and wire going home. there came John Terry to his house to ask for beer and grant was in the streete but afterward departed into the towne, both Johnson and Wire both aferme that when grant was vppon the mayd she cryed out severall times.

> Deborah hadlocke being examined sayth that she mett with the man that
> cals himselfe peeter grant about good prichards that he dogd hir and followed
> hir to hir masters and there threw hir downe and lay vppon hir but had not the
> use of hir body but swore several othes that he would ly with hir and gett hir
> with child before she got home.
>
> Grant being present denys all saying he was drunk and did not know what
> he did. [9]

¶6   The Puritans became inured to sexual offenses, because there were so many. The impression which one gets from reading the records of seventeenth-century New England courts is that illicit sexual intercourse was fairly common. The testimony given in cases of fornication and adultery—by far the most numerous class of criminal cases in the records—suggests that many of the early New Englanders possessed a high degree of virility and very few inhibitions. Besides the case of Peter Grant, take the testimony of Elizabeth Knight about the manner of Richard Nevars's advances toward her:

> The last publique day of Thanksgiving (in the year 1674) in the evening as I
> was milking Richard Nevars came to me, and offered me abuse in putting his
> hand, under my coates, but I turning aside with much adoe, saved my self, and
> when I was settled to milking he agen took me by the shoulder and pulled me
> backward almost, but I clapped one hand on the Ground and held fast the
> Cows teatt with the other hand, and cryed out, and then came to mee Jonathan
> Abbot one of my Masters Servants, whome the said Never asked wherefore he
> came, the said Abbot said to look after you, what you doe unto the Maid, but
> the said Never bid Abbot goe about his businesse but I bade the lad to stay. [10]

¶7 One reason for the abundance of sexual offenses was the number of men in the colonies who were unable to gratify their sexual desires in marriage.[11] Many of the first settlers had wives in England. They had come to the new world to make a fortune, expecting either to bring their families after them or to return to England with some of the riches of America. Although these men left their wives behind, they brought their sexual appetites with them; and in spite of laws which required them to return to their families, they continued to stay, and more continued to arrive, as indictments against them throughout the seventeenth century clearly indicate.

Servants formed another group of men, and of women too, who could not ordinarily find supply for human necessity within the bounds of marriage. Most servants lived in the homes of their masters and could not marry without their consent, a consent which was not likely to be given unless the prospective husband or wife also belonged to the master's household. This situation will be better understood if it is recalled that most servants at this time were engaged by contract for a stated period. They were, in the language of the time, covenant servants, who had agreed to stay with their masters for a number of years in return for a specified recompense, such as transportation to New England or education in some trade (the latter, of course, were known more specifically as apprentices). Even hired servants who worked for wages were usually single, for as soon as a man had enough money to buy or build a house of his own and to get married, he would set up in farming or trade for himself. It must be emphasized, however, that anyone who was not in business for himself was necessarily a servant. The economic organization of seventeenth-century New England had no place for the independent proletarian workman with a family of his own. All production was carried on in the household by the master of the family and his servants, so that most men were either servants or masters of servants; and the former, of course, were more numerous than the latter. Probably most of the inhabitants of Puritan New England could remember a time when they had been servants.

¶8 Theoretically no servant had a right to a private life. His time, day or night, belonged to his master, and both religion and law required that he obey his master scrupulously.[12] But neither religion nor law could restrain the sexual impulses of youth, and if those impulses could not be expressed in marriage, they had to be given vent outside marriage. Servants had little difficulty in finding the occasions. Though they might be kept at work all day, it was easy enough to slip away at night. Once out of the house, there were several ways of meeting with a maid. The simplest way was to go to her bed-chamber, if she was so fortunate as to have a private one of her own. Thus Jock, Mr. Solomon Phipps's Negro man, confessed in court

> that on the sixteenth day of May 1682, in the morning, betweene 12 and one of the clock, he did force open the back doores of the House of Laurence Hammond in Charlestowne, and came in to the House, and went up into the garret to Marie the Negro.
>
> He doth likewise acknowledge that one night the last week he forced into the House the same way, and went up to the Negro Woman Marie and that the like he hath done at severall other times before.[13]

Joshua Fletcher took a more romantic way of visiting his lady:

> Joshua Fletcher . . . doth confess and acknowledge that three severall nights after bedtime, he went into Mr Fiskes Dwelling house at Chelmsford, at an open window by a ladder that he brought with him. the said windo opening into a chamber, whose was the lodging place of Gresill Juell servant to mr. Fiske. and there he kept company with the said mayd. she sometimes having her cloathes on, and one time he found her in her bed.[14]

Sometimes a maidservant might entertain callers in the parlor while the family were sleeping upstairs. John Knight described what was perhaps a common experience for masters. The crying of his child awakened him in the middle of the night, and he called to his maid, one Sarah Crouch, who was supposed to be sleeping with the child. Receiving no answer, he arose and

> went down the stayres, and at the stair foot, the latch of doore was pulled in. I called severall times and at the last said if shee would not open the dore, I would breake it open, and when shee opened the doore shee was all undressed and Sarah Largin with her undressed, also the said Sarah went out of doores and Dropped some of her clothes as shee went out. I enquired of Sarah Crouch what men they were, which was with them. Shee made mee no answer for some space of time, but at last shee told me Peeter Brigs was with them, I asked her whether Thomas Jones was not there, but shee would give mee no answer.[15]

In the temperate climate of New England it was not always necessary to seek out a maid at her home. Rachel Smith was seduced in an open field "about nine of the clock at night, being darke, neither moone nor starrs shineing." She was walking through the field when she met a man who

asked her where shee lived, and what her name was and shee told him, and
then shee asked his name, and he told her Saijing that he was old Good-man
Shepards man. Also shee saith he gave her strong liquors, and told her that it
was not the first time he had been with maydes after his master was in bed. [16]

¶9 Sometimes, of course, it was not necessary for a servant to go outside his master's
house in order to satisfy his sexual urges. Many cases of fornication are on record
between servants living in the same house. Even where servants had no private
bedroom, even where the whole family slept in a single room, it was not impossible to
make love. In fact many love affairs must have had their consummation upon a bed in
which other people were sleeping. Take for example the case of Sarah Lepingwell.
When Sarah was brought into court for having an illegitimate child, she related that one
night when her master's brother, Thomas Hawes, was visiting the family, she went to bed
early. Later, after Hawes had gone to bed, he called to her to get him a pipe of tobacco.
After refusing for some time,

> at the last I arose and did lite his pipe and cam and lay doune one my one bead
> and smoaked about half the pip and siting vp in my bead to guie him his pip
> my bead being a trundell bead at the sid of his bead he reached beyond the pip
> and Cauth me by the wrist and pulled me on the side of his bead but I biding
> him let me goe he bid me hold my peas and folks wold here me and if it be
> replyed come why did you not call out I Ansar I was posesed with fear of my
> master least my master should think I did it only to bring a scandall on his
> brothar and thinking they wold all beare witness agaynst me but the thing is
> true that he did then begete me with child at that tim and the Child is Thomas
> Hauses and noe mans but his.

In his defense Hawes offered the testimony of another man who was sleeping "on the
same side of the bed," but the jury nevertheless accepted Sarah's story. [17]

¶10 The fact that Sarah was intimidated by her master's brother suggests that maidser-
vants may have been subject to sexual abuse by their masters. The records show that
sometimes masters did take advantage of their position to force unwanted attentions
upon their female servants. The case of Elizabeth Dickerman is a good example. She
complained to the Middlesex County Court,

> against her master John Harris senior for profiring abus to her by way of
> forsing her to be naught with him: . . . he has tould her that if she tould her
> dame: what cariag he did show to her shee had as good be hanged and shee
> replyed that shee would run away and he sayd run the way is befor you: . . .
> she says if she should liwe ther shee shall be in fear of her lif. [18]

The court accepted Elizabeth's complaint and ordered her master to be whipped twenty
stripes.

¶11 So numerous did cases of fornication and adultery become in seventeenth-century
New England that the problem of caring for the children of extramarital unions was a
serious one. The Puritans solved it, but in such a way as to increase rather than decrease
the temptation to sin. In 1668, the General Court of Massachusetts ordered:

that where any man is legally convicted to be the Father of a Bastard childe, he shall be at the care and charge to maintain and bring up the same, by such assistance of the Mother as nature requireth, and as the Court from time to time (according to circumstances) shall see meet to Order: and in case the Father of a Bastard, by confession or other manifest proof, upon trial of the case, do not appear to the Courts satisfaction, then the Man charged by the Woman to be the Father, shee holding constant in it, (especially being put upon the real discovery of the truth of it in the time of her Travail) shall be the reputed Father, and accordingly be liable to the charge of maintenance as aforesaid (though not to other punishment) notwithstanding his denial, unless the circumstances of the case and pleas be such, on the behalf of the man charged, as that the Court that have the cognizance thereon shall see reason to acquit him, and otherwise dispose of the Childe and education thereof. [19]

As a result of this law a girl could give way to temptation without the fear of having to care for an illegitimate child by herself. Furthermore, she could, by a little simple lying, spare her lover the expense of supporting the child. When Elizabeth Wells bore a child, less than a year after this statute was passed, she laid it to James Tufts, her master's son. Goodman Tufts affirmed that Andrew Robinson, servant to Goodman Dexter, was the real father, and he brought the following testimony as evidence:

Wee Elizabeth Jefts aged 15 ears and Mary tufts aged 14 ears doe testyfie that their being one at our hous sumtime the last winter who sayed that thear was a new law made concerning bastards that If aney man wear aqused with a bastard and the woman which had aqused him did stand vnto it in her labor that he should bee the reputed father of it and should mayntaine it Elizabeth Wells hearing of the sayd law she sayed vnto vs that If shee should bee with Child shee would bee sure to lay it vn to won who was rich enough abell to mayntayne it wheather it wear his or no and shee farder sayed Elizabeth Jefts would not you doe so likewise If it weare your case and I sayed no by no means for right must tacke place: and the sayd Elizabeth wells sayed If it wear my Caus I think I should doe so. [20]

A tragic unsigned letter that somehow found its way into the files of the Middlesex County Court gives more direct evidence of the practice which Elizabeth Wells professed:

der loue i remember my loue to you hoping your welfar and i hop to imbras the but now i rit to you to let you nowe that i am a child by you and i wil ether kil it or lay it to an other and you shal have no blame at al for I haue had many children and none have none of them… [i. e., none of their fathers is supporting any of them.] [21]

¶12 In face of the wholesale violation of the sexual codes to which all these cases give testimony, the Puritans could not maintain the severe penalties which their laws provided. Although cases of adultery occurred every year, the death penalty is not known to have been applied more than three times. The usual punishment was a whipping or a fine, or both, and perhaps a branding, combined with a symbolical execution in the form of standing on the gallows for an hour with a rope about the neck. Fornication met with a lighter whipping or a lighter fine, while rape was treated in the same way as adultery. Though the Puritans established a code of laws which

demanded perfection—which demanded, in other words, strict obedience to the will of
God, they nevertheless knew that frail human beings could never live up to the code.
When fornication, adultery, rape, or even buggery and sodomy appeared, they were not
surprised, nor were they so severe with the offenders as their codes of law would lead
one to believe. Sodomy, to be sure, they usually punished with death; but rape, adultery,
and fornication they regarded as pardonable human weaknesses, all the more likely to
appear in a religious community, where the normal course of sin was stopped by
wholesome laws. Governor Bradford in recounting the details of an epidemic of sexual
misdemeanors in Plymouth, wrote resignedly:

> it may be in this case as it is with waters when their streames are stopped or
> damned up, when they gett passage they flow with more violence, and make
> more noys and disturbance, then when they are suffered to rune quietly in
> their owne chanels. So wickednes being here more stopped by strict laws, and
> the same more nerly looked unto, so as it cannot rune in a comone road of
> liberty as it would, and is inclined, it searches every wher, and at last breaks out
> wher it getts vente. [22]

¶13 The estimate of human capacities here expressed led the Puritans not only to deal
leniently with sexual offenses but also to take every precaution to prevent such offenses, rather than wait for the necessity of punishment. One precaution was to see that
children got married as soon as possible. The wrong way to promote virtue, the Puritans
thought, was to "ensnare" children in vows of virginity, as the Catholics did. As a result
of such vows, children, "not being able to contain," would be guilty of "unnatural
pollutions, and other filthy practices in secret: and too oft of horrid Murthers of the fruit
of their bodies," said Thomas Cobbett.[23] The way to avoid fornication and perversion was
for parents to provide suitable husbands and wives for their children:

> Lot was to blame that looked not out seasonably for some fit matches for his
> two daughters, which had formerly minded marriage (witness the contract
> between them and two men in Sodom, called therfore for his Sons in Law,
> which had married his daughters, Gen. 19. 14.) for they seeing no man like to
> come into them in a conjugall way . . . then they plotted that incestuous course,
> whereby their Father was so highly dishonoured . . .[24]

¶14 As marriage was the way to prevent fornication, successful marriage was the way to
prevent adultery. The Puritans did not wait for adultery to appear; instead, they took
every means possible to make husbands and wives live together and respect each other.
If a husband deserted his wife and remained within the jurisdiction of a Puritan government, he was promptly sent back to her. Where the wife had been left in England, the
offense did not always come to light until the wayward husband had committed
fornication or bigamy, and of course there must have been many offenses which never
came to light. But where both husband and wife lived in New England, neither had
much chance of leaving the other without being returned by order of the county court
at its next sitting. When John Smith of Medfield left his wife and went to live with
Patience Rawlins, he was sent home poorer by ten pounds and richer by thirty stripes.
Similarly Mary Drury, who deserted her husband on the pretense that he was impotent,
failed to convince the court that he actually was so, and had to return to him as well as
to pay a fine of five pounds. The wife of Phillip Pointing received lighter treatment:
when the court thought that she had overstayed her leave in Boston, they simply

ordered her "to depart the Towne and goe to Tanton to her husband. "The courts, moreover, were not satisfied with mere cohabitation; they insisted that it be peaceful cohabitation. Husbands and wives were forbidden by law to strike one another, and the law was enforced on numerous occasions. But the courts did not stop there. Henry Flood was required to give bond for good behavior because he had abused his wife simply by "ill words calling her whore and cursing of her. "The wife of Christopher Collins was presented for railing at her husband and calling him "Gurley gutted divill. " Apparently in this case the court thought that Mistress Collins was right, for although the fact was proved by two witnesses, she was discharged. On another occasion the court favored the husband: Jacob Pudeator, fined for striking and kicking his wife, had the sentence moderated when the court was informed that she was a woman "of great provocation."[25]

¶15 Wherever there was strong suspicion that an illicit relation might arise between two persons, the authorities removed the temptation by forbidding the two to come together. As early as November, 1630, the Court of Assistants of Massachusetts prohibited a Mr. Clark from "cohabitacion and frequent keepeing company with Mrs. Freeman, vnder paine of such punishment as the Court shall thinke meete to inflict. " Mr. Clark and Mr. Freeman were both bound "in XX £ apeece that Mr. Clearke shall make his personall appearance att the nexte Court to be holden in March nexte, and in the meane tyme to carry himselfe in good behaviour towards all people and espetially towards Mrs. Freeman, concerneing whome there is stronge suspicion of incontinency. " Forty-five years later the Suffolk County Court took the same kind of measure to protect the husbands of Dorchester from the temptations offered by the daughter of Robert Spurr. Spurr was presented by the grand jury

> for entertaining persons at his house at unseasonable times both by day and night to the greife of theire wives and Relations &c The Court having heard what was alleaged and testified against him do Sentence him to bee admonish't and to pay Fees of Court and charge him upon his perill not to entertain any married men to keepe company with his daughter especially James Minott and Joseph Belcher.

In like manner Walter Hickson was forbidden to keep company with Mary Bedwell, "And if at any time hereafter hee bee taken in company of the saide Mary Bedwell without other company to bee forthwith apprehended by the Constable and to be whip't with ten stripes. " Elizabeth Wheeler and Joanna Peirce were admonished "for theire disorderly carriage in the house of Thomas Watts being married women and founde sitting in other mens Laps with theire Armes about theire Necks. " How little confidence the Puritans had in human nature is even more clearly displayed by another case, in which Edmund Maddock and his wife were brought to court "to answere to all such matters as shalbe objected against them concerning Haarkwoody and Ezekiell Euerells being at their house at unseasonable tyme of the night and her being up with them after her husband was gone to bed. " Haarkwoody and Everell had been found "by the Constable Henry Bridghame about tenn of the Clock at night sitting by the fyre at the house of Edmond Maddocks with his wyfe a suspicious weoman her husband being on sleepe [sic] on the bead. " A similar distrust of human ability to resist temptation is evident in the following order of the Connecticut Particular Court:

James Hallett is to returne from the Correction house to his master Barclyt, who is to keepe him to hard labor, and course dyet during the pleasure of the Court provided that Barclet is first to remove his daughter from his family, before the sayd James enter therein.

These precautions, as we have already seen, did not eliminate fornication, adultery, or other sexual offenses, but they doubtless reduced the number from what it would otherwise have been. [26]

¶16 In sum, the Puritan attitude toward sex, though directed by a belief in absolute, God-given moral values, never neglected human nature. The rules of conduct which the Puritans regarded as divinely ordained had been formulated for men, not for angels and not for beasts. God had created mankind in two sexes; He had ordained marriage as desirable for all, and sexual intercourse as essential to marriage. On the other hand, He had forbidden sexual intercourse outside of marriage. These were the moral principles which the Puritans sought to enforce in New England. But in their enforcement they took cognizance of human nature. They knew well enough that human beings since the fall of Adam were incapable of obeying perfectly the laws of God. Consequently, in the endeavor to enforce those laws they treated offenders with patience and understanding, and concentrated their efforts on prevention more than on punishment. The result was not a society in which most of us would care to live, for the methods of prevention often caused serious interference with personal liberty. It must nevertheless be admitted that in matters of sex the Puritans showed none of the blind zeal or narrow-minded bigotry which is too often supposed to have been characteristic of them. The more one learns about these people, the less do they appear to have resembled the sad and sour portraits which their modern critics have drawn of them.

Notes
[1]Samuel Willard, *A Compleat Body of Divinity* (Boston, 1726), 125 and 608–613.
[2]John Cotton, *A Meet Help* (Boston, 1699), 14–15.
[3]*A Meet Help*, 16.
[4]Edward Taylor, *Commonplace Book* (manuscript in the library of the Massachusetts Historical Society).
[5]Records of the First Church in Boston (manuscript copy in the library of the Massachusetts Historical Society), 12.
[6]Middlesex County Court Files, folder 42.
[7]John Cotton, *A Practical Commentary…upon the First Epistle Generall of John* (London, 1656), 126.
[8]*A Practical Commentary,* 126.
[9]Middlesex Files, folder 48.
[10]Middlesex Files, folder 71.
[11]Another reason was suggested by Charles Francis Adams in his scholarly article, "Some Phases of Sexual Morality and Church Discipline in Colonial New England," Proceedings of the Massachusetts Historical Society, XXVI, 477–516.
[12]On the position of servants in early New England see *More Books,* XVII (September, 1942), 311–328.
[13]Middlesex Files, folder 99.
[14]Middlesex Files, folder 47.
[15]Middlesex Files, folder 52.
[16]Middlesex Files, folder 44.
[17]Middlesex Files, folder 47.
[18]Middlesex Files, folder 94.
[19]William H. Whitmore, editor, *The Colonial Laws of Massachusetts.* Reprinted from the Edition of 1660 (Boston, 1889), 257.

[20]Middlesex Files, folder 52.

[21]Middlesex Files, folder 30.

[22]William Bradford, *History of Plymouth Plantation* (Boston, 1912), II, 309.

[23]Thomas Cobbett, *A Fruitfull and Usefull Discourse touching the Honour due from Children to Parents and the Duty of Parents toward their Children* (London, 1656), 174.

[24]Cobbett, 177.

[25]Samuel E. Morison and Zechariah Chafee, editors, Records of the Suffolk County Court, 1671–1680, *Publications of the Colonial Society of Massachusetts,* XXIX and XXX, 121, 410, 524, 837–841, and 1158; George F. Dow, editor, *Records and Files of the Quarterly Courts of Essex County, Massachusetts* (Salem, 1911–1921), I, 274; and V, 377.

[26]*Records of the Suffolk County Court,* 422–443 and 676; John Noble, editor, *Records of the Court of Assistants of the Colony of Massachusetts Bay* (Boston, 1901–1928), II, 8; *Records of the Particular Court of Connecticut, Collections of the Connecticut Historical Society,* XXII, 20; and a photostat in the library of the Massachusetts Historical Society, dated March 29, 1653.

CHAPTER 8   HISTORY ON FILM

"The camera never lies."
                    Conventional wisdom

"Of course the camera lies."
                    The authors

"History is the enemy of art."
                    Edward Anhalt[1]

"Art is the enemy of history."
                    The authors

On December 8, 1941, President Franklin Roosevelt declared to Congress that December 7, the day of the surprise Japanese attack on the U. S. naval base at Pearl Harbor, was "a date which will live in infamy." With that, the United States entered World War II, a titanic struggle that would require the mobilization of millions of American men and women into the armed services.

War is rarely popular, especially in modern democracies. So one of the most urgent tasks faced by the military was to convince an increasingly educated citizenry—especially those involuntarily drafted into the army—that the cause they were fighting for was a just one. At first the army tried lecturing the inductees about the reasons for the war, highlighting the nobility of the Allies' cause (America was now fighting in tandem with Great Britain and Russia against Germany and Japan) and the iniquity of the enemy's cause. The lectures were a total failure. The troops were bored and unresponsive.

At this point the army chief of staff, General George Marshall, decided to try something different: film. In the 1930s *Triumph of the Will* (1935), a German film glorifying Adolf Hitler and the Nazis, had shown the world the effectiveness of film as a propaganda tool. Marshall, deciding to fight fire with fire, asked the already-famous Hollywood director Frank Capra (whose films include *It Happened One Night* and *Mr. Smith Goes to Washington*) to make series of film documentaries to show Americans what they were fighting for—and against. Capra, a Sicilian-born immigrant who passionately believed in the American dream, was reluctant at first, but he finally agreed to make "the best damned documentary films ever made."[2] The result was the *Why We Fight* series, seven films that told the story of the war up to that point in time: *Prelude to War, The Nazis Strike, Divide and Conquer, The Battle of Britain, The Battle of Russia, The Battle of China,* and *War Comes to America.*

---

[1]Quoted in John E. O'Connor, ed. , *Image as Artifact: The Historical Analysis of Film and Television* (Malabar, Fla.: Robert E. Krieger Publishing Co. , 1990), 35.
[2]John Dower, *War Without Mercy* (New York: Pantheon, 1986), 15. On the making of the films see David Culbert, "'Why We Fight': Social Engineering for a Democratic Society at War," *Film and Radio Propaganda in World War II,* ed. by K. R. M. Short (London: Croom Helm, 1983), 173–191.

The series was successful beyond General Marshall's wildest hopes. Capra used Disney maps, witty narration, and miles of graphic war footage—often captured from the enemy—to appeal to the emotions of his audience. The series was based on a strategy of truth: "Let the enemy," said Capra, "prove to our soldiers the enormity of his cause—and the justness of ours."[3] The films were so good that they were shown in public theaters as well as on military bases, and they ultimately were distributed worldwide, with translations in Russian, French, Chinese, and Spanish. The power of the films is most poignantly conveyed by Alfred Kazin, a son of Russian immigrants, who described the affect of seeing *The Battle of Russia* at an army camp in southern Illinois in 1944. "It was a physical shock," recounted Kazin thirty-five years later, "walking out of the theater in the gray dripping twilight, watching the men plodding back to their barracks in the last slant of light, to realize how drained I was, how much I had been worked over, appealed to. In the end, as so often happened to us after a terrific American movie, we were stupefied."[4]

Kazin's experience in 1944 captures perfectly the power of film both to inform and to move us deeply. History, as we have seen, is a discipline primarily based on the written word, and in Kazin's day, history on film was something of a novelty. Not so today. Increasingly people are turning to movies and TV for their entertainment and information, and often what people think they know about history is as likely to have been learned from films and television as from books. This is not altogether a bad thing, given the growing body of respectable historical video and film produced in recent years (e.g., Ken Burns's series on the Civil War). It is not entirely a good thing either, as we shall argue. But whether the trend is welcome or not is immaterial. Moving-image history is here to stay, and history instructors have recognized this by incorporating a variety of films and videos into their history classes.

Historians and students of history should become as adept at "reading" and analyzing film and video history as they are at evaluating the more traditional written historical accounts. In this chapter we will provide a brief introduction to the critical analysis of film documentaries as well as more mainstream Hollywood productions. (Although there are technical and perceptual differences between videotape and film, we include both media in our references to "film.") Although space limitations prevent us from doing more than scratching the surface of this immense topic, interested readers will find more detailed guidance in the sources listed in the footnotes of this chapter.[5]

"A rose is a rose is a rose," said Gertrude Stein. The same cannot be said of a film. Films vary widely in character, and historians use films in quite distinctive ways. Before viewing and analyzing a film it is important to understand the type of film you are viewing and the perspective your instructor wants you to take. To begin it is important to distinguish between film as record, film as representation, and film as cultural artifact.

---

[3]Dower, *War Without Mercy,* 16.

[4]Culbert, "Why We Fight," *Propaganda,* 185–86.

[5]The amount of scholarship devoted to history in films and television programs is growing exponentially, and a single chapter in a book such as this can do no more than provide a few flimsy guideposts for those who want to think more seriously about the merits and drawbacks of moving-image history. Both students and instructors could benefit from reading some of the essays published in O'Connor, *Image as Artifact,* and in Steven Mintz and Randy Roberts, eds., *Hollywood's America: United States History Through Its Films* (St. James, N.Y.: Brandywine Press, 1993). For instructors a place to begin would be John O'Connor and Martin A. Jackson, *Teaching History with Film* (Washington, D.C.: AHA, 1974). An excellent recent addition is Mark C. Carnes, ed., *Past Imperfect: History According to the Movies* (New York: Henry Holt and Co. , 1995).

Film as Record

On the most basic level, film can provide a visual record of an event. Taped footage on the nightly news, amateur videos/films of important events (e.g. Abraham Zapruder's Super-8 film of the Kennedy assassination), and the raw footage taken by documentary filmmakers can provide the historian with an invaluable visual record of the personalities and events that have shaped our century. At this level, film is the equivalent of a primary source—the raw material out of which historians construct their accounts of the past.

However, even when dealing with "actuality footage," historians must not let down their guard, for cameras can indeed lie. First, every piece of film is shot from a specific location, showing some things but not others. Therefore, the historian must always consider what *wasn't* in the viewfinder. Furthermore, it is a rare piece of film that hasn't been edited (cut) to fit time constraints, eliminate unwanted material, or conform to a censor's mandate.[6] Taped television interviews are often edited down from hours of footage to the few minutes that are actually put on the air. In the 1930s and 1940s there was a tacit agreement among news professionals *not* to show that President Franklin Delano Roosevelt was confined to a wheelchair due to an earlier bout with polio. When FDR's disability was filmed, that footage was edited out before the newsreels were released to the public.[7] Finally, visual evidence can be (and has been) falsified. The advent of digital computer technology has made this easier to do today than ever before.

Film as Representation

More complex are those films, crafted by filmmakers, intended to represent a segment of the past. Representational films are carefully scripted and produced historical reconstructions, and, as such, are the visual equivalent of secondary sources. These films attempt to narrate and explain events in a manner analogous to books and essays. Historical *documentaries,* such as Ken Burns's *The Civil War* and *Baseball,* often use actual film footage and photos interlaced with interviews to tell their story. *Docudramas,* on the other hand, attempt to recreate a segment of the past using actors and modern movie-making magic. Some of these films try—sometimes successfully, sometimes not—to tell a "true" story. *The Return of Martin Guerre, Henry V, Reds, The Longest Day, JFK, Malcolm X, Nixon,* and *Titanic* are good examples. We would also include in this category films that, though essentially fictional, attempt to present a defensibly accurate portrait of a piece of the past—*Platoon* (the Vietnam War), *Das Boot* (submarine warfare during World War II), *The Grapes of Wrath* (the Dustbowl migrants during the Great Depression), and *Saving Private Ryan* (the D-Day invasion and the Battle of Normandy).[8]

---

[6]Even in countries that value freedom of the press, there are societal and institutional constraints that have the end result of limiting and coloring what is presented to the public in the mainstream media. For an analysis of the ability of political and economic elites to manage the media, see Daniel Hellinger and Dennis Judd, *The Democratic Facade,* 2nd ed. (Belmont, Calif.: Wadsworth Publishing Co., 1994), chapter 3, *Political Elites and the Media.*

[7]Robert E. Herzstein, "News Film and Documentary as Sources for Factual Information," in O'Connor, *Image as Artifact,* 180.

[8]Historical films have become so popular that various historical journals now feature regular film review sections. The historical accuracy of over seventy such films is discussed by a variety of historians in Mark Carnes, ed., *Past Imperfect: History According to the Movies.*

Many docudramas play fast and loose with the facts, and therefore need to be evaluated carefully and critically. However, we more easily tend to accept documentaries at face value, since they use original film footage, photographs, and interviews with participants, eyewitnesses, and academic experts. But even documentaries must be scrutinized with the same skepticism as Hollywood potboilers. Documentaries are still constructions that present a filmmaker's point of view, and are as much in need of critical analysis and commentary as any written version of history.

Film as Cultural Artifact

Finally, films of all types—whatever their historical content—can be viewed as *cultural artifacts* that can teach us something about the values, behaviors, preoccupations, and myths of the periods in which they were made. Here we have come full circle. Just as raw documentary footage can be considered a primary source, all films, whether made to educate or entertain, are primary sources when used as evidence for the cultural conditions and attitudes of the societies that made and viewed the films. For example, D. W. Griffith's *Birth of a Nation* (1915), which portrays the post–Civil War South and the rise of the Ku Klux Klan, would be a *secondary* source if we were interested in how it represented the Reconstruction period of American history. It would be a *primary* source, however, if we were viewing it a cultural artifact useful for measuring Americans' attitudes toward race relations in 1915.

Thinking About Historical Films

Films have a language all their own, a language that is in some ways similar to the written language of books but unique enough to require very different interpretive and analytical skills on the part of those who want to "read" films as easily as they do books.[9]

Film has certain advantages over the written word. It can communicate the look of people, places, and events in ways that even the best written descriptions cannot. Also, film creates an emotional intensity and immediacy that captures audiences in ways that writers can only envy. "Film can open our minds to another, more vivid and human, less literary understanding of the past."[10] In short, film can make the past come alive.

On the other hand, the emotional power of film is, from the historian's perspective, not always a good thing. Film is inherently manipulative, using clever editing, calculated lighting and camera angles, emotion-laden sound tracks, and special effects of various kinds to create illusions that appeal less to our intellects than our emotions. In fact, film's often nonlinear narrative style (think of the rapid-fire presentation of changing, often unrelated, images on MTV and in many television commercials) might be said to be antithetical to the very enterprise of history. Good historical writing is based on linear thinking. Historians must lead

---

[9]The image here is taken from one of the best summaries of the history and nature of film: James Monaco, *How to Read a Film,* Rev. ed. (New York: Oxford University Press, 1981). See also Art Silverblatt, *Media Literacy: Keys to Interpreting Media Messages* (Westport, Conn.: Praeger Publishers, 1995).

[10]Pierre Sorlin, "Historical Films as Tools for Historians," in O'Connor, *Image as Artifact,* 50.

their readers in a logical sequence from one event to another, or make a systematic argument using linear logic—if A, then B, therefore C. Film need not communicate in this way, leading us to wonder if the meaningful, objective study of history will be possible for people who grow up with the nonlinear visual syntax of moving images.

In comparing words and images, two other points should be made. First, written or spoken language is a medium of *intercommunication* in which an ongoing dialogue is possible. This is not true of film. According to James Monaco, "Cinema is not strictly a medium of intercommunication. . . . Whereas spoken and written languages are used for intercommunication, film, like the nonrepresentational arts in general . . . , is a one-way communication."[11] Additionally, it is much more difficult to check on a film's use of source materials than it is to evaluate the evidence used in a piece of written history. The source citations in history books can be checked for accuracy and contextual legitimacy, but the relationship between content and sources in a film is often difficult to discover. How, for instance, can we find out whether the film footage and interviews in a documentary do justice to the original uncut footage and interviews? How do we discover where docudrama writers get their facts and interpretations? In most cases, the answer is, we can't. For the most part the credibility of a historical film must be tested by using existing written histories.

Asking Questions of Film

When trying to "read" a film, the old cliché still applies: The more you know, the more you will get out of it. And the questions you should ask are the same ones you should ask when analyzing a written document or a history book: What does the content tell us? How was the film produced? How was it received?[12]

Content

Analysis of content is still the heart of the historical enterprise and applies to both the written word and to film. Every documentary or docudrama has a distinctive point of view and often, especially in the case of documentaries, contains an identifiable thesis. Once you identify point of view and thesis, consider the following: Is the reconstruction accurate? What does the filmmaker want the audience to think about the events being presented? What does the filmmaker want the audience to *feel*. Are the film's "conclusions" defensible in the light of what is already known about the event in question? You should also ask yourself how particular techniques—lighting, use of camera position, sound, color, editing—have contributed to the overall message of the film.[13] (See the insert on film language.)

Docudramas pose challenges all their own. Like history books they are historical reconstructions. However, the historian's primary responsibility is to the evidence, whereas the filmmaker's priorities are artistic and financial. Television productions and films must be artistically coherent and entertaining in order to score well in the

---

[11]Monaco, *How to Read a Film*, 132.

[12]The triad of Content, Production, and Reception is based on a number of the essays in O'Connor's' *Image as Artifact*.

[13]Leni Riefenstahl's famous Nazi propaganda film *Triumph of the Will* is an especially interesting example of how the visual language of film can be used to arouse (or intimidate) audiences.

Nielsen Ratings or succeed at the box office. As historians James Davidson and Mark Lytle comment:

> For filmmakers, far different principles of construction are paramount. They involve questions of drama, not fidelity to the evidence. Does the screenplay move along quickly enough? Do the characters 'develop' sufficiently? Does the plot provide enough suspense? These matters dominate the making of a film even when that oft-repeated claim flashes across the screen: Based on a True Story. [14]

Clearly, then, filmmakers alter the historical record in their quest to make artistic and entertaining films. But there are no universally accepted criteria for determining how historically "accurate" a film is. This is so because films (like good historical novels) can communicate two kinds of truth—literal truth and a larger, human, truth that we still recognize as good history. For this reason, individuals may honestly differ on the truth-value of a given film based on how literally they interpret the word "truth." *Platoon* (a gritty, close-up look at the Vietnam War experience through the lives of the members of a single platoon) does not aim for literal truth—the characters are fictional. Yet we would argue that *Platoon* is good history because it captures the larger truth of the war better than most of the other commercially produced films about the war.

A final word about content: though it is important to determine the accuracy of historical films, even inaccuracies can tell us something about a society's cultural myths. As one commentator wrote, "historians who tried to list the historical inaccuracies in *Birth of a Nation* would be ignoring the fact that their job should not involve bestowing marks for accuracy but describing how men living at a certain time understood their own history." [15] While we think it is important to consider the accuracy of a film, we agree that even misrepresentations of history can provide invaluable insights into the minds of those who originally made and viewed a film.

Production and Reception

Effective analysis of books requires that we know something about the times in which the book was written as well as something about the author's values, background, and intent. The same is true of film analysis. [16] *Platoon,* for example, was made at a time (1986) when Americans were finally willing to confront the agonies and traumas of the Vietnam experience, which helps us understand why *Platoon* could portray American soldiers less as mythic heroes (a common approach

---

[14]James Davidson and Mark Lytle, *After the Fact,* 3rd. ed. (New York: McGraw-Hill, Inc. , 1992), 360. This updated edition adds a chapter on "History and Myth in the Films of Vietnam," which provides an excellent essay-length introduction to the analysis of historical films.

[15]Daniel Leab, "The Moving Image as Interpreter of History," in O'Connor, *Image as Artifact,* 89.

[16]Daniel Leab argues, "It is necessary to ask of any visual source how did it come into being, who created it and why, what was or is its impact." "Moving Image," *Image as Artifact,* 88. *(Opposite)*

[17]For a more in-depth discussion see Monaco, *How to Read a Film,* Ch. III, "The Language of Film: Signs and Syntax," or O'Connor, *Image as Artifact,* Ch. V, "An Introduction to Visual Language for Historians and History Teachers."

[18]For the anecdotes about *Hearts and Minds* and *Victory at Sea* we are indebted to O'Connor, *Image as Artifact,* 318, 314.

A Primer on Film Language

Students interested in historical film should know something about film language. Below are a few important terms and concepts used in much formal film analysis.[17]

Shot, Scene, Sequence

The basic unit of a film is the single *shot.* A series of shots make a *scene,* and connected scenes form a *sequence.* Some commentators (e. g. John O'Connor) posit that shot, scene, and sequence can be equated to sentence, paragraph, and chapter in written language. Others (e.g., James Monaco) find the analogy inaccurate and overly simplistic. Whether or not the analogy is appropriate, reasoned critiques of historical films must begin with an analysis of the individual shots (*mise-en-scène*) and how the shots are edited into scenes and sequences (*montage*).

Mise-en-scène

Mise-en-scène (French for "putting together") is a commonly used term in film criticism for the contents and photographic "look" of a single unbroken shot, no matter how long its duration. In evaluating a historical film you should consider the accuracy of the set and costumes, and take notice of how the scene is photographed. Important photographic elements in a single shot are:

•*Duration,* or the length of time a shot is on the screen. A shot can be short and simple or quite long and complex. In *tracking shots* the camera moves while filming, often going from a distance shot to a close-up, or even following an actor or sequence of events without any editorial cutting. Directors occasionally try to enhance a sense of naturalistic realism by filming tracking shots with handheld cameras.

•*Lighting and Color* The intensity and direction of the lighting and the colors that compose each shot, can be powerful evokers of emotion. Dark shadowy images, for example, convey a sense of danger and apprehension. Colors have psychological correlates (red=anger; blue=sadness) as well as culturally significant symbolic meanings.

•*Camera Position* In this category we include a number of elements that film buffs treat independently—composition, camera angle, camera movement. Composition refers to the arrangement of objects and people on the screen, camera angle to how high or low the camera is placed, and camera movement speaks for itself. All of these elements can play a role in influencing the emotions of the audience. The single variable of camera angle, for instance, can influence greatly the audience's reading of a film. Leni Riefenstahl, the film genius responsible for the Nazi propaganda film *Triumph of the Will,* often photographed Hitler, his entourage, and German soldiers from below to make them appear heroic and larger than life.

Montage

Montage, another French term, refers to film editing—that is, the sequencing of the individual shots. If mise-en-scène refers to the modification and manipulation of *space,* montage refers to the filmmaker's manipulation of *time.* Since history is the systematic study of events as they happened *in time,* historians should pay close attention to how filmmakers manipulate emotions through the editing process. *Hearts and Minds,* a 1974 documentary critical of U.S. involvement in Vietnam, includes an interview with U.S. General William Westmoreland in which he states that Asian people don't respect life the same way Westerners do. During this section of the interview the filmmaker, Peter Davis, undercut Westmoreland's credibility by inserting a scene of a Vietnamese woman weeping over the grave of a loved one. Skillful editing can also telescope or compress time in a way that can compromise the historical "truth" of a given sequence or film. Editing can also manipulate your perceptions greatly. In the television series, *Victory at Sea* (1952), a chronicle of the U.S. Navy in World War II, the entire episode on the Battle of Leyte Gulf in the Philippines was created by editing together stock pieces of war footage and adding appropriate narration. There had been no cameras at the actual battle![18]

Sound

Sound is one of the most important weapons in the filmmaker's arsenal of artistic tools. To appreciate this point, compare the emotional impact of the same film viewed with and without the soundtrack. When analyzing a historical film, pay conscious attention to the soundtrack and the feelings it creates.

in dramatic films about World War II) than as frightened, confused, sometimes callous young men who didn't want to be in a war they didn't understand. It is also helpful to know that the film was made by Oliver Stone, a twice-wounded Vietnam veteran, many of whose films (such as *Born on the Fourth of July,* and *JFK*) display a gut-level bitterness about the war as well as a distrust of the U. S. government and military.[19] Stone's worldview explains not only the convincing realism of *Platoon,* but its antiwar message as well.

The popularity of a film or television show also tells us a good deal about the time in which it was made. This is especially important information if we are studying the film as a cultural artifact—i. e. , as evidence for social and cultural history. One could hardly argue that a given television show accurately reflected American tastes if no one watched it, or if it was taken off the air after a few episodes. Similarly, a popular historical film, even if more myth than fact, can tell us how people at the time viewed (or wanted to view) their own history.

Conclusion

Moving-image history is here to stay. The danger is not that we find it enjoyable to watch the magical images, but that we do so casually and uncritically. When the lights go down it is too easy to turn off the brain and wait to be entertained. But what we see on the screen must be analyzed, discussed and challenged if we are to avoid becoming passive receptacles for whatever messages are broadcast in our direction. The critical skills discussed in this book must be used to examine all serious ideas, whatever the medium of their transmission.

EXERCISE

Films can be a component of any segment of a history course. There are no specific exercises for this chapter, but we suggest that you think of classroom films as something more than mere entertainment. The form opposite might be a useful tool for the critical analysis of classroom films or essay assignments.

A Note on Film Research

A legitimate question is: "Where do I go to find out background information on a specific historical film?" A good place to start would be with newspaper and magazine reviews written at the time of the film's release. Also, consult Mark C. Carnes's *Past Imperfect,* John O'Connor's *Image as Artifact,* Steven Mintz's and Randy Roberts's *Hollywood's America*, as well as the bibliographies in each book. Especially noteworthy is the section in O'Connor's bibliography entitled, "Sources on the Connections between History and the Moving Image." The journal *Film & History* is a valuable source, and a number of historical journals have begun to review pertinent films and publish articles on the use of film in the classroom.

---

[19]This discussion of *Platoon* is based largely on Davidson and Lytle, *After the Fact,* 379–82.

PART III
DOING HISTORY

Chapter 9   EVIDENCE

"The documents are liars."

T. E. Lawrence

"The central methodological problem for the historian . . . is to know how to interrogate witnesses, how to test evidence, how to assess the reliability and the relevance of testimony."

Robin Winks

The famous soldier-scholar T. E. Lawrence (Lawrence of Arabia) once wrote a friend: "The documents are liars. No man ever yet tried to write down the entire truth of any action in which he has been engaged."[1] Lawrence exaggerated, but he certainly had a point. Not all documents "lie," but they do not always tell the unalloyed truth either. There exists, says historian Simon Schama, a "teasing gap separating a lived event and its subsequent narration,"[2] and it is that gap which creates a treacherous problem for those who try to wring the truth out of the records of the past.

That "teasing gap" between events and how they are remembered and narrated is familiar to any close observer of courtroom testimony. Witnesses, to the dismay of judges and juries, remember events in very different ways. A startling example of this occurred in an obscure village in the south of France over four hundred years ago. The story so strains credibility that we would dismiss it in a piece of fiction; yet it is true.

The outlines of the story are quite simple. A relatively prosperous peasant, Martin Guerre, one day left his wife and child and village without explanation, and was for years what we would call a missing person. Somehow another man, Arnaud du Tilh, learned of this and, claiming that he was Martin Guerre, one day appeared to reclaim his wife, property, and place in the community. The village, after overcoming some initial suspicions, welcomed the new Martin, and, remarkably, so did his long-suffering wife, Bertrande. A few years later, after a period of domestic happiness, Bertrande and members of her family charged that the new Martin was an impostor. Bertrande said she had been duped. The false Martin was arrested and tried. Just when the judges were about to rule in the imposter's favor—he was an eloquent witness in his own defense—the real Martin appeared. The game was up and Arnaud du Tilh was condemned by the court and executed in 1560.[3]

The soap-opera qualities of this story are evident, and the tale has been told many times in books, plays, novels and in an operetta. Recently the award-winning French film, *Le Retour de Martin Guerre* (1982) and historian Natalie Zemon Davis's book, *The Return of Martin Guerre* (1983), introduced the story to modern audi-

---

[1] Barzun and Graff, *Modern Researcher,* 50.
[2] Quoted in James Atlas, "Stranger Than Fiction," *The New York Times Magazine,* June 23, 1991, 22.
[3] Natalie Zemon Davis, *The Return of Martin Guerre* (Cambridge, Mass.: Harvard University Press, 1983).

ences.[4] Both film and book pose the question, "how, in a time without photographs, with few portraits, without tape recorders, without fingerprinting, without identity cards, without birth certificates, with parish records still irregular—if kept at all—how did one establish a person's identity beyond doubt?"[5] The answer is that the court had to rely on eye-witness testimony. They had to ask the villagers what they remembered of the original Martin Guerre and if they thought the man who returned was the man they remembered twelve years earlier. In the first trial (there were two) about forty-five of the witnesses said that the prisoner was not Martin Guerre; thirty to forty said that "the defendant was surely Martin Guerre; they had known him since the cradle." About sixty witnesses refused to identify him one way or the other.[6]

Let this story serve as an object lesson about the nature of evidence. Even with 150 "witnesses," the court that tried the case of Martin Guerre was left uncertain of the truth. The same uncertainty accompanies events for which we have ample written documents to study. But, whatever the imperfections in the evidence, such documents along with other surviving artifacts are all we have. They are the basic raw materials of history. In this chapter we will consider the types of sources historians use to learn about the past and to write history. We will also examine some of the techniques used by the historian to evaluate and interpret the raw data of the past.

The Sources: Primary and Secondary

The problem of weighing evidence is never an easy one, but the difficulty can be eased by an appreciation of the various types of sources historians rely upon in their work.

A *primary source* (also called an original source) is a piece of evidence written or created during the period under investigation. Primary sources are the records of contemporaries who participated in, witnessed, or commented on the events you are studying. They are the documents and artifacts—letters, reports, diaries, government records, parish registers, newspapers, business ledgers, photographs, works of art, buildings, and a host of others—that make the writing and study of history possible. A note of caution: even though an eyewitness or participant writes down memories many years after the event, the commentary is still a primary source. In sum, a primary source is to the historian what a mountain is to the geologist: the surviving record of events that took place a long time ago.

A *secondary source* is an account of the period in question written after the events have taken place. Often based on primary sources, secondary sources are the books, articles, essays, and lectures through which we learn most of the history we know. Historians take the raw data found in primary sources and transform it into the written histories that attempt to explain how and why things happened as they did.[7]

---

[4] *Sommersby* (1993) was an American adaptation loosely based on the 1982 French film. So much of the original story was changed, however, that *Sommersby* must be considered fiction, not history.

[5] Davis, *The Return of Martin Guerre,* 63.

[6] Davis, *The Return of Martin Guerre,* 67-68.

[7] Textbooks and similar works represent a special category of "tertiary" source. Most general survey texts are not based on research into primary sources so much as they reflect the findings of a wide variety of secondary sources—that is, other history books. An author who attempted to cover American history from pre-Columbian times to the present could not in a lifetime read all the necessary primary sources. Such an author would have to rely on books and articles written by other scholars (i.e., secondary sources) in order to complete the project. Thus textbooks are a step or two further removed from the original sources than are most secondary works.

The distinction between primary and secondary sources is not always as clear as the above definitions imply. For instance, newspapers are definitely primary sources for the periods in which they were published. But newspapers also share many characteristics with secondary sources. Very often journalists are not eyewitnesses to the events they write about. Like historians, journalists must interrogate witnesses—in this case directly—and read pertinent documents in order to construct the story, the "history," that appears in the paper.

Another problematic source is the personal memoir or autobiography written by a politician, military officer, or movie star. Such memoirs often straddle the line that separates primary from secondary sources. While memoirs and autobiographies are first-person narrations of events, their authors rarely rely totally on their memories, as the term "memoir" implies. Authors often "recollect" the events of their public life with the help of a variety of documents, or with previously published accounts of friends and colleagues. In this case the memoir writer is functioning like any other historian, so the memoir must be considered, at least in part, a secondary source.

Also confusing is the fact that many sources can be categorized either as primary or secondary *depending on the subject being studied.* An example is Charles Beard's famous book, *An Economic Interpretation of the Constitution,* published in 1913. Beard's controversial thesis was that the delegates to the Constitutional Convention in Philadelphia designed the Constitution to protect their own personal economic interests. For scholars studying the origins of the Constitution, Beard's book is a secondary source, and its central thesis has been long debated. However, the book would be a primary source for anyone studying the ideas of Charles Beard himself. That is, if Charles Beard and his ideas were the subject of the study, *An Economic Interpretation of the Constitution* would be a primary source; if the origins of the Constitution were the subject, Beard's book would be a secondary source.

Finally, many primary sources have been published in book form. In spite of their resemblance in form to secondary sources, these materials remain primary. Remember, the basic question to ask is: When did the materials originate? Not: When were they published or reprinted? The Declaration of Independence printed in the back of a textbook is still a primary source for the revolutionary period of American history, even though the textbook itself is a secondary source.

Using Primary Sources

However inadequate the surviving store of records related to a specific historical episode, so many documents and artifacts have survived (especially from the more recent centuries) that the task of historians is truly daunting. Before historians can use any body of evidence they must thoroughly sort and sift it. Evidence is found in mixed-up bundles, with relevant and irrelevant information thrown together like kernels of grain and their husks. Only a small part of the existing evidence will be relevant to a particular investigation, and the historian must separate the wheat from the chaff.

Equally daunting is the task of coaxing the truth from the sources. Sources can be seductive or coldly aloof. They can mislead, lie, or lure you into a false sense of security. They can be written in the obscure languages or the incomprehensible jargon of the modern bureaucrat. They can lead the researcher into blind alleys, false turns, and dead ends. For all the frustrations, however, unlocking the secrets of the records of the past can be a fascinating task. The historian is the detective, the primary sources the clues.

Since most primary sources are in written form, historians typically limit themselves to the study of that segment of the past for which we have written records. (The study of preliterate or prehistoric cultures and societies is the domain of cultural anthropologists and archeologists.) Not all primary sources, however, are documents. Remember our definition: A primary source is something that came into existence during the period that the historian is studying. From this perspective, just about anything that has survived (including your Aunt Edna) is a potential primary source—buildings, tools, works of art, weapons, coins, and, more recently, photographs, films, and recordings. The list below should give you a rough idea of the variety of primary sources historians use.

Inscriptions	Works of art
Buildings	Baptismal and burial records
Coins	Newspapers
Royal Charters	Magazines
Tapes of TV shows	Mystery novels
Laws	Autobiographies/Memoirs
Government publications	Legislative debates
Diplomatic dispatches	Maps
Court records	Poetry
Police reports	Films
Advertisements	Your parents
Minutes of organizations	Photographs
Private letters	Folk songs
Diaries	Language
Business records	Furniture
Railroad schedules	Telephone books

A quick review of the list will reveal that not all types of written primary evidence are equally "primary." That is, some primary sources are inherently less useful and less trustworthy than others. Admittedly newspapers are indispensable primary sources, but we have seen that press accounts are frequently written by journalists who are not themselves eyewitnesses to the stories they write. Journalists, like historians, have to piece together stories from many sources, and such stories are often somewhat "distanced" from the events they describe. Also problematical are the memoirs and autobiographies we discussed above. They are often written years after the events they describe; and vanity, personal bias, or failing memory can influence the tale an author has to tell. Even someone who is determined to provide a balanced and accurate account rarely remembers the same event in precisely the same way that someone else does.

Often the most revealing sources are those which were never intended to be made public. "The most primary source of all," says historian Barbara Tuchman, "is unpublished material: private letters and diaries or the reports, orders and messages in government archives."[8] Even here the situation is ambiguous, however, because public figures are now conscious that history will judge them, and even their private correspondence may be written to influence the historians who will one day make those judgments. More on these sources later in the chapter.

---

[8]Tuchman, *Practicing History,* 19.

Primary Sources and Critical Method

The most challenging task of the historian-detective is to draw testimony from the records of the past. Here the historian has two aims, neither of them simple: (1) to determine if a source is *authentic* and, (2) to establish the *meaning* and *believability* of the contents. The first is accomplished through external criticism; the second through internal criticism.

External criticism, in the words of one historian, "authenticates evidence and establishes texts in the most accurate possible form."[9] Many historical records lack precise dates or correct attribution (i.e., who wrote them). Many texts, for various reasons, are inaccurate, and forgeries are not uncommon. Highly specialized techniques are required to authenticate documents and artifacts: carbon dating, linguistic analysis, chemical analysis, and the like. Extensive knowledge of the period in question is also a prerequisite. Beginners rarely have either the background knowledge or the specialized skills for such criticism so that we need not dwell on this aspect of critical method. For present purposes assume that the documents in the exercises and the sources you might be using in a class are authentic.

Once the authenticity of a document has been established, the historian faces the far more important challenge of reading and interpreting the contents. This is called *internal criticism,* and the techniques involved are much less mysterious. More than anything else, the process requires a healthy skepticism. We have an innate tendency to believe anything if it is written down, and, the older the document or more ornate the script, the more we tend to believe it. Therefore, it is important to remind ourselves that our venerable ancestors could lie, shade the truth, or make a mistake, just as we can.

Documents do not reveal their secrets easily. You must learn to question the evidence like an attorney in a courtroom—from different angles, from different perspectives, relentlessly, suspiciously. Even an account written by an individual of unimpeachable honesty can be marred by error and half-truth. It is the historian's job to separate the true from the false. What sort of questions should you ask of the evidence? Below is a partial list of some of the most important.[10]

1. What exactly does the document mean?

Often the literal meaning differs from the real meaning. Diplomatic communications, for example, are notorious for veiling harsh international disagreements in extremely polite language. Diplomats are trained to phrase messages in such a restrained fashion that even an impending war can be made to sound no more threatening than a neighborly disagreement over the backyard fence. Because of this, the historian must become familiar with the conventions of diplomatic correspondence in order to understand the real meaning of the dispatches.

Another problem facing the historian is that words change meaning from one age to the next. A nineteenth-century reference to a "gay" person means something quite different from a similar reference in the 1990s. Likewise, the word "enthusiasm" meant something quite different in the eighteenth century, when the connotations were largely pejorative. To discover these sorts of differences

Copyright © 2000 Harlan Davidson, Inc.

---

[9]R. J. Shafer, ed., *A Guide to Historical Method* (Homewood, Ill.: Dorsey Press, 1969), 100.
[10]These questions are based on those printed in Shafer, *Guide to Historical Method,* 137–38.

you have to know as much as possible about the cultural and political context of the period you are studying.

2. How well situated was the author to observe or record the events in question?

Here there are a number of subsidiary questions. What was the author's physical location? Was he or she a direct eyewitness or did the information come from someone else? What was the author's *social ability* to observe? That is, might the person's social or economic position in the society have influenced how an event or situation was seen? A middle-class English woman, for example, would view the agitations of the early-twentieth-century suffragettes quite differently than the male Members of Parliament who were convinced that women lacked the capacity to be trusted with the right to vote. Finally, did the witness have *specialized knowledge* that might enhance the credibility of the testimony? A lawyer's report of a murder trial might be far more insightful than that of a casual observer in the audience. On the other hand, the causal observer might be able to report on things the lawyer missed.

3. When, how, and to whom was the report made?

Obviously, the longer the time between the event and the report, the greater the chance a witness's memory will play tricks. In addition, you should ask what the intended purpose of the report was. An army officer reporting to a superior may tell what the commander wants to hear rather than a more disappointing truth. The number of casualties inflicted by American soldiers on the enemy during the Vietnam War (1961–1975) was constantly exaggerated as field commanders turned in unrealistically high "body counts" to please their superiors at headquarters.

4. Is there bias that must be accounted for?

Personal bias can be the enemy of truth on two levels. It is, of course, common for a piece of testimony to be colored by an author's personal beliefs and convictions. In the same way, however, your own biases can often blind you to much that the sources reveal. Knowing as much about the person who left the account will help you recognize and compensate for the first sort of bias. Knowing yourself is the only way to insure that your own prejudices don't get in the way of understanding.

5. What specialized information is needed to interpret the source?

Many times you will have to look up names, places, dates, and technical terms to get the full meaning of a statement.

6. Do the reported actions seem probable in the light of informed common sense?

Here the significant words are "probable" and "informed common sense." We can never get absolutely conclusive answers for many questions in history. The test of the believability of a given piece of testimony is the inherent probability of

‗‗‗‗‗ 3. Konrad Heiden, *Hitler* (1936).

‗‗‗‗‗ 4. *The Goebbels Diaries,* edited by Louis P. Lochner (1948). [Joseph Goebbels was one of Hitler's original followers and became Nazi propaganda minister in 1933.]

‗‗‗‗‗ 5. A. J. P. Taylor, *The Origins of the Second World War* (1961).

‗‗‗‗‗ 6. *The Speeches of Adolph Hitler, 1922-29,* edited by Norman H. Baynes, 2 vols. (1942).

‗‗‗‗‗ 7. Gerhard L. Weinberg, *A World At Arms: A Global History of World War II* (1994).

‗‗‗‗‗ 8. *The Times* (London), 1933-39.

‗‗‗‗‗ 9. Adolf Hitler, *Mein Kampf* [My Struggle], 1939.

‗‗‗‗‗ 10. Winston Churchill, *The Second World War,* Vol. I, *The Gathering Storm* (1948). [Churchill was a member of the British Parliament when the war broke out and in 1940 became Britain's prime minister.]

Exercise 2: Types of Primary Sources

See Exercise 2 in Set A.

Exercise 3: Inference

Inference, as we noted, is a major tool in the interpretation of evidence. Because the questions that interest historians are often quite different from the objectives of those who created various pieces of primary evidence, historians constantly have to make logical deductions that may not be provable in any absolute sense. Below are a number of short statements followed by some possible inferences. After reading a statement, indicate for each inference whether it is a "Valid" inference ("V"), an invalid or "False" inference ("F"), or an inference for which we have Insufficient Data ("ID") to determine its validity or invalidity. If you label an inference "F" (False/Invalid), indicate your reasons on the lines provided at the end of each unit.

For the purposes of this exercise assume that the statements reflect the best judgment of the speaker or writer. Also assume that for any statement of fact there exists corroborating evidence. For a completed sample see Item A, Set A, page 161.

A. *Declaration of Sentiments* from the women who met at the Seneca Falls Convention in 1848. (Reprinted in David Burner, et al., eds., *America Through the Looking Glass,* Vol. I, Prentice-Hall, 1974, 280-81.)

> When, in the course of human events it becomes necessary for one portion of the family of man to assume among the people of the earth a position different from that which they have hitherto occupied, but one to which the laws of nature and of nature's God entitle them, a decent respect to the opinions of mankind requires that they should declare the causes that impel them to such a course.
>
> We hold these truths to be self-evident: that all men and women are created equal; that they are endowed by their Creator with certain inalienable rights; . . .
>
> The history of mankind is a history of repeated injuries and usurpations on the part of man toward woman, having in direct object the establishment of an absolute tyranny over her. To prove this, let facts be submitted to a candid world. [There follows a specific list of grievances.

* * *

In entering upon the great work before us, we anticipate no small amount of misconception, misrepresentation, and ridicule; but we shall use every instrumentality within our power to effect our object. We shall employ agents, circulate tracts, petition the State and National legislatures, and endeavor to enlist the pulpit and press in our behalf.

Possible Inferences:

_____ 1. The authors of this document probably were middle- and upper-class women.

_____ 2. The women who wrote this were extreme radicals who were willing to resort to violence to achieve their ends.

_____ 3. The authors were familiar with the events of the American Revolution.

_____ 4. Political activism among women was unusual at this time.

_____ 5. This protest resulted in a number of important reforms.

Reasons for "F" labels:

_____

_____

B. General Dwight Eisenhower's reflections on his World War II experiences. From Dwight Eisenhower, *Crusade in Europe,* (1948).

Except during World War I, the U.S. public has habitually looked upon Europe's quarrels as belonging to Europe alone. For this reason every American soldier coming to Britain was almost certain to consider himself a privileged crusader, sent there to help Britain out of a hole. He would expect to be treated as such. On the other hand, the British public looked upon itself as one of saviors of democracy, particularly because, for an entire year, it had stood alone as the unbreakable opponent of Nazism and the European Axis. Failure to understand this attitude would of course have unfortunate results.

Possible Inferences:

_____ 1. Eisenhower feared U.S. and British troops would not get along.

_____ 2. Eisenhower feared that arrogance in American troops would create conflicts with the British public.

_____ 3. Eisenhower saw no reason why Americans and Britons could not get along well.

_____ 4. Eisenhower had studied American history at some time in his life.

_____ 5. There were many conflicts between British troops and American troops during the latter stages of World War II.

Reasons for "F" labels:

_____

_____

C. Letter from a warehouse worker in England to the *Nottingham Daily Guardian* in 1863. From E. R. Pike, *Golden Times* (1972).

> Sir,—I have been a lace warehouse girl about 13 years, and should know a little about the regulations of warehouses. Is there not an Act which compels the masters of factories to let children leave their employment at six o'clock at night? If there is, can any one tell me why this Act is not applied to lace warehouses, which are heated with steam, for children and young women are kept there at work from 8 in the morning till 7, 8, and 9 o'clock at night, for about 3s 6d to 8s per week, which, in my opinion, is worse than slavery in South America, for I do not think they work above 12 hours a day; and if they do, they are better off than a portion of the warehouse girls of Nottingham, who have to work in cellars not fit for pigstyes, much more for human beings.

Possible Inferences:

_____ 1. Even members of the working class who worked very long hours somehow learned how to read and write.

_____ 2. Child labor was still common in the England of the 1860s.

_____ 3. The government had taken no action to correct ill-treatment of workers.

_____ 4. Apparently there had already been an attempt to limit the length of the working day for some workers in some industries.

_____ 5. Only women and children worked in lace warehouses.

Reasons for "F" labels:

_____

_____

D. A scholar's statistical summary of the role of women in medicine in the nineteenth century. From Paul Starr, *The Social Transformation of American Medicine (1982)*.

> By 1893–94, women represented 10 percent or more of the students at 19 coeducational medical schools. Between 1880 and 1900, the percentage of doctors who were women increased nationally from 2.8 to 5.6 percent. In some cities the proportion of women was considerably higher: 18.2 percent of doctors in Boston, 19.3 percent in Minneapolis, 13.8 percent in San Francisco. With more than 7,000 women physicians at the turn of the century, the United States was far ahead of England, which had just 258, and France, which had only 95.

Possible Inferences:

_____ 1. In the United States a higher percentage of women studied medicine than in western Europe during the twenty years after 1880.

_____ 2. Women had an easier time becoming doctors in the United States because women's rights were more widely recognized in America than in Europe.

_____ 3. American women were smarter than European women.

_____ 4. A lower percentage of American women is studying medicine in the United States today than in 1900.

_____ 5. More women could study medicine in the United States (as opposed to Europe) because there were more medical schools in the United States.

Reasons for "F" labels:

_____

_____

Set B, Exercise 4: Analysis of Evidence

The Kent State Incident, May 4, 1970

One of the most tragic and controversial events in Vietnam era America was the violent confrontation between the Ohio National Guard and a large group of students at Kent State University on May 4, 1970. On that day four students were killed and nine wounded. What exactly happened at Kent State, and why, will never be known with absolute certainty. In spite of reams of testimony, Kent State remains a highly controversial subject.

The late 1960's were a time of increasing unrest on America's college campuses. The Vietnam War spurred student protests all over the country, and radical student political groups (like the SDS—Students for a Democratic Society) proliferated on many campuses. Student outrage over the U.S. failure to get out of Vietnam peaked when President Richard Nixon announced, on April 30, 1970, that he had ordered U.S. troops into Cambodia, thus apparently expanding the war.

The next four days were marked by escalating student unrest on the campus of Kent State University and in the town of Kent itself. On Friday, May 1, there were disorders in the city; on Saturday a group of students burned the campus ROTC building and the authorities requested troops from the National Guard; on Sunday the first confrontations between the Guard and the students took place; on Monday, the fateful day, the accumulated tensions climaxed with the killings that shocked and aroused the nation.

How could such a thing happen? This question led to newspaper investigations, grand jury proceedings, civil suits, the creation of a government commission on student unrest, and many books and articles. It is not our purpose to answer that question. But by examining some of the eyewitness testimony we can get a better idea of how the historian "questions" evidence. The evidence below relates to one very specific question that many investigators tried to answer after the shootings: was the National Guard endangered by the student mob on May 4? Was the Guard justified in firing at the students in self-defense?

In this exercise your task is not to determine whether or not the National Guard was threatened by the students. Instead you should try to note any facts about each piece of evidence that would help you to assess its believability. Make pertinent observations concerning the authorship, circumstances of com-

position, content, and potential credibility of each piece of testimony. Use the seven questions on pages 00-00 as a basis for your analysis.

The Evidence

1. Statement of General Robert Canterbury, Assistant Adjutant General of the Ohio National Guard, to the President's Commission on Campus Unrest, August 25, 1970. (From *The Report of the President's Commission on Campus Unrest,* 1970, pp. 269-70.)

> As the troop formation reached the area of the Pagoda near Taylor Hall, the mob located on the right flank in front of Taylor Hall and in the Prentice Hall parking lot charged our right flank, throwing rocks, yelling obscenities and threats, 'Kill the pigs,' 'Stick the pigs.' The attitude of the crowd at this point was menacing and vicious.
>
> The troops were being hit by rocks. I saw Major Jones hit in the stomach by a large brick, a guardsman to the right and rear of my position was hit by a large rock and fell to the ground. During this movement, practically all of the guardsmen were hit by missiles of various kinds. Guardsmen on the right flank were in serious danger of bodily harm and death as the mob continued to charge. I felt that, in view of the extreme danger to the troops at this point, that they were justified in firing.

Analysis: _____

_____

_____

_____

_____

2. Observations of Charles Brill, a Kent State professor, as reported in *Time,* May 18, 1970.

> "They are shooting blanks—they are shooting blanks," thought Kent State Journalism Professor Charles Brill, who nevertheless crouched behind a pillar. "Then I heard a chipping sound and a ping, and I thought, 'My God, this is for real.'" An Army veteran who saw action in Korea, Brill was certain that the Guardsman had not fired randomly out of individual panic. "They were organized," he said. "It was not scattered. They all waited and they all pointed their rifles at the same time. It looked like a firing squad." The shooting stopped—as if on signal. Minutes later, the Guardsmen assumed parade-rest positions, apparently to signal the crowd that the fusillade would not be resumed unless the Guardsmen were threatened again.

Analysis: _____

_____

_____

_____

_____

3. Testimony of Claudia Van Tyne, a 20-year-old junior at Kent State at the time of the shootings. (From *The Middle of the Country: The Events of May 4th As Seen By Students and Faculty at Kent State University,* ed. by Bill Warren, June, 1970, pp. 119–121.)

> For what occurred on Kent State University's campus I can only give one term-murder.... The area was filled with students in the middle, many spectators on the outskirts and the pigs were lined-up waiting. I don't like the expression 'pig' but it is the only word I shall ever use again to refer to law officials.... The pigs then informed us that we must disperse over their bull horn. In our response, we informed them that they, not us, should get off our campus and we began to chant 'Power To The People—Off The Pigs' etc., etc. They then began making their advance and everyone walked, telling others not to run but to walk, up the hill. We were all choking and sputtering because the tear gas (pepper pellets) had already been shot.... The pigs advanced, came up the hill and marched down into the old football practice field behind Taylor Hall (architecture building) where they gassed us again. Many of us picked up the cannisters and tossed them back. Finding themselves out of teargas, the pigs retreated followed by jeers and a few rocks. I was next to the architecture building, about twenty feet away from them, when suddenly they turned and fired. I was stunned to say the least. We all were. No one expected it....

Analysis: _____

_____

_____

_____

4. Report (October 17, 1970) of the special grand jury that investigated the Kent State tragedy. The grand jury was composed of 15 middle-aged local residents. The grand jury began meeting on September 14. (Copyright © 1970 by *The New York Times.* Reprinted by permission.)

> Those orders [to disperse], given by a Kent State University policeman, caused a violent reaction and the gathering quickly degenerated into a riotous mob....
>
> Those who acted as participants and agitators are guilty of deliberate criminal conduct. Those who were present as cheerleaders and onlookers, while not liable for criminal acts, must morally assume a part of the responsibility for what occurred....
>
> It should be made clear that we do not condone all of the activities of the National Guard on the Kent State University campus on May 4, 1970. We find, however, that those members of the National Guard who were present on the hill adjacent to Taylor Hall on May 4, 1970, fired their weapons in the honest and sincere belief and under circum-

stances which would have logically caused them to believe that they would suffer serious bodily injury had they not done so. They are not, therefore, subject to criminal prosecution under the laws of this state for any death or injury resulting therefrom.

It should be added, that . . . the verbal abuse directed at the guardsmen by the students during the period in question represented a level of obscenity and vulgarity which we have never before witnessed!

Analysis: _____

_____

_____

_____

_____

_____

5. Testimony of unnamed Guardsman—a 23 year-old, married machinist. (Reported in a Special Report by the Akron *Beacon Journal,* May 24, 1970. Quoted in I. F. Stone, *The Killings at Kent State*, 1970, p. 125.)

Q.—Did you shoot to save your life?

A.—No. I didn't feel that. Because, like it was an automatic thing. Everybody shot, so I shot. I didn't think about it. I just fired. . . .

Q.—Did you feel threatened?

A.—No. I didn't think they' try to take our rifles, not while we could use the bayonets and butts. . . . The guys have been saying that we got to get together and stick to the same story, that it was our lives or them, a matter of survival. I told them I would tell the truth and couldn't get in trouble that way.

Analysis: _____

_____

_____

_____

_____

6. Testimony of Richard Schreiber, Assistant Professor of Journalism. Shreiber had been in the army and was a life member of the National Rifle Association. (From James Michener, *Kent State: What Happened and Why*, 1971, p. 359.)

I went out on the south porch of Taylor with my binoculars and saw something which has caused a lot of discussion. While the Guard was pinned against the fence, the students kept throwing rocks, but they were rather far away and most of the rocks were falling short. I happened to have this one Guard in my glasses and I saw him raise his revolver and bang away. I've fired many hundreds of rounds with a .45 and I know a shot when I see one. There can be no question but that he fired the first round of the day. But the damnedest thing happened. Even while he was firing, some student ran up with a gas grenade and threw it at him. Where could he have possibly got it? Didn't look like the ones the Guards had been using. One of the Guardsmen, foolishly I thought, picked up the grenade and threw it back. It seemed like horseplay, so I turned away.

Analysis: _____

_____

_____

_____

_____

_____

For Discussion

1. Which pieces of evidence do you find most convincing? Which do you find least convincing? Why?
2. On which "facts" does there seem to be general agreement?
3. What are the central points of disagreement?

Exercise 5: Essay

Based on the evidence above, write a paragraph-length account of the incident at Kent State. In your paragraph take a position on the question at issue: Was the National Guard or the students most responsible for the violence? In your paragraph you might want to help the reader understand what can be established beyond doubt (assume the excerpts above are all the sources you have available to you), what is *probable* given the above evidence, and what cannot be established with certainty. In your account, include direct quotations from the documents. Read Writing Capsule 5 (on page 160) before you begin.

CHAPTER 10 ORAL HISTORY AND STATISTICS

"We have agencies aplenty to seek out the papers of men long dead. But we have only the most scattered and haphazard agencies for obtaining a little of the immense mass of information about the more recent American past—the past of the last half century—which might come fresh and direct from men once prominent in politics, in business, in the professions, and in other fields; information that every obituary column shows to be perishing."

Allan Nevins[1]

"Historians deal with a universe not of absolutes but of probabilities, and for a world conceived in these terms statistics are the appropriate tool."

William O. Aydelotte[2]

Richard Goodwin, a White House advisor and speechwriter during the early 1960s, related an unforgettable episode when he wrote his political memoir, *Remembering America.* In April of 1964 he got a call from his colleague, Bill Moyers, saying "Come on, Dick, the president wants to see us."

"In his office?" Goodwin replied.

"Nope, in the pool. He's swimming and so are we."

"I don't have a bathing suit."

"You don't need one."

At that Goodwin says he realized he had been summoned for a skinny-dip with the president. "We entered the pool area," Goodwin continued, "to see the massive presidential flesh, a sun-bleached atoll breaching the placid sea, passing gently sidestroke, the deep-cleft buttocks moving slowly past our unstartled gaze. Moby Dick, I thought, being naturally inclined to literary reference." The president called across the pool: "Come on in, boys. It'll do you good." Goodwin and Moyers stripped on the spot and joined the president, circling the pool in the buff, with the president discussing his plans for the future of the country.[3]

The president was, of course, Lyndon Baines Johnson (1963–69), surely one of the most colorful, larger-than-life individuals ever to play on the stage of American politics. Johnson was a big man from a very big state. In the words of one writer he "seemed like the quintessential Texan to many Americans: big, loud, brash, friendly, informal, folksy, pushy, vulgar, and combative."[4] He was also intelligent, superhumanly energetic (he once gave twenty-two campaign speeches in a single day), and a temperamental and uncompromising taskmaster who worked his staff until they were ready to drop. "I don't have ulcers," he said. "I give 'em!"[5]

[1] *Gateway to History,* 1938. Quoted in Louis Starr, "Oral History," *Oral History: An Interdisciplinary Anthology,* ed. by David K. Dunaway and Willa K. Baum (Nashville, Tenn.: American Association for State and Local History, 1984), 8.
[2] Quoted in Robert P. Swierenga, ed., *Quantification in American History* (New York: Atheneum, 1970), xi.
[3] Richard N. Goodwin, *Remembering America* (New York: Harper and Row, 1988), 267–68.
[4] Paul F. Boller, Jr., *Presidential Anecdotes* (New York: Penguin, 1981), 307.
[5] Quoted in Boller, *Presidential Anecdotes,* 309.

By many measures Lyndon Johnson was an effective president (his administration passed much landmark social and civil rights legislation), but he was never popular. Even before the Vietnam War destroyed his presidency, he had failed to "connect" with most Americans. Many were repelled by his folksy country manner, uninspiring speaking style, and penchant for the outrageous—e.g., showing reporters his scar from a gall bladder operation, and scaring them half to death by racing them around his ranch in his car at ninety miles an hour while sipping beer from a can.

Johnson, like other modern presidents, was very conscious that his reputation was ultimately in the hands of historians. As plans for the Lyndon Johnson presidential library were being made, the White House staff was ordered to save every note, memo, and scrap for the library. One day Johnson's personal secretary reprimanded Bill Moyers, one of Johnson's most trusted aides, for throwing things away in his wastebasket. Later, Moyers dumped some chicken bones on her desk, saying, "Here's something else for the library. These are leftovers from the President's lunch today."[6] In contrast, we know that much important information from the Johnson years has effectively been lost forever. Johnson was a master of political persuasion, and as he tried to build Congressional majorities for his programs he spent countless hours on the telephone. Johnson, Richard Goodwin notes, "labored, often far into the night, telephone constantly in hand, to persuade, seduce, coerce congressional leaders, committee chairmen, and, it seemed, most of an entire membership. . . ."[7] What historian wouldn't love to have transcripts of those calls!

Johnson's desire to save every piece of paper for future historians, and his constant use of the telephone to get things done illustrate some of the frustrating ambiguities faced by historians of the twentieth century: on one hand there is too much information, and, on the other, there is too little. We generate and save so much information that no mortal has time to read it all. At the same time some of the things we would most like to read—the substance of the countless phone conversations that shape the world in which we live—were never recorded. Increasingly, information that used to be written down is now communicated by phone or e-mail, and, unless someone has made a point of preserving this material, it is lost to the historian forever.[8]

If the twentieth century has presented historians with new challenges, it also has given them some powerful new tools. In the last chapter we discussed the analysis of documentary evidence, the most traditional and important type of evidence used by historians. Yet two other types of evidence—oral interviews and statistics—have become increasingly important in recent decades, giving rise to *oral history* on the one hand and *quantitative history* (i.e., history grounded in

---

[6]Boller, *Presidential Anecdotes,* 311.

[7]Goodwin, *Remembering America,* 260.

[8]As it turns out, shortly after this passage was originally written, the public learned that many of Lyndon Johnson's private phone conversations had not been lost after all. For years, even before he became president, LBJ kept records of his phone calls, first by having an aide take shorthand notes, and then by tape recorder. Johnson originally intended that the recordings be locked away until the year 2023, but they were released early. The first installment is available in audio and print versions in Michael Beschloss's *Taking Charge: The Johnson White House Tapes, 1963–1964* (Simon and Schuster, 1997). These tapes, which cover the period November 1963, to August 1964, interestingly dramatize the point made above: They are a very rare exception to the reality that the great majority of phone messages are lost to historians forever. And, if LBJ had had his way, no historian would have listened to those tapes until well into the twenty-first century.

numbers and statistics) on the other. Ironically, oral history is as old as quantitative history is new, but both owe their prominence to the emergence of technologies that didn't exist a century ago: the tape (and later video) recorder and the computer. Even if you never try to do either type of history, you should be aware of the strengths and potential pitfalls of each.

Oral History

Oral history is older than the practice of writing about the past, and, at the same time, a true child of the last half of the twentieth century. Historians have always interviewed living witnesses, as any reader of Herodotus or Thucydides can testify. Yet, as an organized enterprise, oral history dates from the government-sponsored interview projects of the New Deal and from Allan Nevins's 1938 plea (quoted above) for the collection of the living memories of important individuals.

Oral history weds the ancient practice of interviewing witnesses to the modern technology of the tape and video recorder. Defined as "recorded interviews which preserve historically significant memories for future use,"[9] oral history provides the contemporary historian with a wealth of source materials that simply did not exist fifty or sixty years ago.

Oral history refers to the source materials—the evidence—not the final product created by the historian. Recorded interviews, even if transcribed, are oral documents roughly equivalent to the printed and manuscript sources that have for generations been the lifeblood of historical scholarship. Historians must sift, analyze, and interpret oral sources in precisely the same manner as they would scrutinize diaries, letters, or government documents. As Barbara Tuchman pointed out, "The memories of the living, one soon discovers, are no more reliable or free of wishful recollection and the adjustments of hindsight than the memoirs of the dead."[10] Thus, when students do an oral history project, they are (1) collecting sources in the interviewing process and (2) actually doing history when they critically evaluate those sources and write a narrative or commentary.

As Allan Nevins's 1938 plea implies, oral history projects first targeted the prominent individuals who had always been the objects of historical scholarship: politicians, intellectuals, business leaders, generals, etc. But it was not long before historians realized that the magic of the tape recorder opened up dramatic new possibilities. It was now possible to tape the remembered experiences of the not-so-famous people who had previously slipped through history's net: the poor, the illiterate or uneducated, marginalized members of minority groups, women, workers who rarely wrote journals or diaries, the anonymous soldiers and sailors who usually bear the brunt of war—in short, people like most of us.

Critics have argued that the quest to interview anyone who would sit still in front of a microphone has created a mountain of trivia of questionable accuracy and merit that few historians will ever use. While there is some truth to the charge, the influence of the telephone and rapid air travel make oral sources increasingly important to historians of the twentieth century. Whereas political leaders in the past wrote lengthy letters and kept extensive diaries, today they pick up the phone or fly a few hours to have a person-to-person conference. Oral history, then, necessarily replaces the manuscript sources that have disappeared in our high-technol-

---

[9]Dunaway and Baum, *Oral History,* xix.

[10]Barbara Tuchman, "Distinguishing the Significant from the Insignificant," in Dunaway and Baum, *Oral History,* 76.

ogy age. Further, oral history is something even novice historians can get involved in. It is personally satisfying and can render a valuable community service.

Doing Oral History: Interviewing

Oral history involves much more than turning on a tape recorder in front of an interviewee. In this section we will attempt to single out the most important considerations fledgling oral historians should keep in mind. For a more detailed discussion of the process of oral history, however, and for project suggestions, we recommend that you turn to one of the many guides written to help teachers and students get started.[11]

The scouting motto, "be prepared," is triply relevant for oral history. After making sure that your tape/video recorder works (are the batteries fresh?), you have to (1) choose with care the people you intend to interview, (2) do background research on your subject and prepare for the interview, and (3) familiarize yourself with the legal and ethical constraints that responsible interviewers observe.

1. Choosing Narrators

Almost anyone, young or old, can be a good source for the oral historian, depending on the subject under investigation. Still, you will want to select interview subjects with care. Choose individuals who have good memories (to the extent that can be determined) and who have the potential of making a valuable contribution to your particular study. Build a list of prospects by soliciting suggestions from parents, friends, and teachers. If you are studying events a few decades in the past, inquire at retirement centers, local churches, and nursing homes. Excellent possible sources are members of your own family, whose testimony might be incorporated into a family history project.[12]

2. The Interview

Never do an interview unless you have done some preliminary research on the topic in question. It is difficult to ask meaningful questions about the Depression, Vietnam War, or the Flood of '48 unless you know something about them prior to conducting the inverview. Background reading allows you to test the generalizations you find in textbooks against the individual experiences of the people you interview.

You should also prepare yourself to be an effective interviewer. One expert notes, "The interviewer's paramount objective is to help the narrator reconstruct his/her personal history with as much accuracy and vivid detail as possible."[13] To accomplish this it is wise to prepare some questions in advance. Then, at the interview itself:[14]

[11]For example, Cullom Davis, Kathryn Back, and Kay MacLean, *Oral History: From Tape to Type* (Chicago: American Library Association, 1977); Thad Sitton, George L. Mehaffy, and O. L. Davis, Jr., *Oral History: A Guide for Teachers* (and Others) (Austin: University of Texas Press, 1983); James Hoopes, *Oral History: An Introduction for Students* (Chapel Hill: University of North Carolina Press, 1979). Section V ("Oral History and Schools") of Dunaway and Baum, *Oral History* (1984) is also valuable. The bibliography of this work lists a large number of additional oral history manuals.
[12]See David E. Kyvig and Myron A. Marty, *Your Family History: A Handbook for Research and Writing* (Wheeling, Ill.: Harlan Davidson, 1978).
[13]Davis, et al., *Oral History,* 20.
[14]These questions were drawn from lists suggested in Davis, et al., Oral History, 20–21, and William Bruce Wheeler and Susan D. Becker, *Discovering the American Past: A Look at the Evidence,* Vol. II (Boston: Houghton Mifflin, 1986), 228.

- Ask provocative questions—Who? What? Where? When? How? Why? Keep questions broad and general so that interviewees have to do more than answer "yes" or "no."
- Ask about specific events or experiences. "Why did you vote as you did in the 1968 election?" "Where were you when you watched the telecast of the first moon landing?" "What was it like to work on the Ford assembly line in the 1940s?"
- Elicit emotions. Ask the person to recall actual feelings about the events and experiences you are discussing.
- Ask your narrator to reconstruct specific conversations and physical locations. Asking for such concrete details often helps people recall a wealth of interesting particulars.
- Don't argue with the person you are interviewing. You are there to solicit their experiences and opinions, not convert them to your way of thinking.
- Save controversial issues until the end of the interview. By that time the narrator may feel more comfortable talking about sensitive matters.
- Make sure you have written down all pertinent personal information: name, age, educational and family background, occupation at time of events being investigated, etc.
- Make sure the interviewee signs a proper release form.

3. Ethical and Legal Considerations

At some point in the interviewing process, preferably at the beginning, it is necessary to obtain the interviewee's signature on a legal release. The legal release (see Appendix B) "acknowledges the legal (and legitimate) rights of interviewees to shield themselves from public ridicule or the betrayal of confidences. Generally, legal releases either give complete access to an interview or stipulate the conditions under which all or portions of the interview will be released."[15] Without such a signed release you do not have the legal right to allow others to have access to the collected materials.

There are other rules that, though not mandated by law, are dictated by common sense and good manners. The Oral History Association, founded in 1967, encourages practitioners to "recognize certain principles, rights and obligations for the creation of source material that is authentic, useful and reliable."[16] See the Appendix B for a copy of the Oral History Association guidelines.

Doing Oral History: The Narrative

Oral testaments are pieces of evidence—not history as we have defined it in this book. The most important goal of an oral history project is to use your newly created sources to write some history. The length and nature of what you write depends on individual classroom circumstances, but something should be written, however brief or tentative. It is at this point that you actually do the work of the historian, and, it is the most meaningful phase of the project.[17] That said, have fun.

---

[15]Sitton, et al., *Oral History,* 78.

[16]Reprinted in Dunaway and Baum, *Oral History*, 415–416.

[17]Another important aim of oral research projects is to catalog and store the oral histories (often in written transcriptions) for the use of future historians. Given the nature of this book, these elements have not been discussed. See the sources in Note 4 for further information.

History by the Numbers: Quantitative History

Like oral testimony, historians have, of course, always used quantitative (i.e., numerical) evidence in their work. They tell us how many soldiers died in the battle of Waterloo, what percent of the population voted for the Republicans in the presidential election of 1992, and how many people lived in Great Britain in 1871. They tell us how Congress voted on the Compromise of 1850, how much steel was produced at the turn of the century, and how many immigrants from Ireland came to North America after the Irish potato famine of the 1840s. On the other hand, the most casual glance at the average history book will show that numerical evidence usually takes a distinct back seat to literary or written evidence. Historians, and students of history, are generally more comfortable with words than with numbers.

There are those who argue, however, that in this age of the computer, history should become much more quantitative (number oriented). Numerical data and statistics are necessary, they say, if history is to become more rigorous, systematic, and "scientific." Quantification, they say, will help us move beyond the vague and impressionistic style that characterizes so much traditional historical writing.

To this, many traditionalists have reacted with barely controlled outrage. The historian Oscar Handlin lamented that "we have long known the danger of depending on translators; we must now learn the danger of depending on programmers." The eminent intellectual historian Jacques Barzun said that when a person examines a chart [of numbers], "he is not *reading history*.[18]

The details of the debate between the quantifiers and traditionalists need not detain us. However, it is important to understand both the advantages and disadvantages of using numbers in history. After all, graphs, tables, and opinion polls have become so common that individuals who desire to understand the world in which they live will have to be able to interpret simple numerical data.

On the positive side, numerical evidence can make history much more precise. Historians talk about quantities all the time, but often in a vague and shapeless manner. We talk about majorities who support such-and-such a proposition; about social classes that are *growing* in strength (the "middle classes were on the rise"); about a *rising tide* of antigovernment opinion, and the like. Our history would be much more convincing if, when possible, some precise numbers could be attached to these statements—a 54 percent majority; a middle class than numbered 37 percent of the population; 63 percent opposed the government on a specific measure.

Statistical data and computer calculations are useful in other areas of historical study. Many issues in modern social history—the study of people as groups, not individuals—can be approached only if we have some meaningful numbers with which to work. Quantification is essential if we are to find answers to such questions as: At what age did people get married in England in the seventeenth century? What was the average life expectancy in Boston, New York, and Charleston in 1850? What percentage of the population lived on family farms in the pre–Civil War South? Were illegitimate births a serious problem in pre–industrial France?

In asking these questions we are trying to understand the history of the great mass of people—people like most of us—who lived and died without leaving a written legacy. And we cannot answer such questions by studying individuals one

---

[18]Quotations are from Richard E. Beringer, *Historical Analysis: Contemporary Approaches to Clio's Craft* (New York: John Wiley and Sons, 1978), 193-94.

by one. We can begin to get answers only when we use parish records, census data, and court records to count heads and compile a collective portrait of a group of people at a given time and place. We can never know these people as individuals, but statistics can provide countless clues to the very real lives they lived.

On the other hand, although we should welcome the precision and social insights quantification can provide, "history by the numbers" should not be embraced uncritically. Three objections to quantification in history are worth noting here. First, most historical evidence is still in the form of written records. Since quantifiable evidence is simply not available for many questions, most history will still have to be based on the written record.

Second, many important historical questions cannot be answered with numbers or statistics. Arthur Schlesinger, Jr., pointed out in 1962 that "most of the variables in an historical equation are not susceptible to commensurable quantification." Further, said Schlesinger, "almost all important questions are important precisely because they are *not* susceptible to quantitative answers."[19] We might say that, while quantification can provide many valuable insights, it is necessary to know when such evidence is and is not appropriate to the task at hand.

Finally, numbers can be seductively misleading. Given the scientific bias of our age, many people have a tendency to trust numbers over more literary formulations. Statistics carry weight in debates and discussions, and effective politicians, journalists, and social reformers are quick to cite relevant figures in support of their positions. The problem for the historian is that numbers, like other forms of evidence, do not speak for themselves. Numerical evidence must be analyzed and interpreted by the historian. Note the difference between saying that "one-quarter of southern white families owned slaves in 1860," versus saying that "only one-quarter of those families owned slaves." The first statement is more-or-less neutral, while the second includes a very clear judgment that slave holding was concentrated in a small minority of families.[20] And notice what a different impression would be created if we said, "fully one-quarter of Southern white families owned slaves." In each case 25 percent carries a different connotation.

It is also useful to pay attention to the source of the numbers you are reading. The way numbers are presented can influence the way they are interpreted, or, in the case of modern opinion polls, the wording of the questions can have a significant impact on the answers people give. And, sad to say, sometimes people lie to poll-takers for a variety of reasons. The point is, quantitative information that appears in books and in the press should never be accepted uncritically.

To see how the presentation of data can influence its interpretation, compare the two (fictitious) graphs in Figure A. Both show the identical information: that the unemployment rate for the State of Clio went up three percent in a six year period (1985–1991). Graph I uses a percentage scale that begins at 0 percent and ends at 8 percent; Graph II, however, uses an expanded amount scale and grounds the graph at the original 3 percent unemployment rate. Note how much more severe the rise in unemployment appears in Graph II. Yet the "numbers" are identical. How might unwary readers react differently to the two graphs?

[19]Quoted in Beringer, *Historical Analysis,* 195.
[20]See Peter J. Parish, *Slavery: History and Historians* (New York: Harper and Row, 1989), 28.

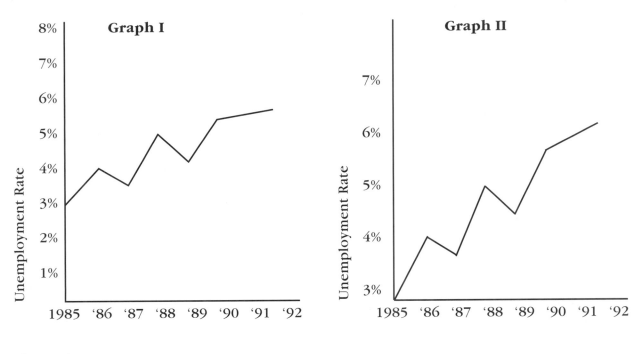

Figure A

In sum, quantification in history is here to stay. Computers and statistical techniques have enriched and will continue to enrich our understanding of the human past. On the other hand, instead of eliminating the need for historians to draw "legitimate inferences" from the raw, undigested evidence, numerical data demands even more sophisticated inference-making skills.

EXERCISES

Set A, Exercise 1: History by the Numbers

Although history remains a discipline primarily grounded in a literary tradition, a significant number of historians use numerical and statistical evidence in their work. Moreover, since much of the history and journalism read by the general public is accompanied by tables, graphs, opinion polls, and statistical assertions, it is important for students of history to be able to read and interpret evidence that comes in numerical form.

It is not our aim to provide an in-depth immersion in the techniques of quantification and the interpretation of numerical evidence. But the exercise below will provide a taste of the sort of reasoning and analysis that the use of statistical evidence requires. The tables reproduced below do not represent primary sources in the purest sense. The historian who drew up the charts, John Demos, has culled the information from many original documents and has done the counting for you. Moreover, the organization of the information reflects the questions that Demos wished to investigate.[21] Nevertheless, the charts do represent raw data that does not "speak for itself." It must be interpreted by the historian.

[21]John Demos, "Witchcraft in Seventeenth-Century New England," *American Historical Review* (June, 1970), 1311–26. Statistical tables reprinted by permission of the author.

The tables printed below categorize by age, sex, and marital status those people who, during the infamous Salem witchcraft trials in 1692, were either accused of being witches or who accused others of witchcraft. On the basis of the evidence presented, what general conclusions can be made concerning the "types" of people most likely to be accused of witchcraft (group I) compared with the "types" of people who accused others of witchcraft (group II)?

I. Persons accused of being witches:

Age	Male	Female	Total
Under 20	6	18	24
21–30	3	7	10
31–40	3	8	11
41–50	6	18	24
51–60	5	23	28
61–70	4	8	12
Over 70	3	6	9
Total	30	88	118

Marital Status	Male	Female	Total
Single	8	29	37
Married	15	61	76
Widowed	1	20	21
Total	24	110	134

II. Persons who accused others of witchcraft:

Age	Male	Female	Total
Under 11	0	1	1
11–15	1	7	8
16–20	1	13	14
21–25	0	1	1
26–30	0	1	1
Over 30	0	4	4
Total	2	27	29

Marital Status	Male	Female	Total
Single	5	23	28
Married	0	6	6
Widowed	0	0	0
Total	5	29	34

1. General characteristics of persons in group I:

_____

_____

_____

_____

2. General characteristics of persons in group II:

_____

_____

_____

_____

Set A, Exercise 2

Refer back to the tables on the accusers and accused in the Salem witch trials. Using the letters A, B, C, indicate whether each statement below:[22]

A. Can be *proved* using the data in the tables.
B. Can be *neither proved nor contradicted* using the data in the tables.
C. Can be *contradicted* using the data in the tables.

Be prepared to defend your answer orally.

Statements:

_____ 1. Most of the men accused of being witches were middle-aged or older.
_____ 2. Most of the men accused of witchcraft were economically well off.
_____ 3. A majority of those accused were between the ages 41 and 60.
_____ 4. Three times as many women as men were accused of witchcraft.
_____ 5. The young women who accused other women of witchcraft were envious of the status and power of the older women.
_____ 6. Men made accusations of witchcraft almost as often as women did.
_____ 7. Most of those accused of witchcraft were married.
_____ 8. Most people in Salem believed that witches made pacts with the devil.
_____ 9. Twenty-four of those accused of witchcraft were teenagers.
_____ 10. The accusers tended to be very religious people.

Set A, Exercise 3: Oral History (Optional)

Even a modest oral history project can be very time consuming, so many instructors may decide to pass it by. If circumstances permit, however, the following exercise can be an interesting introduction to doing history from the ground up.

Oral history is written from the recorded interviews of people who actually witnessed and experienced the history later generations can only read about. Obviously, to do oral history you have to interview people who are still alive, which limits your pool of interviewees to those from relatively few generations.

To do oral history even moderately well you have to prepare thoroughly and allot sufficient time. Therefore, begin this exercise by rereading the information

---

[22]The inspiration for this exercise came from Horace T. Morse and George H. McCune, *Selected Items for the Testing of Study Skills and Critical Thinking* (Washington, D.C.: National Council for the Social Studies, 1964).

on pages 172–173. A full-fledged oral history project involves the collection, transcribing, editing, dissemination, and storage of the interviews.[23] For the purposes of this exercise we will limit the activity to interviewing subjects and disseminating the findings in a written paper or oral report.

Oral history projects take many forms, but for this exercise we suggest that you attempt an oral history of a significant theme or local or national event—a flood, an election, experiences, at home or abroad, in a war (World War II, Korea, Vietnam, the Persian Gulf), etc.[24] After making the preparations outlined in this chapter, you should record an interview with at least two individuals who can comment on your chosen event or theme. The interviews will constitute the evidence from which a paper, as assigned by the instructor, will be written.

An abbreviated exercise could take the form of (1) a group interview (in the classroom) of a person who has useful firsthand knowledge to share, or, (2) an oral autobiography assignment in which each student is expected to prepare an account based on an interview with another student in class. In both cases questions and expectations would have to be thoroughly discussed beforehand. Both of these options allow students to practice, and instructors to critique, interviewing skills.

Set B, Exercise 1: History by the Numbers

Although history remains a discipline primarily grounded in a literary and humanistic tradition, a significant number of historians use numerical and statistical evidence in their work. Moreover, since much of the history and journalism read by the general public is accompanied by tables, graphs, and statistical assertions, it is important for students of history to be able to read and interpret evidence that comes in numerical form.

It is not our aim to provide an in-depth immersion in the techniques of quantification and the interpretation of numerical evidence. But the exercise below will provide a taste of the sort of reasoning and analysis that the use of statistical evidence requires. The tables produced below do not represent primary sources in the purest sense; they were compiled by the author, James Bonner, in his article on the social history of the white farmers in one slave-holding region (Hancock County, Georgia) before the Civil War.[25] The tables represent, in short, the questions Bonner chose to ask and the categories he used to display the data he had gathered.

The tables show the average ages, occupations, and economic status of the nonslave population of Hancock County in 1860. "Realty" refers to landed property, or "real estate." "Personalty" refers to other forms of personal property.

---

[23] See Cullom Davis, Kathryn Back, and Kay MacLean, *Oral History: From Tape to Type* (Chicago: American Library Association, 1977).

[24] For a list of many oral history project options, see Thad Sitton, George L. Mehaffy, and O. L. Davis, Jr., *Oral History: A Guide for Teachers* (and Others) (Austin, Texas: University of Texas Press, 1983), Ch. 2. To do your project as family history, see David E. Kyvig and Myron A. Marty, *Your Family History: A Handbook for Research and Writing* (Wheeling, Ill.: Harlan Davidson, 1978).

[25] James C. Bonner, "Profile of a Late Ante-Bellum Community," *American Historical Review* (July, 1944), 663–80. The tables are from pp. 671–72.

Table I: Economic Status of Occupational Groups, 1860

Occupational Group	Number	Total in families	Percent owning realty	Percent owning slaves	Percent owning other personal property
Planters and farmers*					
$10,000 and above	56	267	100.0	100.0	100.0
$9,999 to $1,001	220	1,049	100.0	92.2	100.0
$1,000 and under	85	379	100.0	41.6	91.7
Professional class	48	195	62.4	54.1	77.1
Merchants	29	101	50.0	45.0	75.9
Tradesmen	116	414	13.7	7.7	26.9
Overseers	139	367	1.4	6.4	20.8
Farm laborers	198	610	1.2	0.016	8.4
Factory workers	96	157	0.9	0.0	0.0**
All others	110	276	—	—	—

*While the landowning agricultural subdivision (those whose land was valued at $1,000 and under) is placed third from the top in this table, it is evident that its position would be lower when measured by other criteria. For example, see the values of land and personalty assigned to various groups in Table II.

**The absence of personal property assigned to factory workers is explained by the failure of enumerators to list personal property evaluations of less than $100.

Table II: Economic Status of Occupational Groups in 1860

Occupational Group	Average age of each group	Percent owning slaves	Average value of realty	Average value of personalty	Ratio of personalty to realty
Planters and farmers*					
$10,000 and above	49.7	100	$21,786	$45,434	1.99
$9,999 to $1,001	45.8	92.2	4,268	12,904	3.02
$1,000 and under	44.9	41.6	719	2,348	3.26
Professional class	34.85	54.1	2,844	8,025	2.82
Merchants	33.5	45	1,862	5,848	3.14
Tradesmen	38.03	7.7	216	874	4.04
Overseers	28.8	6.4	72	1,524	21.16
Farm laborers	30.0	6.01	15	44	2.87
Factory workers	24.09	0	4	0	0

Using the letters A, B, C, indicate whether each statement below:

A. Can be *proved* using the data in the tables.
B. Can be *neither proved nor contradicted* using the data in the tables.
C. Can be *contradicted* using the data in the tables.

Be prepared to defend your answer orally.

Statements:

Unless stated otherwise, assume all statements refer to Hancock County, Georgia in 1860.

_____ 1. Planters and farmers constituted the majority of the nonslave population of Hancock County.
_____ 2. The largest single occupational group was that of farm laborers.
_____ 3. Generally, the younger people were the less well-off economically than the older people.
_____ 4. The majority of employed whites owned slaves in 1860.
_____ 5. The economic position of farm laborers in Hancock County was the same as the economic position of farm laborers in all of Georgia.
_____ 6. All planters and farmers owned slaves.
_____ 7. The majority of the non-farmers supported the institution of slavery.
_____ 8. Industry was as important to the economy of Hancock County as was agriculture.
_____ 9. The same percentage of people in the North as in the South owned real estate in 1860.
_____ 10. Some merchants and members of the "professional class" were better off economically than were some farmers.

Set B, Exercise 2

Using the same numerical tables, write a paragraph in which you try to make some generalizations about class relationships in Hancock County in 1860. Your generalizations should be those statements that are either absolutely true or probably true in light of the evidence.

Set B, Exercise 3: Oral History (Optional)

For potential oral history projects, see Set A, Exercise 3.

CHAPTER 11 INTERPRETATION

"The writing of history reflects the interests, predilections, and even prejudices of a given generation."

John Hope Franklin

"[Y]ou cannot see things till you know roughly what they are."

C. S. Lewis

History has many "villains," among them Nero of Rome, Attila the Hun, Oliver Cromwell in Ireland, Henry VIII of England, and General William T. Sherman in Georgia. But in the mind of most people alive today, none of them is as steeped in evil as is Adolf Hitler (1889–1945). Even in the twentieth century, when villains have been relatively easy to come by (Lenin, Mussolini, Stalin, Idi Amin, Saddam Hussein), Hitler far overshadows the rest.

From every source come accounts of Hitler's depravity. Biographers provide a glimpse of the Austrian's boyhood and adolescence: his ungovernable temper; his laziness and habitual lack of self-discipline; his hostility to correction of any kind; his psychological brutality toward his peers; his way of lying with utter conviction of manner; his loutishness in the presence of women; his poorly formed moral conscience. Historians of his political career catalog his single-minded pursuit of power, his viciousness toward Jews and political rivals, his foreign policies built on lying and deception, his bull-headedness as a military warlord. Psychiatrists call him a diseased personality, describe him as a neurotic psychopath, and speak of his messiah complex. Occultists conjecture about a diabolical nature shaped and controlled by Satan himself.[1] Such images of personified evil have led most historians to charge Hitler with being the dominant, if not sole, cause of World War II.

But there are exceptions. In 1961 British historian A. J. P. Taylor published *The Origins of the Second World War,* an account of Hitler and World War II that differs from the rest. Though no admirer of Hitler, Taylor attacks the common view that World War II was "Hitler's War." Hitler, says Taylor, sought no more (perhaps even less) than earlier German leaders sought, or should have sought, to restore the Germany that had been destroyed by the hated Versailles Treaty of 1919. This included regaining lost German territory on its eastern borders, reestablishing German preeminence in Central Europe, and returning Germany to a position of military strength. These were, in Taylor's opinion, logical, legitimate, perhaps even necessary goals for Hitler to seek. Hitler in the 1930s, says Taylor, was not so much a warmonger as an opportunist willing to take advantage of the "stupidity" and timidity of British and French leaders. He had no long-term plan for war; it was the

---

[1]Trying to explain Adolf Hitler has been a preoccupation of countless historians for the last half century. For an overview of the many varying interpretations of Hitler's character and deeds see Ron Rosenbaum, *The Search for Hitler* (New York: Random House, 1998). This is not so much a study of Hitler directly as a study of the myriad interpretations of Hitler that scholars have offered over the years.

last thing he wanted. In short, says Taylor, World War II was not "Hitler's War," but the consequence of the Versailles Treaty, the geopolitics of Central Europe, German nationalism, and the naiveté of the Western powers. Hitler was but the "fuel to an existing engine."[2]

Such is Professor Taylor's interpretation of the origins of World War II, an interpretation that has been ferociously attacked by many historians.[3] This is not the time or place to debate the merits of Taylor's position, only to observe that it is the product of *his* reading of the source materials relating to the origins of World War II—and, we might add, of his delight in challenging conventional wisdom. Just as a portrait painters seek not photographic realism but special insight into the nature of their subjects, so too historians seek to portray events according to their best understanding of the historical situation. All of us do fundamentally the same thing many times a day. When we are asked to evaluate a teacher, or a job situation, or the quality of the automobile we drive, we review the record and respond with an *interpretation* based on the range of our experience and the depth of our understanding, though perhaps not as systematically as in Taylor's case.

The primary purpose of this chapter is to give you a clear idea of this vital term, for interpretation is the most basic and final product of historical study. Its clear-cut presence and development makes any student paper an intellectual achievement; its absence reduces a paper to an empty recital of facts.

Interpretation is, in its most fundamental sense, *generalization*. It is that mental act in which one rises above the details of a given experience and makes a statement that characterizes the entire experience according to its principal elements. Such a simple statement as "I had a great time last night" can illustrate the essential nature of generalization. What the speaker has done—in an instant—is recall elements of the evening, including the personality and appeal of the person one was with, the food and drink consumed, the warmth felt, the quality of the music heard, the level of conversation shared. Finding that all of these elements reflect a pattern, the speaker can summarize the whole experience as "a great time." The speaker can then, if asked, supply corroborating detail to support the generalization offered.

So it is with history, though the raw materials you work with are usually historical sources rather than personal experience. A generalization (interpretation) about George Washington's military role in the American Revolution might read: "Washington's military genius manifested itself repeatedly in his avoidance of defeat rather than in a string of victories." Many of us might be inclined to accept that statement. But we should not do so until we are supplied with corroborating details such as Washington's refusal to commit his full army to a frontal battle at Boston, his dilatory campaign around New York, his withdrawal at Monmouth, his patience at Philadelphia, etc. In other words, just as a listener expects to hear certain details that can justify the "great time" one claims to have had last night, so, too, does a reader expect a historian to provide detailed support for any generalizations he or she makes.

---

[2]A. J. P. Taylor, *The Origins of the Second World War* (Greenwich: Fawcett Books, 1961), 292. See also, Gertrude Himmelfarb, "Taylor-Made History," *The National Interest,* No. 36 (Summer 1994).
[3]See Gordon Martel, *The Origins of the Second World War Reconsidered: The A. J. P. Taylor Debate After Twenty-Five Years* (Unwin Hyman, 1986).

Types of Generalization

"All learning of history," says historian Robert Daniel, "is learning about generalizations—how to form them, how to understand and remember them."[4] For our present purpose, a generalization can be treated as belonging at one of three levels: summary, limited interpretive, and broad interpretive. A *summary* generalization is essentially a statement that is so obvious and basic that it requires very little proof or argumentation to convince people that it is true: e.g., "The Democratic party won the presidential election of 1992." (This statement is a generalization because it summarizes the Electoral College results of the individual state elections.) A *limited interpretive* generalization is more sophisticated. It makes a claim that must be supported with evidence and argument in order to convince others that it is true. This type of generalization is also concrete enough to be susceptible to a convincing proof: e.g., "The Democratic party won the presidential election of 1992 *because Ross Perot split the opposition votes to Bill Clinton.*" (The clause that begins with "because" makes this a generalization that requires the support of evidence.)

Finally, *broad interpretive* generalizations are so grand and all-encompassing that they are exceedingly difficult to validate with any amount of evidence or argument. Broad generalizations often try to explain so much that even with a massive accumulation of evidence they remain quite speculative. Karl Marx's "all history is the history of class conflict," or Arnold Toynbee's generalizations about the rise and fall of civilizations, or Frederick Jackson Turner's claim that "the primary factor in shaping the American character was the two-hundred year frontier experience of its people" belong to this category. Generalizations of such magnitude, though often very thought-provoking, are best left to philosophers.

Most worthwhile historical interpretations are generalizations at the limited level. They provide truths of a manageable size, modest units of knowledge that can be supported by citing the particulars on which the generalization is based. For example, a carefully written student essay on Franklin Roosevelt's first term in office (1933–1937) might set forth the generalization: "The emergence of radical political movements in the mid-thirties brought a leftward shift in New Deal policy." The writer could then make such a statement plausible by examining some specific "radical political movements": Huey Long's "Share Our Wealth" crusade, Francis Townsend's over-sixty scheme, Father Charles Coughlin's attack on Roosevelt's monetary policy, followed by a discussion of the new direction signified by the Wagner Labor Act and the Social Security Act.

Limited interpretive generalizations and their supporting elements are the "meat-and-potatoes" of historical discourse: they compel assent; they advance understanding; they deepen knowledge; they give a signal that the writer knows the subject. How much better is such a student generalization than a vague and almost meaningless statement like "Roosevelt had trouble in the late years of his first administration," a thesis that seems suspended in midair, suggesting little connection to events and developments of the times.

In addition to being supportable, limited interpretive generalizations should also add to the readers' (or listeners') *understanding*. They should provide an explanation of how and why something happened as it did; they should explain the causes behind the event. To do so, one need not kill a mosquito with a sledge-

[4]Robert V. Daniel, *Studying History* (Englewood Cliffs, N.J.: Prentice-Hall, Inc., 1966), 37.

hammer, that is, bring into play all possible remote, proximate, underlying, or indirect "causes." Such an approach only diminishes the limited interpretive generalization and makes it insupportable.

Developing Interpretations

The reader might ask "Where are we at this stage?"—a good question. To summarize briefly, in order to understand any historical development you must ask the questions described in Chapter 4, consider the context—the cultural and intellectual setting in which events took place (Chapter 5), read what other historians have said about the topic (Chapter 7), and closely study the available evidence (Chapters 9 and 10). Now comes the difficult but rewarding step of trying to interpret the evidence you have found. In essence, you will be trying to answer the questions—What happened? How did it happen? Why did it happen?

We cannot emphasize enough that interpretation is a process not a singular episode. Usually you begin an investigation with some preliminary and tentative conjectures about why things happened the way they did. As one of C. S. Lewis's characters noted in *Out of the Silent Planet,* "[Y]ou cannot see things till you know roughly what they are."[5] These initial conjectures may have to be modified or cast aside as you dig deeper into the evidence, and new ideas may be "tried on for size." In essence, you are creating a *preliminary hypothesis* that will allow you to begin your research with a sense of direction and purpose. At each stage of your project, you will have to refine your interpretation as new evidence comes to light and as your understanding of the material becomes more sophisticated. In the end, your final interpretation, or thesis, must be constructed so that it does justice to all the evidence you have discovered.

In this section, we've described a special kind of intellectual experience, and we'd like to pause and reflect on it a bit. In essence, the historian first lifts an event from its temporal surroundings, and then examines those surroundings for elements that bear a crucial relationship to the event under scrutiny. In a way it is like unraveling a snarled skein of yarn. Perhaps the real source of the difficulty is that the historian is attempting to turn the world, complex and multilayered, into language, which is linear and can express only one idea or relationship at a time. The process is one of mental reconstruction. Eventually the hours of reading, mental shuffling, and reorganizing pay off: there emerges a *synthesis*, a mental image that combines elements experienced separately. Some would use the term "pattern," others "insight," instead of synthesis. Whatever word is used, the exact processes of the mental experience described here remain a mystery to psychologists. Sometimes the synthesis builds slowly, often laboriously, occasionally with a sudden flash. Whichever the case, undue haste in trying to "make it come" can be counterproductive. Understanding relationships seems to have a slow-paced chronology, a point brilliantly made by novelist Eudora Welty in a recent work.

> Connections slowly emerge. Like distant landmarks you are approaching, cause and
> effect begin to align themselves, draw closer together. Experiences too indefinite of
> outline in themselves to be recognized for themselves connect and are identified as a
> larger shape. And suddenly a light is thrown back, as when your train makes a curve,

---

[5]Quoted in David Lowenthal, *The Past is a Foreign Country* (Cambridge, Mass.: Cambridge University Press, 1985), 39.

showing that there has been a mountain of meaning rising behind you on the way you've come, is rising there still, proven now through retrospect.[6]

Thus, after studious and extended consideration of the historical situation in which an event is contained, the historian sees (or begins to see) that event as part of a larger whole. The event is like a piece of jigsaw puzzle, which suddenly makes sense when seen in the context of other pieces. For example, Adolf Hitler's confidence that his invasion of Poland in 1939 would not be seriously challenged makes sense when seen in the context of his experience of the repeated British and French pacifism of the preceding years. Basically, the historian comes to see an event as part of a whole composed of numerous individual acts, of certain prevailing conditions, and certain action-producing pressures.

It is important to reiterate that an interpretation does not jump out of an assembled body of factual data nor does the historian passively await a moment of inspiration. In contrast, interpretations are aggressively sought. Historians approach historical situations with certain expectations about how human affairs work: what moves human beings, typical tendencies of motivation, relations between economic and political power, the relations between geography and economic development—generally all manner of regularities that experience has reinforced. They then actively use these expectations to develop their interpretations. What this means, of course, is those with wide experience in human affairs have something of a head start in historical interpretation. But however wide one's experience, the rules of the game require that one's expectations serve as a guide not as an inflexible formula, as a tool that may (or may not) prove useful in explaining the event under consideration.

Variations in Interpretation

All that we have said leads us to a crucial question: What can one say about the validity of interpretations? It is best to avoid a counsel of perfection on this matter. For one thing, all historical generalizations are probabilistic rather than certain. That is, if generalizations are rooted solidly in evidence, they are *probably* valid. Scientists may say with certitude that all physical objects must descend according to a mathematically predictable rate of acceleration. Historians are in no such position, because their evidence is never complete and they can never be sure that the evidence they do have is representative. The historian is more or less in the situation of a person driving down a street, who, seeing five black cats, is tempted to conclude that all cats on that street are black. Perhaps it is so, but there are likely a number of cats on the block that haven't been seen. As a rule most generalizations—in day-to-day life, in the social sciences, and in history—have a "rickety" quality. They are usable as effective but temporary ways of organizing information: rarely can they be regarded as absolute truth. For exactly this reason, some historians prefer to use the term "construct" to describe a historical generalization. A "construct" is a mental representation that organizes data into a thought unit that is both manageable and convincing while maintaining a certain tentative quality.

---

[6]Eudora Welty, *One Writer's Beginning* (Cambridge, Mass.: Harvard University Press, 1984), 90.

Thus, the issue of validity must be viewed within the context of the limited, or probabilistic, character of historical generalization. However, there is another, equally important side to the matter. *Any historical occurrence may be interpreted in a variety of ways.* In this respect mental functioning parallels perceptual functioning. The following figures (over) were taken from a psychology textbook that deals with perceptual variations.

Figure A   **Figure B**[7]

Some see in Figure A the cheek of a well-dessed young woman; others see an elderly peasant woman with a large nose and pointed chin. We'll let you ascertain the possibilities of Figure B.

The point of view also makes a big difference in historical interpretation. Because historians approach the past with different interests and goals, they may differ greatly in how they "locate" an event in the broad context of the period they are studying. Thus an event may plausibly be seen as the end event of an economic sequence, or of a political sequence, or of an ideological sequence, or of a combination of such factors. For example, the election of Franklin D. Roosevelt in 1932 can legitimately be regarded as part of the public's reaction to economic distress, as the product of a series of political failures by Republicans, as part of an ideological shift by the American people, or (in a more sophisticated way) as a combination of all three. Behind each of these interpretations (patterns) is a particular frame of reference and point of view. As we have seen, when historians start from different places, they necessarily travel different roads to the same destination. Nowhere is this basic feature of history better expressed than in Patrick Gardiner's *The Nature of Historical Explanation*:

---

[7]From *Mind Sights* by Shepard © 1990 by Roger N. Shepard. Used with permission by W. H. Freeman and Company.

There are no absolute Real Causes waiting to be discovered by historians with sufficiently powerful magnifying-glasses. What do exist are historians writing upon different levels and at different distance, historians writing with different aims and different interests, historians writing in different contexts and from different points of view.[8]

Thus, readers of history should not only get used to but come to expect major differences in the way several historians interpret a single event. Such difference is well illustrated in the discussion of the Social Security Act of 1935 in the following passages, each of them written by historians highly respected within the profession. Please note the comments below each selection.

1. William E. Leuchtenburg, *Franklin D. Roosevelt and the New Deal* (New York: Harper & Row, 1963), 129–30.

> By predepression standards, Roosevelt's works program marked a bold departure. By any standard, it was an impressive achievement. Yet it never came close to meeting Roosevelt's goal of giving jobs to all who could work. Of the some ten million jobless, the WPA [Works Projects Administration] cared for not much more than three million. Workers received not "jobs" but a disguised dole; their security wage amounted to as little as $19 a month in the rural South. The President split up the billions among so many different agencies—the Department of Agriculture got $800 million of it—that [WPA head Harry] Hopkins had only $1.4 billion to spend for WPA. By turning the unemployables back to the states, he denied to the least fortunate—the aged, the crippled, the sick—a part in the federal program, and placed them at the mercy of state governments, badly equipped to handle them and often indifferent to their plight.
>
> Roosevelt's social security program was intended to meet some of the objections to his relief operations.

Comment: *As seen by Leuchtenburg, the Social Security Act was part of the pattern of "doing something for everybody" that FDR had adopted early in his administration. This passage is preceded by descriptions of various relief agencies, such as the WPA and the NYA (National Youth Administration). But these agencies, and others like them, missed a good many Americans; hence, the Social Security Act.*

2. Oscar Theodore Barck, Jr., and Nelson Manfred Blake, *Since 1900,* 4th ed. (New York: Macmillan, 1965), 479.

> Another foundation stone of the Second New Deal was the Social Security Act of August, 1935. Behind its passage lay a reversal in prevailing American opinion. Old-age pensions, unemployment insurance, and provisions for sickness and accident benefits under government administration had been commonplace in Europe before World War I. But most Americans persisted in the belief that saving against old age and misfortune was an individual problem. The depression provided a cruel disillusionment. Thrifty citizens saw their life savings swept away by bank failures, while the average individual's inability to guarantee his own security in a complex economic system was demonstrated in many other ways as well. By 1932 there was a widespread demand for government action. The AFL [American Federation of Labor] passed resolutions asking unemployment insurance

---

[8]Patrick Gardiner, *The Nature of Historical Explanation* (London: Oxford University Press, 1963), 109.

with compulsory payments by employers and the state—reversing its earlier hostility to the proposal—and the Democratic National Platform included a plank advocating both unemployment and old-age insurance under state laws.

But building a social security system exclusively on state legislation offered many difficulties. . . . Some Federal program to coordinate action on a national basis seemed to be required. . . . In January, 1935, the President transmitted to Congress . . . recommendations for joint Federal-state action.

Comment: *Emphasizing ideological factors, the authors of this passage see the depression experience as having eroded traditional American individualistic ideas. The change in national ideology was manifested early in the 1930s by the AFL resolutions and by a plank in the Democratic National Platform. Here the Social Security Act is seen as part of that same pattern of ideological change.*

3. Henry J. Carman, Harold C. Syrett, and Bernard W. Wishy, *A History of the American People,* Vol. II (Philadelphia Book Co., 1967), 634.

For the first two years of its existence, the New Deal did little to provide long-range protection against the risks of a private economy for working people. But in 1935, it set up a social security program for the care of dependent children, the aged, the handicapped, and the temporarily unemployed. This move was long overdue. . . .

Throughout the 1930s, but especially during the first years under the New Deal, the bitterness and frustration built up by the depression provided fertile grounds for demagogic movements and quackery of various sorts. . . .

Some of the panaceas hawked for the illnesses of depression were harmless, but others were dangerous because of both their simplification of complex issues and their openly antidemocratic bias. . . . Senator Huey Long, dictator of Louisiana and self-styled "Kingfish," had promised to make "every man a king"; Dr. F. C. Townsend had assured his aged followers that his plan would give them $200 a month; and demagogues like Father Coughlin and Gerald L. K. Smith had outlined programs that were startlingly similar to those of Nazi Germany and Fascist Italy. The popularity of these and similar proposals among the poor as well as humanitarian considerations, convinced Roosevelt that the national government could no longer put off the adoption of social-security legislation.

Comment: *This is a most interesting passage that not only presents a pattern clearly different from the preceding two but also reflects an evident authors' bias. Note the editorial in line 5—"This move was long overdue." Note also the usage of such emotion-charged words as "quackery," "hating," "demagogues," and "Nazi Germany." The authors reflect a liberal, perhaps class-conscious point of view. As to the pattern they present, they see the Social Security Act as politically necessary because of the popularity of extremist proposals, including those of Huey Long, Francis Townsend, and Father Coughlin. The Social Security Act was part and parcel of the "turn to the left" of the Roosevelt administration in 1935.*

Nothing is more typical than difference in historical interpretation, an axiom that returns us to the question of validity with which we began this section. Simply because interpretations reflect individual points of view and must always be considered tentative does not mean that any and every interpretation is acceptable. Evaluation of interpretations remains an important intellectual task. Judging the soundness of a historical interpretation can be a complex and time-consuming endeavor, but that sober reality should not keep you from trying. From a practical, day-to-day standpoint, historians ask two things when evaluating an interpretation.

1. **Does the author adequately support the interpretation with evidence?** What we as readers want is a generalization clearly tied to the reality being described. We want the particular segment of the past about which the author is writing to "make sense" once we have finished our reading. We expect the author to have taken a reasonably wide look at the evidence and sought out the points essential to support the generalization. We want the author to avoid providing information extraneous to the interpretation presented. We are willing to recognize that no one can cover everything and that the author is obligated only to cover the material relevant to the interpretation being developed. In short, we want a limited interpretive generalization that is manageable within the limits of a book, article, or research paper.

2. **Does the author avoid being overwhelmed by personal intellectual preoccupations or theories?** All of us are aware that we have certain biases, be they political, national, racial, class, religious, or moral. We know that they can decisively shape our viewpoint, leading to a refusal to look honestly at evidence that does not fit our point of view. Perhaps it is true that history is "neither made nor written without love or hate," but we must distance ourselves from our personal attitudes as much as possible and recognize the inherent dangers in letting them pervade our work. This process is a matter of intellectual honesty as much as anything else. Just as an advertiser can distort the qualities of a product, so too can a historian distort the reality of the past. In fact, the world's libraries have many books full of misrepresentations founded on misplaced nationalism, political ideology, or similar preoccupations.

Interpretation is the centerpiece of the historian's work. In this chapter we have discussed the meaning of interpretation; the levels of summary, limited interpretive, and broad interpretive generalization; the importance of hypothetical generalizations; the chronology of development of an interpretation; and finally, the variations of interpretation. The next chapters will examine the culminating step of the historian's labor, putting it all on paper.

EXERCISES

Set A, Exercise 1: Classification

Effective interpretation requires that you put information into manageable units of analysis. This process, *classification,* is fundamental to the study of history, and vital if you intend to write intelligibly about human affairs. The past, as a whole, is so complex and confusing that it is incomprehensible unless broken into small, digestible pieces. The pieces must be *organized* into patterns that make sense to the researcher. Just as books in a huge library are of little use without a clear classification scheme to help you find the book you need, the "facts" of history are useless without similar systems of classification.

Whether classifying books or historical data, the choice of a classification system is often quite arbitrary. The needs and perceptions of the classifier determine the most appropriate classification system. Furthermore, classification systems are trial-and-error undertakings. As we proceed from ignorance to comprehension most of us find ourselves using tentative categories or names that later prove to be inexact or imprecisely phrased. When this happens, we have to alter our classification scheme. Finally, to classify effectively you have to use a "part-whole" mentality. That is, somewhere along the way you need to establish some major categories (often three or four), along with a number of subcategories appropriate to each.

Since classification schemes are created by the historian, there is the ever-present danger of trying to shoe-horn information into configurations that distort more than they clarify. The other extreme, approaching historical data with a totally blank mind, is also unsatisfactory (not to mention impossible), as you lack the beginnings of a classification system to make the data manageable. Since you cannot totally eliminate the influence of personal values and biases when creating a classification scheme, at least you can avoid the twin dangers mentioned above if you take to heart the words of Barzun and Graff: *"To be successful and right, a selection [i.e., pattern or scheme of classification] must face two ways: it must fairly correspond to the mass of evidence, and it must offer a graspable design to the beholder."*[9]

The most basic and obvious of the categories used by historians to classify information are the time periods—decades, reigns, centuries, eras—that constitute the organizational units of history books and college curricula. Period labels are convenient but no more than a starting point. To set off the 1930s, for example, from the rest of the twentieth century does not tell us anything other than these years somehow "belong" together. To give that period a name, in this case "The Depression Thirties," helps but not much. The name provides only a general theme, which may or may not be entirely applicable. Much more needs to be done in order to advance our understanding and insight of this particular decade.

Second, period labels, like all classification schemes, are the invention of the historian, a point clearly made by British historian G. J. Renier: "It cannot be stated with sufficient emphasis that the historian's principles of serialization are introduced into history by him, not deduced from it...."[10] The first tick of the clock on January 1, 1930, did not usher in a totally new era called "The Depression Years," nor did the final days of 1939 end the patterns of life as they had existed throughout the 1930s. There are no absolute openings and closings in history. To think otherwise is fundamentally anti-historical—remember what was said about change and continuity. Historical pots generally boil slowly, so the assigned dates of a historical "period" must be treated with flexibility.

Third, and this is the most important point of all, periods vary widely as to the unity that characterizes them. At one end of the spectrum we find "periods" that seem to have the quality of a three-ring circus: lots of events with little relationship to each other. Still, a textbook (or a professor) might give us such a time unit just to break down the task of learning into digestible pieces. Division of a segment of twentieth-century American history into a 1910–1920 period might be regarded as such a case. In that time span there was little relationship between diplomatic developments, economic achievements, government policies, and ideological attitudes. At the other end of the spectrum there are periods that seem to have deep and pervasive cultural unity. In these periods, politics, the arts, eco-

---

[9]Jacques Barzun and Henry Graff, *The Modern Researcher,* rev. ed. (New York: Harcourt Brace & World, 1970), 179.
[10]G. J. Renier, *History: Its Purpose and Method* (New York: Harper and Row, 1965), 176.

nomic life, religion, ideology, and social structure are profoundly affected by some powerful underlying current and are therefore interrelated in identifiable ways. The fifth century B.C. in Greece might be cited as an excellent example and so, too, the American South of the 1850s. Between these two ends of the spectrum are periods that have a good deal of integrity. The main events share similar attributes, making it fruitful to study the period following strong thematic lines. The Depression Thirties, for instance, is a good example of this middle type.

Classification is a natural inclination of the mind, but, like any other human capability, this inclination must be disciplined and thus expanded. Such is the purpose of the exercise that follows. Earlier (in Chapter 6) you were asked to classify some book titles into the categories of political, economic, social, and ideological. The next stage of difficulty is that of finding your own headings. All of the information given below relates to the Confederate States of America, 1861–1865. Your task is to classify the information into four categories, using your own headings, except for the first, which we have provided as an example. There should be three items in each category.

a. The Confederate dream of revolutionizing New Mexico and California ended in March 1862, when a rebel force was defeated at Pidgin's Ranch, just east of Glorieta Pass in the territory of New Mexico.

b. The Constitution of the Confederacy provided for a cabinet of six members, who were to serve as administrators of their departments and advisors to the president.

c. The Confederacy sent John Slidell as an envoy to France, but he was unable to secure French recognition of the Confederation as an independent government.

d. A stunning loss for the South occurred in mid-1863 when Vicksburg on the Mississippi fell to General Grant, causing him to telegraph Lincoln that "the Father of Waters again flows unvexed to the sea."

e. In 1861 the seceding southern states formed the Confederated States of America and elected Jefferson Davis as the first president.

f. Though Confederate commissioners were received cordially in London, British dealings with them were minimal because of the strong antislavery feelings of the British common people.

g. In the early stages of the Civil War the Southern government had to refuse the enlistments of tens of thousands of young men because there were no firearms for them.

h. The Southern victory at Chancellorsville in 1863, while decisive, was also extremely costly, as one of the South's greatest field commanders, General "Stonewall" Jackson, lost his life there.

i. Estimates of the total number of men in Confederate uniform during the four years of the war run from 700,000 to 900,000.

j. The first Confederate effort at diplomacy failed when U.S. Secretary of State Seward refused to see the Southern commissioners sent to establish peaceful relations with the United States government.

k. By the mid-point of the war, Southern recruitment of soldiers was bolstered by conscription of able-bodied men between the ages of eighteen and forty-five.

l. Because of the opposition of states' righters, who feared its appellate jurisdiction, the Confederate governmental system had to get along without a supreme court.

Category 1: Basis/Label: *Diplomacy/International Relations*

1. *Envoy Slidell unsuccessful in obtaining French recognition of
   independence (c).*
2. *Confeds. received cordially in London but little accomplished (f).*
3. *U.S. government refuses to see Southern diplomats (j).*

Category 2: Basis/Label: _____

1. _____

2. _____

3. _____

Category 3: Basis/Label: _____

1. _____

2. _____

3. _____

Category 4: Basis/Label: _____

1. _____

2. _____

3. _____

Set A, Exercise 2

We're now going to call upon you to interpret an array of facts. For each set of statements below write a carefully worded topic sentence that could serve as a lead-in to the specific pieces of information you are attempting to synthesize.

Note: *At this point we want to remind you of our earlier distinction between "summary" generalizations and "limited interpretive" generalizations. Broadly speaking there are two types of generalization: (1) those that summarize, such as: "It was a very hot day" (based on high temperature readings for several hours) and (2) those that show causal relationships, such as: "High temperatures prevailed today because a lingering low pressure area brought southerly winds." Both of these types of generalization are common in historical discourse. By far the most important of them is the causal, explanatory generalization (type 2).*

A. Using the following statements about the impact of the Model-T automobile in America in the 1920s, write a topic sentence (summary generalization) in the spaces provided below the statements.

- The Model-T ended the social isolation of the American farmer.
- By enabling children to get away from their parents, the automobile affected American family life.
- The automobile influenced romantic relationships, as now lovers could have a privacy not possible before.
- One of the factors contributing to the weakening of neighborhood relationships in America was the car, which enabled people to travel easily outside the neighborhood.

_____

_____

B. Using the following statements about various pieces of British legislation relating to the American colonies in the years preceding the Revolution (which began in 1775), write a summary generalization to serve as the topic sentence.

- American debtors bitterly opposed the Currency Act of 1764, which outlawed paper money issues thus deflating money values.
- The Quartering Act (1765) permitted public housing facilities in the colonies to be taken over for usage by British troops.
- By the provisions of the Stamp Act of 1765, American merchants found themselves having to purchase a government stamp for each and every business contract into which they entered.
- The Sugar Act of 1764, if enforced (and British officials said it would be enforced strictly), meant highly irritating losses to American shippers engaging in trade with the West Indies.
- Western settlers hotly resented the Proclamation Act of 1763, which prohibited colonial settlers from moving to attractive lands beyond the Appalachian Mountains.

_____

_____

C. The following statements relate to German plans to repulse the anticipated Allied invasion of Western Europe in 1944. At that point in World War II, the German leader, Adolf Hitler, knew that the Allied invasion would determine Germany's fate. If the invasion could be repulsed, he thought, Germany might yet win the war. Using the following items, write an *interpretive* sentence that explains why the Germans failed to repulse the invasion that came in June 1944. You should organize the statements chronologically and topically before you decide on the best topic sentence.

- Sent from Italy in early 1944 to inspect German defenses against invasion, General Erwin Rommel (the famed Desert Fox of the North African campaign) found them uncoordinated and undermanned.
- Shortly after his arrival in Normandy, General Rommel initiated extensive improvement of waterline defenses, including underwater obstacles, concrete dragon's teeth, and offshore mines.

- German western military commander Field Marshal Von Rundstedt saw no hope of preventing an Allied landing; however, he believed a German counterattack could throw them back to the beaches.
- German dictator Adolf Hitler, though agreeing with Rommel on where the Allies would strike (in Normandy), thought important diversionary activity would occur in the Calais sector, which was well north of Normandy.
- Rommel believed that once ashore the Allies could not be stopped; therefore, they must be stopped at the water's edge.
- Rommel was convinced that the main Allied invasion effort would be mounted in Normandy, which, as distinct from Calais, had not been mined by the Allies.
- Von Rundstedt, no admirer of Hitler, thought the main invasion strike would be in the Calais area.
- During the invasion itself, Allied air supremacy, destroying German transportation and communication facilities, immobilized German forces.
- Hitler compromised between the Von Rundstedt view and the Rommel view; though believing Rommel to be correct, he allowed large army groups to remain committed to the Calais area.

D. In the mid-1950s a new music widely known as "rock and roll" (rhythm and blues in the black community where it originated) began to displace in popularity older musical forms, such as crooning and the big band style. Write an *interpretive* topic sentence about that development based on the following statements.[11]

- One of the attractions of rock is that it makes few if any intellectual demands on the listener.
- Earlier popular black performers, such as Nat King Cole and Duke Ellington, adjusted their performances to white norms, as contrasted with black rock and rollers, who cared little for white gentility in clothing, dance, and language.
- Sam Phillips, a Memphis recording executive, was heard to say (in 1953), "if I could find a white man who had the Negro sound and the Negro feel, I could make a million dollars."
- As a group, teenagers of the 1950s had more money, more freedom, and less family orientation than any of their predecessors.
- As contrasted with earlier "white" popular music, rock featured hard-driving rhythm, shouted, repetitive lyrics, heavy dependence on guitar and drums, all this with ear-popping amplification.
- Pat Boone, a clean-cut college educated white, also did a few rock songs, thus giving the music a respectability to those who did not care for the ribald antics of Elvis Presley and various black performers.
- Widely popular in the 1930s, "swing" music had lost its momentum by the late 1940s, and had also lost much of its earlier audience to newly emerging television and to the movies.

---

[11]These statements, some quoted and some paraphrased, were drawn from Daniel P. Szatmary, *Rockin' In Time* (Englewood Cliffs, N.J.: Prentice-Hall, Inc., 1987); and James L. Baughman, *The Republic of Mass Culture* (Baltimore: The Johns Hopkins University Press, 1997).

- The white popularizer of rock, Elvis Presley "created a definitely 'antiparent' outlook. . . . His music and he, himself—appeared somewhat insolent, slightly hoodlum."
- Regarded as the "first" rock and roll song, "Rock a Beaten Boogie" was written by Bill Haley, a white band leader who with his "Comets" performed it for white audiences thus breaking the color line for this new music.
- Expressing the view of older Americans, popular crooner Frank Sinatra described rock music as "phony and false, and sung, written and played for the most part by cretinous goons."

Set A, Exercise 3

On a separate sheet of paper, write a full paragraph that synthesizes the information found in *either* Item C (German plans to repulse an Allied invasion) or Item D (the rise of rock and roll) from Exercise 2 above. Begin with your topic sentence (which should be a "limited interpretive"—explanatory—generalization) and support it with evidence drawn from the informational statements provided in Exercise 2. You need not use all of the statements in your paragraph, but it is important that you take account of them.

Set A, Exercise 4

A famous historian, Fénelon, once said, "The good historian belongs to no time or country: though he loves his own, he never flatters it in any respect. The French historian must remain neutral between France and England. . . ." Difficult counsel indeed. What Fénelon was talking about is bias, a crucial issue in any discussion of interpretation.

Earlier in this chapter we discussed the matter of the historian's "intellectual preoccupations"—the biases that might be national (despite the above advice), political, racial, class, religious, or moral. Remember, all interpretations reflect, to some extent, the historian's frame of reference. But bias is more than an acceptable intrusion of the historian's point of view; bias is, in the words of Barzun and Graff, *"an uncontrolled form of interest"* (italics ours). The presence of bias does not automatically mean a piece of history is worthless. But it is important that you develop the ability to identify obvious intrusions of bias so that you are better able to weigh the credibility of what you read.

Below are some examples of history writing that reflect authors' biases. Your task with the following excerpts is to identify in each passage any kind of bias you detect. Note each author's choice of words, emphasis, tone, and the like. Under each passage record the type(s) of bias you detect (political, racial or ethnic, class, national, religious, moral) along with your reasons for thinking so. *In choosing your labels decide what particular religion, class, etc. the historian is biased for or against.*

1. Cuba, our land, emerged from the condition of being a Spanish colony at the close of the past century, only to become a protectorate and semi-colony of the United States.

The efforts of the Cuban people to gain full independence and sovereignty—the heroic sacrifices of the Ten Years' War, the little Way, the War of [18]95, the aspirations expressed . . . above all by Antonio Maceo and by Jose Marti—were frustrated and flouted by North American intervention in the Cuban-Spanish War at a time when the Cubans had practically defeated Spanish colonialism and were on the verge of gaining full independence.

In 1902 it was said that Cuba was a free and sovereign republic. It had an anthem and a flag. But above these symbols of sovereignty . . . we had the Platt Amendment, an instrument of oppression and of foreign domination over the country. . . .

The United States imperialists had militarily occupied the island. They maintained here their army of occupation; by trickery they had disarmed the Army of Liberation and had organized a rural militia and a police force under their command. . . .

_____

_____

_____

2. Eisenhower and his administration have lived off the accumulated wisdom, the accumulated prestige, and the accumulated military strength of his predecessors who conducted more daring and more creative regimes. If our margin for error is as great as it has traditionally been, these quiet Eisenhower years will have been only a pleasant idyll, an inexpensive interlude in a grim century. If our margin for error is much thinner than formerly, Eisenhower may join the ranks of history's fatal good men, the Stanley Baldwins and the James Buchanans. Their intentions were good and their example is pious, but they bequeathed to their successors a black heritage of time lost and opportunities wasted.

_____

_____

_____

3. The first element in the negro problem is the presence in America of two alien races, both practically servants. The Indians were savages, and helped to keep alive savage traits in the souls of white settlers; but there was no considerable number of mixed bloods, and the Indians faded away as the white people advanced. The original slaves were also savages, just out of the jungle, who required to be watched and handled like savages, but they steadily increased in numbers, and from the beginning there was a serious race admixture. Their descendants in the second and third generation were milder in character, and were much affected by at least a surface Christianity; but their standards of character were much lower than those of the dominant white community, and tended to pull the superior race down. To the present day the low conditions of great numbers of negroes has a bad effect on the white race.

_____

_____

4. In pride and vanity, he [Henry VIII] was perhaps without a parallel. He despised the judgment of others; acted as if he deemed himself infallible in matters of policy and religion; and seemed to look upon dissent from his opinion as equivalent to a breach of allegiance. He steeled his breast against remorse for the blood which he shed, and trampled with out scruple on the liberties of the nation. When he ascended the throne, there still existed a spirit of freedom, which on more than one occasion defeated the arbitrary measures of the court; but in the lapse of a few years that spirit had fled, and before the death of Henry, the king of England had grown into a despot, the people had shrunk into a nation of slaves.

5. During the last century the [New England] manufacturer imported the Irish and Fr[ench] Canadians . . . thus the American sold his birthright in a continent to solve a labor problem. Instead of retaining political control and making citizenship an honorable and valued privilege, he intrusted the government of his country and the maintenance of his ideals to races who have never yet succeeded in governing themselves, much less anyone else.

Associated with this advance of democracy and the transfer of power from the higher to the lower races, from the intellectual to the plebian class, we find the spread of socialism and the recrudescence of obsolete religious forms.

Sources
1. Donald Robinson, ed., *As Others See Us* (Boston: Houghton Mifflin, 1969), 108–109.
2. William V. Shannon, "Eisenhower as President," in *Perspectives on 20th Century America*, Otis L. Graham, Jr., ed. (New York: Dodd, Mead, 1973), 323.
3. Albert B. Hart, "Negro Problem," *Cyclopedia on American Government* (Chicago: Appleton, 1914), 513.
4. John Lingard, *History of England*, Vol IV (Paris: W. Galignani, 1840), 215.
5. Madison Grant, "The Passing of the Great Race," in *Antidemocratic Trends in Twentieth-Century America*, Roland L. DeLorme and Raymond G. McInnes, eds. (Reading, Mass.: Addison-Wesley, 1969), 45.

Set B, Exercise 1: Classification

See discussion under Set A, Exercise 1.

All the information given below relates to Adolf Hitler's Germany (1933–45) and World War II (1939–45). Your task is to classify the information into four categories, using your own headings, except for the first, which we have provided as an example. There should be three items in each category.

a. Though he lacked the qualities of a statesman, Hitler shaped events by the force of his personality. He exuded personal magnetism.
b. In September 1939 the world saw a new form of military power, as the German *blitzkrieg* (lightning war) smashed through Poland in a matter of days.
c. At Munich, in September 1938, the leaders of Germany, France, Italy, and Great Britain "solved" the Czechoslovakian problem with an international agreement that gave the Sudetenland to Germany.
d. By the Nuremberg decree of 1935, German Gentiles were forbidden not only to marry Jews but even to touch them.
e. The Austrian *Anschluss* (union with Germany) in 1938 had been signaled earlier by German-Austrian diplomatic negotiations concerning trade relations.
f. One of the most brilliant achievements of the German *Wehrmacht* (army) was its "end run" around the French Maginot Line, leading to the destruction of the French army as a fighting force.
g. Because he thought in black-and-white terms, Hitler had no difficulty in perceiving those who opposed him as wholly evil.
h. Extensive German demands on Poland in 1939 led to a flurry of diplomatic negotiation between Germany and Russia, culminating in the Nazi-Soviet Pact of that year.
i. Exercising the power given him in the Enabling Act, Hitler decreed that all political parties but his own Nazi party were to be abolished.
j. The German Fuehrer (Hitler) was an opportunist, a man who knew clearly what he wanted and patiently waited for a chance to strike.
k. In 1933 Hitler maneuvered the German Reichstag into passing the Enabling Act, which gave him the power to pass laws without consent of the Reichstag, thus making him a dictator.
l. After a highly successful campaign in North Africa, General Erwin Rommel's *Afrika Korps* was repulsed and thrown back at El Alamein, the first major defeat of a German army in World War II.

Category 1: Basis/Label: *Aspects of Hitler's personality*

1. *Influenced events by blunt force of personality rather than statesmanship (a)*
2. *Not a subtle thinker—thought in categorical terms (g)*
3. *Had clear goals and patiently awaited opportunities (j)*

Category 2: Basis/Label: _____

1. _____

2. _____

3. _____

Category 3: Basis/Label: _____

1. _____

2. _____

3. _____

Category 4: Basis/Label: _____

1. _____

2. _____

3. _____

Set B, Exercise 2

For each set of statements below write a carefully worded topic sentence that could serve as a lead-in to the specific pieces of information you are attempting to synthesize. Before beginning, review the note on summary and limited interpretive generalizations in the directions of Set A, Exercise 2.

A. Using the following statements concerning the technological development of the United States in the late nineteenth and early twentieth centuries, write a summary topic sentence in the space provided.

• In 1879, Thomas Edison perfected the light bulb and three years later, in 1882, developed the first power transmitting station, thus bringing a major new form of power to U.S. industry.
• In the late nineteenth century the "open hearth" process of steelmaking was developed, marking a notable advance in machine tool production.
• By the early years of the twentieth century, American industrial production vastly exceeded that of her nearest rival.
• Development of the internal combustion engine in the late 1800s greatly increased the market for industrial products.
• Continuing development of petroleum products in the years after 1870 significantly influenced American industrial markets.

_____

_____

B. These statements relate to events in Eastern Europe at the end of World War II and in the years following. Write a summary topic sentence in the space provided.

• In January 1944, following the great Russian World War II victory over Germany in Eastern Europe, Yugoslavia adopted a new constitution that closely resembled that of the Soviet Union.
• Influenced by the presence of Russian armies, Bulgaria in 1944 formed a government with Communists in key positions.
• In 1947, Rumania's foreign minister resigned and was succeeded by Communist Ana Pauker.
• In 1948, the refusal of [Catholic] Cardinal Mindszenty in Hungary to make church

concessions to the Marxist government led to his trial and conviction, bringing a sentence of life imprisonment.
• Because of the government attempt to destroy the Catholic Church in Czechoslovakia, the Vatican in 1949 excommunicated all active supporters of communism in Czechoslovakia.

C. The following statements relate to the rejection of the Versailles treaty by the U.S. Senate in 1919–1920. President Woodrow Wilson had gone to Versailles and personally negotiated this treaty ending World War I. The treaty he brought home called for American acceptance of League of Nations participation. Write an interpretive topic sentence in the space provided.

• Though temporarily sidetracked in 1917–1918 by anti-German feeling, traditional American isolationism remained strong.
• In 1918, Americans elected a Republican Senate, an ominous sign for the Democrat Administration of President Woodrow Wilson.
• Americans of German and of Irish ethnic background opposed the League of Nations, although for different reasons.
• The wrangling of European diplomats at the Versailles Peace Conference of 1919 confirmed many Americans' view of European countries as narrow and self-serving.
• To get the League of Nations principle accepted in the peace treaty, President Wil-son had to compromise several of his ideals.
• The chairman of the Senate Foreign Affairs Committee was Republican Henry Cabot Lodge, a major political enemy of President Wilson.
• Wilson's peace treaty incorporating the League of Nations principle, which had to be approved by the Senate, was eventually decisively rejected.
• Wilson's refusal to take any Republican with him to the Versailles Peace Conference eventually proved costly to his hopes of Congressional acceptance of the treaty.

D. During the 1960s rock and roll music became something of a national passion. Using the following statements as the base, write an interpretive topic sentence in the space provided.[12]

• Emerging as rivals to the Beatles were the Rolling Stones, who cultivated a rebel image and whose songs represented more overt sexuality through pornographic lyrics.

---

[12]These statements, some quoted and some paraphrased, were drawn from Szatmary, *Rockin' In Time,* and Baughman, *The Republic of Mass Culture.*

- Acid rock as played by such drug-influenced groups as the "Jefferson Airplane" and the "Grateful Dead" had taken over much of American airwaves by 1968.
- Even Bob Dylan, whose protest songs infused with a folk style had gained a wide following among better-educated teens, saw the Beatles as the wave of the future.
- During the early sixties the Presley fan following was diluted when the musical tastes of rural and blue-collar youth shifted to country music.
- The Beatles' popularity was partly traceable to their somewhat more moderate image: their tailored suits, their mod haircuts, and their self-mocking style.
- As measured by record sales, rock and roll appeared to be on the way out in the early 1960s.
- By 1969 the "rock revolution" had become the staging area for drug addiction, indiscriminate sex, and full-scale rejection of traditional American values.
- In 1964 the Beatles, already popular in England, became an American sensation when they appeared on the Ed Sullivan show, followed by two concerts at Carnegie Hall.

Set B, Exercise 3

On a separate sheet of paper, write a full paragraph that synthesizes the information found in *either* Item C (U.S. rejection of the Versailles Treaty) or Item D (rock and roll music) from Exercise 2 above. Begin with your topic sentence (which should be a "limited interpretive"—explanatory—generalization) and support it with evidence drawn from the informational statements provided in Exercise 2. You need not use all of the statements in your paragraph, but it is important that you take account of them.

Set B, Exercise 4

See comments introducing Exercise 4 of Set A.

Below are some examples of history writing that reflect authors' biases. Your task with the following excerpts is to identify in each passage any kind of bias you detect. Note each author's choice of words, emphasis, tone, and the like. Under each passage record the type(s) of bias you detect (political, racial or ethnic, class, national, religious, moral) along with your reasons for thinking so. *In choosing your labels decide what particular religion, class, etc., the historian is biased for or against.*

> 1. We love to indulge in thoughts of the future extent and power of this [American] Republic—because with its increase is the increase of human happiness and liberty.... What has miserable, inefficient Mexico—with her superstition, her burlesque upon freedom, her actual tyranny by the few over the many—what has she to do with the great mission of ... the New World....

_____

_____

_____

2. God has not been preparing the English-speaking and Teutonic [Germanic] peoples for a thousand years for nothing but vain and idle self-contemplation and self-admiration. No, He has made us master organizers of the world to establish system where chaos reigns. [Hint: "Religious Bias" is not the answer!]

_____

_____

_____

3. The Romanism [Catholicism] of the present day [late nineteenth century] is a harmless opinion, no more productive of evil than any other superstition, and without tendency, or shadow of tendency, to impair the allegiance of those who profess it. But we must not confound a phantom with a substance; or gather from modern experience the temper of a time when words implied realities, when Catholics really believed that they owed no allegiance to an heretical sovereign, and that the first duty of their lives was to a foreign potentate. This perilous doctrine was waning, indeed, but it was not dead. By many it was actively professed.

_____

_____

_____

4. An underlying weakness of his [F. D. Roosevelt's] leadership lay in his acceptance of the pragmatic approach to the solution of both domestic and foreign problems. In essence, it was a refusal to take the stand for a distinctively American approach to the basic problems of capitalism. No political program that emerged in the Roosevelt administration was distinctly the expression of the American tradition. In the course of twelve years, at home and abroad, the President stood with the radicals, using the political party parlance of the "middle way" in both instances.

_____

_____

_____

5. In fighting the War for Independence in North America, the bourgeoisie led the popular masses of the colonies against the English landed aristocracy and against the colonial yoke of England. This war of the colonies for independence was a bourgeois revolution which overthrew the landed aristocracy and brought to power the American

bourgeoisie in union with the slaveholders. The American bourgeoisie used the struggle of the popular masses against the English as a means of achieving power; then, having come to power, like the English bourgeoisie of the seventeenth century, they oppressed the popular masses. In North America under the title "sovereignty of the people," (democracy), a so-called bourgeois democracy (in actual fact, the power of the bourgeoisie), was established.

_____

_____

_____

Sources

1. Walt Whitman, editorial, "Brooklyn Daily Eagle" (July 7, 1846), in *The Mexican War,* Ramon Ruiz, ed. (New York: Holt, Rinehart and Winston, 1963), 8.
2. Albert J. Beveridge, *The Meaning of the Times and Other Speeches* (Indianapolis: Bobbs-Merill, 1908), 84–5.
3. James A. Froude, *History of England,* Vol. II (New York: Charles Scribner, 1872), 321.
4. Edgar E. Robinson, *The Roosevelt Leadership, 1933–45* (New York: Lippincott, 1955), 404.
5. Donald Robinson, ed., *As Others See Us* (Boston: Houghton Mifflin, 1969), 321.

CHAPTER 12 WRITING: THE HISTORY PAPER

"Writing is easy. All you do is stare at a blank sheet of paper until drops of blood form on your forehead."

Gene Fowler

"Who does not know the first law of historical writing is the truth?"

Cicero

Most students spend their college days going from class to class, usually without appreciating the close relationships between the different subjects they are studying. These relationships are especially pronounced when the courses are in literature, journalism, and history. All three disciplines focus on writing, and they all require the completion of certain processes, excellently illustrated by the career of American author Truman Capote.

Capote emerged as a writer of some importance on the New York scene in the late 1940s. Over the next thirty-six years he produced several novels and many short stories, but in time it was as a journalist that he achieved the greatest fame. In 1965 he published what would prove to be his best-known work, *In Cold Blood,* a six-year project that was the hit of that year's literary scene.[1] *In Cold Blood* was a 343-page account of the murder of four members of the Clutter family in Holcomb, Kansas, an account distinctive because it was presented as a "non-fiction novel." To some observers the term "non-fiction novel" is self-contradictory, but many others credit Capote with having created a new art form. Essentially what Capote did was to use the conventions of the novel to tell a true story. What resulted was a book that read like engrossing fiction but was historically accurate down to the last grisly detail. According to one literary critic, it is "quite possibly the best piece of artistic journalism ever written."[2] What is important to us in the present context is that Capote's *In Cold Blood* clearly illustrates four processes essential to effective writing: research, analysis, organization, and composition.

Research

Capote could not have been more thorough in his exploration of the facts of the Clutter case. He was interested not only in the physical setting of Holcomb, Kansas, but also in the mentality of the local citizenry. Further, since in the first stages of his research the prevailing town opinion was that the murderer was likely a local person, he found it necessary to interview everyone with even the remotest connection to the murder victims. His passion for accuracy was shown in his avoidance of using a tape recorder in his interviews. Finding that such equipment made interviewees nervous and uncommunicative, he trained himself in total recall,

---

[1]Truman Capote, *In Cold Blood* (New York: Random House, 1965).
[2]William L. Nance, *The Worlds of Truman Capote* (New York: Stein and Day, Publishers, 1970), 178.

becoming "his own tape recorder" as he put it.[3] Within three hours of the interview he would write out in longhand the interview contents, label its various points, cross index the material with earlier interviews, and next morning type up the previous day's material.

The search for the Clutter family killer soon widened beyond the town of Holcomb. After six weeks of Kansas Bureau of Investigation work two transients in a Las Vegas, Nevada, cell were charged with the murders, and within a few days had confessed to them. Now Capote entered a new phase of research: lengthy, repeated interviews with the killers in an attempt to understand their motivations and outlook. These interviews continued through the trial (both were convicted and sentenced to hang) and for five years afterward during the long appeal process. Over this period Capote conducted over two hundred intensive interviews with the killers, and carried on a weekly correspondence with them as well. He came to know them "as well as I know myself," and when the time came for their execution, they asked for their new "best friend" to be present. He was there. He said he threw up a "whole two days before the execution" and "cried for two and a half days afterward." Yet, despite this emotional involvement, Capote remained cool and detached in his professional mind, and continued writing his story.[4]

This account of Capote's work is intended to illustrate two aspects of the research process. (1) Research is a frequently arduous undertaking: It requires an understanding of the context of the event being studied; it calls for thoroughness in the search for evidence, and (sometimes) a resourcefulness in adapting to the medium in which the evidence is found (in this case, interviewing); it often takes time for the researcher to achieve a strong focus on what really is vital to the undertaking; it benefits from a more-or-less continuous effort to relate a new piece of evidence to what is already known. (2) Research and writing frequently require an ability to distance oneself from emotional leanings and sentimental attachments.

Analysis

By the time Capote neared the end of his project, he had accumulated about six thousand pages of typewritten notes in addition to boxes and boxes of pertinent documents. You can bet that he did not at that point sit down and say to himself, "Well, now I've got to sit down and *begin* to analyze this stuff." This stage of writing doesn't work that way. Analysis begins early and is an *ongoing process* throughout a project. In Capote's case it perhaps began with his second interview during which he realized he was heading down a blind alley with this particular interview subject. Analysis is like that, yet even the negatives often help in focusing inquiry, letting the researcher know what is *not* involved. Capote's undertaking achieved an enhanced definition when interview subject Susan Kidwell, best friend of the murdered Nancy Clutter, described in detail the habits of the Clutters, their recent experiences as a family, and the identity of their closest associates in town. Slowly the pieces began to fit together—remember the counsel of the last chapter: "connections emerge slowly."

---

[3]To develop this ability he would have a friend read to him for a certain length of time—without Capote's taking notes—and tape record the reading at the same time. Then, when the friend finished, Capote would write down his recall of what had been said, after which he would compare what he said with the tape record. At last, Capote said, he was able to achieve nearly 100 percent accuracy.

[4]Nance, 175, 176, 169.

Capote's investigation took a big step forward with the arrest and confessions of the killers. Still, much remained unanswered, chiefly: What could possibly have motivated them to slaughter an entire family? The months and years of personal contact with the killers eventually brought Capote to conclude the reason for the murders was that Perry Smith, the trigger-man it seems, saw the middle-class Clutters as symbols for the many ways in which American middle-class society had wronged him in his life. This essentially was Capote's final piece in his structure of analysis—his interpretation.

What we have done above is take a closer look at this process called analysis, which often may begin during the research process, although in the main Capote speaks of it as a separate phase: "I worked for a year on the notes before I ever wrote a line."[5] Analysis is basically a mental sorting out process. Most of all it is a gradual process, sometimes sluggish, sometimes leaping ahead, sometimes trying out alternative hypotheses, often frustrating, but eventually, patience observed, leading to an interpretation—a sense of how the pieces fit together into a whole.

Organization

Organization, as we are using the term here, refers to the development of an overall plan for the composition that will follow. The importance of such a plan can be seen in Capote's remarks about *In Cold Blood*: "[W]hen I wrote the first word, I had done the entire book in outline, down to the last detail."[6] Historians proceed in much the same way. A piece of writing should have a determinable beginning (Introduction), a developmental middle (Body), and an identifiable end (Conclusion).

1. The Introduction

The introduction is a critically important part of every paper. It is usually a paragraph that provides a gradual lead-in, something of a broad, stage-setting orientation to the subject of the paper. Remember that having done your research you are now quite familiar with that certain segment of the past but your reader is probably not. You must describe, at least in broad terms, the context of the event you are exploring.

Next, either as a part of such a paragraph or in a paragraph immediately following it, you should unequivocally state the basic interpretive generalization you intend to support in the pages to follow. This interpretation, which, as we have seen, is developed during the analysis process, is the cornerstone of any effective history paper. A major misconception of many students is that history papers merely present "facts." Not so. The historian, more than simply reciting facts, tries to explain them with a thoughtful generalization. As historian G. R. Elton said: "What distinguishes history from the collection of historical facts is generalization."[7] Facts have no meaning apart from the generalization (interpretation) the historian supplies. So it makes sense that the first order of business in organizing a paper is to make sure you have a clearly expressed, carefully stated generalization that you intend to prove true through the course of your paper.

---

[5]Nance, 180.
[6]Nance, 180.
[7]Quoted in E. H. Carr, *What is History* (New York: Alfred A. Knopf, 1967), 82.

This is no minor point. Professors may use different terms to refer to this vital ingredient, such as thesis, main point, controlling idea, unifying theme, but these are all simply different ways of saying that which makes a paper a pleasure to read: a clearly expressed generalization that will be given substance in the pages that follow it. Unless this generalization is in the forefront of a writer's mind, there will be no clear basis for deciding what goes where in the body of the paper, and the result is, inevitably, chaos. Knowing what you mean to prove is so important that many professors refuse to accept a history essay unless it is accompanied by a cover page stating the main point along with the supporting points that make it believable.

2. The Body

The body (middle) of the paper is where you set down those main supporting points, along with necessary corroborative detail, that make your thesis believable. Some writing coaches speak of the body of the paper as its *proof structure* wherein you make the paper's main point convincing. Harry James Cargas, a colleague and much-published writer, says this about the developmental section of the paper:

> Here is where you present powerful arguments to support your thesis. Here is where you prove you are right. As in all parts of your paper, write clearly and simply and be sure that you follow this guide: overprove rather than underprove your point. So often students will try to buttress an argument with a quotation or two on the topic in question when in fact, ten or fifteen references or examples would be better.[8]

3. The Conclusion

The end (conclusion) presents, briefly—a paragraph or two is usually sufficient, a restatement or reemphasis of the thesis along with a summary of the major points made in the paper.

This overall structure of beginning, middle, and end may seem simplistic, but it remains the organizational plan that experienced historians follow, principally because it is the form that is most comfortable and the one readers expect.

Composition

One of our favorite comments about writing is that its success is determined by "the length of time one can keep the seat of his pants in contact with the seat of his chair." Pretty good counsel, that, but not enough to insure quality work. Therefore, we offer a few items of more specific advice, as follows.

1. Writing Coherent Paragraphs

In many sports an athlete's success is dependent on how well the person carries out the sport's body mechanics, sometimes called "keys" (as in golf: firm left side, hip rotation, full follow-through, etc.). The term can also be used to describe the right mechanics of history paper work: in research, the key is thoroughness; in analysis, the key is patience; in organization, the key is supporting evidence; in

---

[8]Harry James Cargas, "The Term Paper: An Overview," published in Michael Salevouris and Conal Furay, *Learning American History* (Wheeling, Ill.: Harlan Davidson, 1997), 167.

The Formal Outline
If you do choose to use a formal outline, keep the following in mind:[9]

1. Put the thesis (your unifying generalization) at the top.
2. Use parallel grammatical structure for parallel ideas.
3. Use sentences or fairly complete phrases in the outline. (This helps you keep clear the logical structure of the paper.)
4. Use the conventional outline format, which allows you to subordinate less-general concepts to more general concepts—e.g.,

I. National government

    A. State government

        1. County government

            a. Local government, Etc.

The traditional outline format is as follows.

I. First major point/unit

    A.
    B.

        1.
        2.

            a.
            b.

                (1)
                (2)

                    (a)
                    (b)

II. Second major point/unit

    A.
    B.

        Etc.

Note, each level of generalization—I, A., 1., a., etc.—must have at least two subordinate points under it.

---

[9] Diana Hacker, *A Writer's Reference,* 3rd ed. (Boston: St. Martin's Press, 1995), 10.

composition, the key is strong paragraphing. The paragraph is the basic unit of all effective writing, since it constitutes the *thought-unit* that enables the reader to follow the writer's train of thought.

Strong paragraphing can be achieved *only* by a writer's creation of meaningful topic sentences. To put it more exactly, each paragraph must have a *controlling* sentence, which, in nearly all cases, should initiate it. The controlling sentence is followed by several sentences that elaborate and develop its meaning. Whether phrased in a narrative mode (this happened, then this happened) or an analytical mode (describing effects, structures, and segments) the controlling sentence points to a cluster of related elements. It is something like a master chord that resonates and reverberates throughout a paragraph. It is the most vital factor in the readability of a passage, an essay, or a research paper.

Just as an essay or paper must be clearly organized, so too the paragraph. Organization involves putting ideas and elements in proper relationship to one another, i.e., putting smaller details where they belong—under larger ideas. Readers have a right to expect this basic arrangement and get understandably irritated when they do not find it. Consider this simple illustration:

> We've been having trouble with the family car during the past few weeks. In learning to drive my most difficult task was shifting gears smoothly. My parents didn't allow me to take driving lessons until I was seventeen. Our car seems to vibrate when its speed gets over thirty-five. My driving instructor told our class that we should learn on stick-shift automobiles because it would mean a saving when we get our own cars.

This is an almost ridiculous example of a paragraph that combines several elements that don't clearly relate to each other. Truman Capote said it best: "That's not writing, that's typing!" Yet such arrangements of ideas are common in history papers and account for much of the red ink that stains work returned to student writers.

To summarize, ordering your ideas is a basic task. When you write a paper begin by putting down your basic generalization in an explicit statement, followed by the two or three or four supporting points that make the generalization plausible. When writing paragraphs on each supporting point, add the detail necessary for that point to make sense. This is the fundamental principle of organization.

2. Transitions

Well-organized paragraphs are the essential building blocks writers use to develop supporting points for their interpretation. But just as building blocks have to fit together, so too do paragraphs. In other words a careful writer must give attention to the flow between paragraphs. Quite often, as you know, a new paragraph shifts to a different facet of the subject—a turn around a corner, so to speak. It is exactly at such points that readers often get lost unless the writer gracefully steers them into the turn. Many experienced writers do this by making the final sentence "lean" in the direction of the forthcoming shift. Sample expressions they use might be something like: "But a different factor soon made its appearance" or "As important as this development was, it was not the only influence involved." Other writers prefer a very short two- or three-sentence *transitional* paragraph (distinct from the developmental paragraph described above). This type of paragraph first summarizes then redirects the reader's attention by announcing that a new aspect of the subject is about to be discussed. Such transitional paragraphs can add greatly to the continuity of a narrative. Writers of history should use them whenever there is a danger that the reader will get lost.

3. Story Shifts

We have just emphasized the theme of continuity within a paper—the importance of making sure that paragraphs have an internal consistency, and the importance of paragraphs connecting to each other. But there are times in most history papers when a straightforward narrative flow must be broken in order to give the reader a more nuanced grasp of the historical situation.

- *Managing Historical Time:* A historian is something like a wilderness guide who takes a tenderfoot through the woods to view a backwoods stream—the stream of time. The reader is invited to step into the stream to meet some of the people there, and then, stepping back on the bank, to look upstream and downstream to see a broader panorama.

  Here we are speaking of the importance of managing historical time. The reader is willing to stay in the stream for awhile and follow the struggle going on there, or to get back on the bank, or to look upstream, or downstream—all provided the narrator gives the proper signals. Suspension of the story for political analysis, or sociological commentary, or psychological insights, or geographical fact are all tolerable interruptions provided the writer gives signals of the shift in attention. It is perfectly acceptable for a writer to break the flow of action, as long as it is done with careful concern about the reader's switch in mental orientation, and as long as the writer remembers to return gracefully to the main story line.

- *Shift in perspective:* Given the fact that one person's path often crosses another's, a story of the past is very often a story of conflicting individuals and groups. But the dramatic values evident in conflict will remain dormant unless clearly developed by the narrator. That is, the narrator (you) must shift at critical points in the story from a description of the viewpoint or perspective of one historical figure (or group) to that of another with whom there is conflict. Thus, after discussing, say, American military initiatives at a given point in the Vietnam War, a historian might immediately switch focus and discuss the same events from the perspective of the North Vietnamese and South Vietnamese. Doing so enhances the quality of the account, again as long as it is done with a sensitivity to the reader's perceptions.

4. How Much Detail is Enough?

When writers adhere to the foregoing principles, their readers begin to relax a little, knowing that a considerate hand is guiding them. Yet something more is necessary. An effective writer must not overburden the account with excessive detail, lest readers get to the point where they fail to see the larger picture. Experienced historians make this point over and over: Too much detail can obscure any argument and ultimately confuse the reader. Barbara Tuchman, a superb historian and a fine writer, expresses the same idea in this way:

> The writer of history, I believe, has a number of duties vis-à-vis the reader, if he wants him to keep reading. The first is to distill. He must do the preliminary work for the reader, assemble the information, make sense of it, select the essential, discard the irrelevant—above all, discard the irrelevant. . . . To offer a mass of undigested facts, of names not identified and places not located, is of no use to the reader and is simple laziness on the part of the author, or pedantry to show how much he has read. To discard the unnecessary requires courage and also extra work. . . .[10]

Thus, too much information is the enemy of form. In the next breath, however, we must also warn against overcorrecting in the opposite direction.[11] As we stated earlier in this chapter, it is important to "overprove rather than underprove your point." The key principle must be that of selectivity, which, as a famous ballerina once said, is "the soul of art."

Documentation: Footnotes and Bibliography

The quirks and eccentricities of English kings, aristocrats, and politicians have long intrigued the history-reading public. In the period during and after World War I there was an especially interesting collection of British public figures who loved to ridicule each other's weaknesses with witty barbs. Lord Kitchener, for instance, said: "My colleagues tell military secrets to their wives, except X who tells them to other peoples wives." X, it has been suggested, was Prime Minister H. H. Asquith. And Asquith, as historian A. J. P. Taylor notes, "was the first prime minister since the younger Pitt who is said to have been manifestly the worse for drink when on the Treasury Bench.

This type of detail makes history come to life. What is curious about the above stories is that they were drawn from footnotes in the first chapter of A. J. P. Taylor's, *English History, 1914–1945.*[12] Taylor was an eminent historian and a master of the informational footnote. Reading some of Taylor's works, which are uniformly provocative and well written, can be slow going since the reader doesn't want to miss the interesting tidbits that Taylor imbeds in his footnotes. Where else might we learn that King George V creased his trousers at the sides, not front and back? Or that General Haig said of the Earl of Derby: "like the feather pillow he bears the mark of the last person who sat on him"?[13]

In light of this we might be tempted to say: "Footnotes can be fun." We hardly think you would believe it, but such a thought shouldn't be rejected out of hand. What is indisputable is that the use of footnotes is not an affectation or a sign of snobbish pedantry. In history writing, footnoting is essential. (A footnote, by the way, is placed at the "foot" of the page. If the notes are all collected at the end of the paper they are called "endnotes." We use the term "footnote" to refer to both variations.)

There are two types of footnotes. The first, the *informational footnote,* you are already familiar with from the examples above. Often you have information

---

[10]Barbara Tuchman, *Practicing History* (New York: Knopf, 1981), 17–18.

[11]As was the case with a nineteenth-century railroad supervisor named Finnegan, who, after having been cautioned against excessive wordiness, sent railroad headquarters the following message after one in a series of derailments: "Off again, on again, gone again, Finnegan."

[12]A. J. P. Taylor, *English History, 1914–1945* (Oxford: Clarendon Press, 1965), 3, 15.

[13]Taylor, *English History,* 2, 53.

that could clarify or expand remarks in the text, but would interrupt the flow of the narrative if actually put in the body of the paper. Such footnotes provide a sort of running commentary on the material that forms the central core of your work. Very few students, in our experience, take advantage of the opportunities presented by the informational note. Give them a try, since explanatory footnotes allow you to include a good deal of important information that otherwise might have to be left out.

The informational footnote is optional; the second type, the *source reference footnote,* is not. Source references record the origin of, or authority for, material in the text of the paper. The credibility of a piece of historical writing depends on the integrity of the historian, which, sadly, is not something accepted on trust. It is through source references (footnotes or endnotes) that we can hold writers accountable and verify the accuracy and legitimacy of their facts and generalizations. Documentation of this sort allows the reader to follow better the reasoning processes of an author; it allows the reader to test the links between fact and conclusion. From the author's standpoint, footnotes acknowledge the intellectual debt every writer owes to those who have gone before.

All *direct* quotations, of course, need be footnoted—remember the verse: Every quote, requires a note! But there is more. You also need to cite the sources of paraphrases (*indirect* quotations) and unique pieces of information. If you owe a debt to a specific author, whether you quote directly or not, you should provide a source reference.

How do you know if you have too many or too few citations? Alas, there is no universal standard on this matter. Footnoting, like much else in the world of scholarship, is as much art as it is science. Gradually, through practice, you will get a "feel" for what is appropriate. You will want to avoid littering your writing with an avalanche of references, or leaving the reader with the feeling that key references have been left out. Two to four references per typed page is probably adequate. Less or more than that and you flirt with doing your reader an injustice. Ultimately, though, the number of citations depends on the type of paper you are writing, the nature of the sources, and the expectations of your reader. Just remember, as our colleague Harry James Cargas puts it, "your paper is your whole presentation. You will not be there to amplify or to clarify when your reader is looking it over. Cite as many sources as necessary to leave no doubt in the reader's mind that what you say is absolutely true."[14]

Every paper should also include a *bibliography.* A bibliography (list of the sources you consulted) serves a different function than footnotes or endnotes. A source reference tells the reader the specific location (author, title, date and place of publication, and page number) of a quotation or piece of information used in the text of a paper or book. A note has a one-to-one relationship with a particular segment of the text. A bibliography, on the other hand, gives the reader, in one place, a complete list of all the sources that were used by the author, whether they were cited in the notes or not. In some large works, authors list only the most valuable sources. This is called a "selective bibliography." In other cases there is a "Works Cited" page, which lists only those works actually mentioned in the source references themselves. Whatever the case, the works listed in bibliographies or works-cited pages are alphabetized according to the first letter of the authors' last names. It is common, in larger bibliographies to divide the sources according to

---

[14]In Salevouris and Furay, *Learning American History,* 167.

type: books, articles, manuscripts, government documents, etc., or according to whether they are primary or secondary sources. In such cases, each section is alphabetized according to the aforementioned categorization.

It is not our purpose to teach you proper bibliographic and footnote style. Suffice it to say, the forms for both are highly standardized and used universally by scholars all over the world. You will find slight differences in format depending on what sort of style manual you consult. But the differences are less obvious than the similarities. In your own work the thing to remember is that you *should consult a style manual* and then follow the same format consistently throughout your paper.

The Elements of Style

The points made above are those most essential to success in writing a history paper. But what often separates the merely good paper from the memorable one is something less concrete: style. Author Truman Capote brought a novelist's perspective to his account of the Clutter murders. What this meant in practice was a richness of style that much enlivened the pages of *In Cold Blood*. His description of Holcomb, Kansas, the setting of the murders, evokes a sense of prairie loneliness: "Holcomb, too, can be seen from great distances. Not that there is much to see—simply an aimless congregation of buildings divided in the center by the main-line tracks of the Santa Fe Railroad, a haphazard hamlet bounded on the South by a brown stretch of the Arkansas. . . ." His physical characterization of the murderer forebodes the doom that awaited the Clutters: "It was a changeling's face, and mirror-guided experiments had taught him how to ring the changes, how to look now ominous, now impish, now soulful; a tilt of the head, a twist of the lips, and the corrupt gypsy became the gentle romantic."[15] At this point it is worthwhile to discuss history in the context of fiction at one end of a spectrum and empirical studies (economics, political science, etc.) at the other end, for history lies between them. It is not an empirical study (that is, one in which the researcher can directly observe, measure, or retest through experimentation) for it is predominantly concerned with past events, each of which is in some sense unique and thus unrepeatable. Nor is history fiction, since its characters and actions are taken from reality rather than from imagination.

Still, while distinct, written history does have a good deal in common with fiction. Both historical narratives and novels deal with the gradual unfolding of a causally connected series of incidents (i.e., they both have a "plot"); both must make human acts meaningful within the context of the central values of the society in which the acts take place; both must blend description and background with action in order to make their accounts understandable. Many historians do not understand or fully appreciate these parallels, and all too often they write accounts that dull the intellect as well as the imagination. Not surprisingly, students find such writing boring and put it aside with relief when the required reading is finished.

---

[15]Capote, *In Cold Blood*, 3, 15–16.

Set B, Exercise 2

This is another form of exercise aimed at enhancing the ability to subordinate specific ideas to more general ones. What follows is a scrambled paragraph; unscramble it, using numbers ("1" for the first sentence, "2" for the second, etc.) to indicate proper sentence order. Keep in mind that the first sentence or two must provide the framework for the entire paragraph.

_____ The administration quickly disposed of most of its war plants, usually by turning them over to private interests on very generous terms.

_____ Under such pressure, the politicians of both parties simply collapsed.

_____ Business was permitted to move ahead quickly into civilian production.

_____ The pressures for a return to civilian life were overwhelming by mid-1945.

_____ In November 1945, Congress approved a $6 billion tax cut, even though it would obviously contribute to inflation.

_____ Business interests demanded lower taxes, immediate demobilization, and the end of lend-lease and other measures assisting other foreign competitors in international markets.

_____ The armed forces, 12 million strong in 1945, had only 3 million by mid-1946, and but 1.6 million by mid-1947.

_____ Lend-lease shipments were cut.

_____ And—feeling secure with an atomic monopoly—it brought the boys home.

_____ Soldiers insisted on being allowed to come home, and officeholders were swamped with postcards from Asia labeled, "No boats, no votes."

Set B, Exercise 3

This exercise is a somewhat more complex version of the one you just completed. You must do two things: (1) work out the relations between the general and the specific and (2) organize the pieces so they are logically related. Use number "1" for the first sentence, "2" for the second, etc., to indicate the proper sentence order. Again, remember that the first sentence provides the framework for the entire paragraph.

_____ Surface raiders, such as the pocket battleships _Graf Spee_ and _Deutschland_ caused much concern.

_____ But the enduring enemy was the U-boat [submarine].

_____ But later in the war U-boats found it very difficult to operate, as the British used a version of sonar, and American hunter-killer groups sent many submarines to the bottom.

_____ The Germans successfully planted magnetic mines that did much damage to British shipping in coastal waters.

_____ If, in 1940 the defeat of France had been offset by the British success in the Battle of Britain, in 1941 the defeat of Great Britain became once more a possibility to be reckoned with.

_____ In 1940, however, the U-boat fleet, reinforced by a production drive, began to score abundantly.

_____ One British convoy lost thirty-two ships in a U-boat attack that continued through four consecutive nights.

_____ In the first year of the war, 1939, the German U-boat fleet had been small and was not particularly successful.

_____ Because Britain was an island nation she was especially vulnerable to German sea warfare, which included mines, surface raiders, and U-boats.

Set B, Exercise 4

One of the ways to secure good coherence within each paragraph is to remain conscious throughout its writing of the key words of the topic sentence. These words contain the controlling idea for the paragraph. In Exercises 2 and 3 you worked on two paragraphs. Specify the key words of the topic sentence of each one.

Exercise 2 paragraph: _____

Exercise 3 paragraph: _____

Set B, Exercise 5

The following exercise presents ten pieces that, when put together correctly, represent a simplified sentence outline for a short essay. Though much is missing, we specifically include a main thematic statement (topic sentence), three main points, five subpoints belonging somewhere under the main points, and a summary statement. Put all the pieces in their proper places (by number) in the form provided below.

1. A powerful new military bureaucracy developed during the war, with in creasingly strong links to major industrial firms.
2. During the war more than a million Blacks moved out of the South to north ern cities seeking a better life than they had known on southern farms.
3. The deficit mentality lingered on after the war, and contributed to the acceptance of new governmental programs in later years.
4. Indeed these three changes brought by the war affected American society permanently.
5. The war also deepened public willingness to accept enormous government deficits as the national debt doubled and redoubled from 1941 to 1945.
6. Huge numbers of civilians migrated to ship and aircraft production facilities, seeking the high wages paid there.
7. World War II brought deeper changes in American life than any other develop ment since the Civil War.
8. In fact much later, President Dwight Eisenhower, himself a military man, was to warn the nation of the dangers of this combination of interests, often called the "military-industrial complex."
9. First and foremost it caused a vast uprooting of Americans from their tradi-tional homes.
10. Millions of men and women became temporary citizens of military camps all across America

_____ Main thematic statement

_____ A. Supporting point
      _____ 1. Subpoint
      _____ 2. Subpoint (if any)
      _____ 3. Subpoint (if any)

_____ B. Supporting point
      _____ 1. Subpoint
      _____ 2. Subpoint (if any)
      _____ 3. Subpoint (if any)

_____ C. Supporting point
      _____ 1. Subpoint
      _____ 2. Subpoint (if any)
      _____ 3. Subpoint (if any)

_____ D. Summary statement

Set B, Exercise 6

See the commentary for Exercise 6 of Set A. Your task here is to indicate after each sentence in the space provided whether it is "Narrative" (using an "N") or "Analytical" (using an "A"). The passage concerns the domestic legislative program of the Johnson administration during the 1960s.[17]

> Lyndon Johnson sponsored the most advanced program of social reform in history of the republic._____ Congress responded to his leadership by enacting an extraordinary burst of social legislation: civil rights, the war on poverty, Medicare, aid to education, housing and urban development, increased social security benefits, conservation measures, a new immigration law, and even the subsidization of American "culture." _____ The Great Society sought to correct old racial wrongs, to provide badly needed educational and medical services, to advance social justice by mounting a broad-based attack on poverty and urban blight, and to demonstrate man's capacity to master his environment._____ There were genuine successes in moving toward greater racial equality, in offering expanded educational opportunities and better health care, and in launching important federal programs in such areas as the war on poverty and environmental control._____ If the Great Society was a failure in many respects, it was nevertheless an audacious failure. A leader of uncommon ability and impressive accomplishments, Johnson set his sights on becoming a great president._____ The tragedy was that he lacked the capacity to inspire the confidence and trust of the people._____

Set B, Exercise 7: The History Paper

See instructions under Set A, Exercise 7.

---

[17]Dewey W. Grantham, _Recent America_ (Wheeling, Ill.: Harlan Davidson, Inc., 1987), 281.

PART IV:
HISTORIOGRAPHY

Chapter 13 THE HISTORY OF HISTORY

"History does not repeat itself. The historians repeat one another."

Max Beerbohm

"History has to be rewritten because history is the selection of those threads of causes or antecedents that we are interested in."

Oliver Wendell Holmes, Jr.

A university professor once berated a young graduate student for what he termed "stale historiography. "A fellow student later said this sounded something akin to bad breath. What the professor meant, of course, was that the student was not familiar with the most recent scholarly interpretations in a particular subfield of history.

"Historiography" is not a word normally found in everyday reading, but you probably already know the concept even if the word itself is unfamiliar. Literally the word means "the writing of history." In modern usage, however, the word refers to the study of the way history has been and is written—the history of historical writing, if you will. When you study "historiography" you are studying how individual historians have interpreted and presented specific subjects, such as the collapse of the Roman Empire, the causes of the industrial revolution, or the end of the Cold War. For example, to learn about the variety of ways historians have tried to explain the coming of the American Civil War is to become familiar with the "historiography" of that subject.[1]

It is our purpose in this chapter to provide a thumbnail sketch of the history of historical writing in the West in order to acquaint you with some of the defining moments in the evolution of the discipline. Keep in mind, however, that such a brief survey can only trace the faint outlines of a subject that is rich in both variety and complexity. In addition, be warned that you should view with suspicion any secondhand summary—including ours—of another historian's work. If you want to know what a historian says about a subject, you should read that historian's work yourself. As a final caution, remember that we discuss historiography in terms of exceedingly broad trends and patterns, but few individual works will ever fit the pattern exactly.

History: The Beginnings

The Western tradition of historical writing began with the ancient Hebrews (Jews) and Greeks. The Jews, in their long struggle for freedom and autonomy, developed the belief that they were special in the eyes of God and that their historical expe-

---

[1] Some historians see that war as a conflict between an agrarian economy (the South) and an industrializing economy (the North); others emphasize slavery as the primary cause; still others see states' rights versus federal sovereignty as the issue at stake.

riences reflected God's will. Conscious of their role as God's "chosen people," the Jews wrote history as a chronicle of their continuing and evolving relationship with the Creator. Essentially the books of the Old Testament of the Bible (some elements of which may date as far back as 1000 B.C.) constitute a written history of the Jewish people and Hebrew nation. This God-centered historical perspective of the Old Testament was destined to have a long and influential run in Western intellectual history, as we shall see.

If Jewish historical writing was "God-centered," it was the ancient Greeks who first wrote history in self-consciously human terms. At first the Greeks saw both their own past and the workings of the physical universe as the products of supernatural forces and the intervention of the gods. Later, in the sixth century B.C., a number of Greek philosophers began to reject supernatural explanations in favor of natural ones. They saw nature as functioning according to concrete "natural" laws that could be comprehended through human reason. Likewise, in the realm of human affairs, the Greeks increasingly saw history as the product of human actions and decisions, and believed that accounts of the past should be based on solid evidence, not legend or myth.

Herodotus (ca.484–ca.425 B.C.), often called the "Father of History," wrote the first systematic historical work based on personal observations and the examination of witnesses and surviving records. In his account of the Greek wars against the Persians he admittedly included many fanciful myths and unsubstantiated legends, but essentially his was a history of human actions told in human terms. Thucydides (ca.460–400 B.C.), who, a generation later, wrote a justly famous history of the Peloponnesian Wars (431–404 B.C.), was even more careful in his use and analysis of evidence. He insisted that his history include only relevant, verifiable facts, and that it explain events only in ways that could be substantiated by the evidence. (The English word "history" comes from the Greek word for "research.") In Thucydides' work we first see what moderns would call a true historical spirit.

There was little change in the nature of written history after Greece succumbed to the power of Rome in the second century B.C. However, during the European Middle Ages (ca. A.D. 500–1400) a change of some magnitude took place. With the triumph of Christianity, history writing again became more concerned with the relationship between the human experience and Christian perceptions of God's eternal plan. Christian historiography mirrored that of the Jews, not that of the Greeks and Romans, although Greek and Roman influences were still evident. To Christian writers in the Medieval period, human experiences on earth were but a minor part of a larger drama—the unfolding of God's divine plan for humanity. It was the job of written history, therefore, to find and reveal the transcendent design of God hidden in the chaos of day-to-day events. That is why many histories written in the Middle Ages began with the biblical story of creation and incorporated that part of the Jewish Old Testament tradition that fit the redemptive message of Christianity. The proper subject of written history, in the eyes of the Christian monks who wrote it, was not the earthly fate of a particular state or people, but the universal drama of humanity's quest for salvation. We might note in passing that those very monks were also the inventors of the conventional western calendar that distinguishes between the events that occurred before the birth of Christ (B.C.) and those that came after (A.D., Anno Domini, "in the year of the lord").

Only in the Renaissance (the 1400s and 1500s) did historians return to the more secular, humanistic style of the Greeks. Especially important were a number of Italian historians, Niccolò Machiavelli (1469–1540) and Francesco Guicciardini (1483–1527) being the best known. Although the Renaissance historians were Christians, they believed that the function of history was to narrate the experiences of particular states and individuals, not to reveal God's designs in the earthly affairs of humanity. The Renaissance also saw the gradual emergence of new critical standards for collecting, reading, and interpreting evidence. History was not yet recognized as an independent field of study (like theology or law), but the path was now clearly marked.

In spite of the long tradition of history writing in the West, history emerged as a formal academic study only in the early nineteenth century. Of course, there were many pre-nineteenth-century historians who produced works of great power and sophistication, as any reader of Gibbon (*The Decline and Fall of the Roman Empire*) or Thucydides can attest. On the whole, though, such works were few and far between, for history still lacked a coherent and workable critical methodology. Much history was written, but seldom did the historians actively consider the criteria for writing good history. Many pre–nineteenth-century historians handled evidence with a cavalier disregard for critical standards. Often they cited no sources whatever; on other occasions they accepted myth, legend, and gossip as established fact; on yet others, they read or interpreted records with too much credulity and too little skepticism.

In another way, the pre-nineteenth-century historians had a blind spot. They did not fully understand that in some respects past ages differed from their own; they had difficulty realizing that styles, habits, and values changed over time. For instance, even though a number of Renaissance scholars became increasingly conscious that the classical past that they studied was radically different from their own time, this insight was never fully internalized. There are many Renaissance paintings, for example, that portray biblical scenes in which individuals from the time of Christ are dressed as fifteenth-century Florentines and surrounded by buildings constructed in the architectural styles of the Italian Renaissance. The equivalent today would be a painting of George Washington crossing the Delaware River in a car ferry while dressed in a double-breasted pin-striped suit.

Conversely, when many of the early historians did perceive differences between their age and another, their response was not to try to understand that which was different, but to denounce it. Thus did Voltaire, in the eighteenth century, dismiss the Middle Ages as unworthy of study because medieval men and women were not "enlightened," as he felt himself to be.] Such an attitude, as we have seen is ahistorical. (See Chapter 5, "Context.")

Leopold Von Ranke and the Rise of Modern History

Historical studies came into their own following the immense political and social upheavals associated with the French Revolution (1789–1815). The French Revolution represented a massive break with the past and, paradoxically, made people much more "history-conscious" than ever before. Thus, it was in the nineteenth century that history became the "Queen of the Sciences" and earned a permanent place in the academy.

The man most responsible for elevating the study of history to a new plateau was the German historian Leopold von Ranke (1795–1886). Ranke's contributions were threefold: (1) he played a leading role in establishing history as a respected discipline in the universities, (2) he firmly established the notion that all sound history must be based on primary sources and a rigorous methodology, and (3) he reflected the broader nineteenth-century attempt to define the concept of "historical-mindedness." Of these, the latter two points require further elaboration.

Ranke and Historical Method

Previously, as we mentioned above, much history was written, but "there was no systematic use of sources and no accepted methodological principles."[2] Many pre-Rankean historians relied heavily on the work of other authors (secondary sources) rather than going to the original documents, or primary sources. Ranke (pronounced "Ronkuh"), on the other hand, stressed the importance of basing any historical narrative firmly on the reading of primary sources. Furthermore, he insisted that the historian constantly inform the reader of the specific sources upon which a given point was based. Hence the central importance, after Ranke, of thorough footnotes (or endnotes) and bibliographies. (Now you know whom to blame.) In a word, Ranke popularized the idea that history could be "scientific"—not in the sense that history could discover general laws of behavior, but in that historical writing should be based on rigorous critical standards.

Ranke and Historical Mindedness

Ranke also contributed to the rise of the conviction that one should not study a past age in terms of one's own values and culture but in terms of the values and realities of the age itself. According to Ranke, one should not make moral judgments on past individuals and past cultures but try to understand them on their own terms. To Ranke, every age and individual was "immediate to God" (did not need to be justified) and worthy of our sympathy and understanding. Ranke appreciated the fact that things do change over time, and this basic insight is central to the whole process of thinking historically.

Ranke, then, and many other eminent scholars, established the study of history on a firm methodological foundation. But what sorts of things did these pioneers write about? Space forbids a detailed treatment of history and historians in the nineteenth century, but two general points can be made:

1. Most nineteenth-century history was political, legal, or diplomatic in emphasis, as historians began to get access to government archives that had hitherto been closed to researchers. Their work, which reflected the character of the documents, naturally focused on the actions of kings, parliaments, law courts, armies, navies, and diplomats—"drum and trumpet" history as it came to be called. The nineteenth-century historians also studied and wrote about the history of ideas—especially the political and legal ideas that had played a role in the evolution of nations and legal systems.

2. Nineteenth-century history, especially in Europe, tended to have a national focus—more in the sense of "nationality" than "nation-state." During that era a number of "new" nations, or ethnic groups, perceiving their cultural and historical uniqueness, began to explore their own historical roots with great vigor. Even history coming out of the more established nations, such as England and France, reflected this compulsion to probe the depths of their national experience. Much the same could be said of the histories produced in nineteenth-century America.

---

[2]Arthur Marwick, *What History Is and Why It Is Important* (Bletchley, England: Open University Press, 1970) 42.

Across the board, historiography during this period tended to be ethnocentric and nationalistic.

Karl Marx and History

If Ranke and his contemporaries saw only politics and diplomacy as worthy of the historian's attention, it was the German economist and revolutionary philosopher Karl Marx who opened historians' eyes to the importance of social and economic forces in human affairs. Marx (1818–1883) is widely recognized as one of the most influential thinkers of the last one hundred and fifty years. Much modern scholarship in history, economics, political theory, sociology, and philosophy cannot be fully appreciated without some understanding of Karl Marx's ideas. This is not the place to discuss Marx's system in detail, but a few words concerning his impact on the discipline of history are in order. It should be noted from the start, however, that a consideration of Marx the historian can be effectively divorced from consideration of Marx the prophet of socialism. In the latter guise Marx, and his collaborator, Friedrich Engels, postulated a broadly "progressive" theory of history, which held that human societies would evolve through a number of stages culminating in the establishment (through revolution) of a "dictatorship of the proletariat" and, eventually, a classless society. This was a secular version of the medieval Christian conviction that the human race was moving toward a "preordained goal."

More important for our purposes is the fact that Marx opened new intellectual vistas by breaking out of the political-diplomatic straitjacket that had bound most historical investigations before his time. Marx, says one American historian, "became the first to formulate, in explicit fashion, the economic interpretation of history."[3] Marx (and Engels) argued that, at any given point in time, the mode of economic production determined, to a great extent, the character of the entire society—its ideas, values, political structure, and social relations. To some of Marx's more dogmatic followers, this insight was converted into a thoroughgoing economic determinism. That is, economic forces were seen to determine totally the nature of society, and changes in the economic structure were considered the sole engine of historical change. Marx himself never went so far; late in life he even commented: "I am not a Marxist." Marx and Engels did not deny that noneconomic factors could be contributing causes of events. They simply asserted that economic factors were of primary importance.

Within this general framework, the history of economic and social classes was more relevant than the history of great men or ruling elites. "The history of all hitherto existing society," wrote Marx and Engels in *The Communist Manifesto,* "is the history of class struggle." This, of course, is a debatable conclusion. Of significance though is the fact that Marx and Engels saw class interests as a vital element in any historical equation.

Marx's impact on politics and political thought has been immense and requires no further comment. But what of Marx's impact on the writing of history?

In communist countries, of course, where Marxism in some form or another was (and, in a few cases, still is) an official ideology, historical writing has been "Marxist" in the extreme. And, quite frankly, much of it is not very good history. Evidence was chosen, organized, analyzed, and interpreted more with an eye to

---

[3]Allan Nevins, *The Gateway to History* (Chicago: Quadrangle Books, 1963), 268.

validating the ideology than establishing the best true account of the past. Much official communist history written before 1989 in Russia and eastern Europe, and elsewhere even today, suffers from this defect.[4] In fairness, we should also note that noncommunist history is not immune from this failing, and any time scholarship is subordinated to the dictates of an ideology—Marxism or any other—it is truth that suffers.

In the noncommunist West the influence of Marx, while great, has been less direct. In the broadest sense Marx is significant because, by emphasizing the importance of economic factors in history, he opened the door to a new approach to the past. Few historians today, whatever their political orientation, would deny the validity of exploring the role of social classes, economic interests, and modes of production in the historical process. Economic interpretations have, in fact, become a staple of American historiography. A famous (and controversial) example is Charles A. Beard's *An Economic Interpretation of the Constitution of the United States* published in 1913. In that work Beard examined the economic interests of the framers of the Constitution and concluded that the Constitution was designed more to protect property rights than political rights. Whatever the accuracy of this interpretation (and it has been vigorously challenged), the important thing to note is the explicitly economic focus of the work. Beard was no Marxist, but he acknowledged a debt to Marx just the same. Few historians have gone as far as Beard in emphasizing economic factors so single-mindedly, but even fewer would deny that the economic "question" is one that must be asked in order to understand any given segment of the past.[5]

The Twentieth Century

The twentieth century, especially since 1945, has witnessed a "knowledge explosion" of sorts. Books, articles, reviews, and reports have been pouring off the presses in ever-increasing numbers. This "explosion" has been most dramatic in the sciences, but the generalization is applicable to history as well. Moreover, recent historical writing has displayed such kaleidoscopic diversity that history is a more exciting field than ever before. Unfortunately, the mass and diversity of recent historical scholarship also makes it impossible to summarize neatly even the most prominent trends in twentieth-century historiography. What follows, therefore, is a very selective sampling of what we see to be some of the defining characteristics of recent historiography—especially American historiography.

---

[4]David Remnick says of the Soviet Union and its distaste for open inquiry: "The regime created an empire that was a vast room, its doors locked, its windows shuttered. All books and newspapers allowed in the room carried the Official Version of Events, and the radio and television blared the general line day and night." It was Mikhail Gorbachev who finally decreed that the time had come to fill in the "blank spots" of history and, in so doing, precipitated the collapse of the USSR (see Chapter 1). *Lenin's Tomb: The Last Days of the Soviet Empire*, 4.

[5]For some Western scholars the Marxian impact has been more direct. There are many scholars, historians among them, who consciously call themselves "Marxists," and they have adopted an explicitly Marxian approach to the study of history and society. Such scholars are a distinct minority within the profession, yet many of them have published solid scholarly works that have greatly enriched our understanding of the past. Remember, the test of good history is not the author's ideology or bias, but the thoroughness, accuracy, and soundness of the research and the argument.

The New Social History

There is nothing especially "new" about social history. Social history, simply put, is the history of life in the broadest sense: the history of the everyday experiences of "average" men and women. It is the history of social and economic classes, occupations, life-styles, leisure activities, family structures, eating habits, sexual practices, reading preferences, beliefs, and values; it is "grass roots" history; it is, in the memorable words of G. M. Trevelyan, history "with the politics left out"—or, to the irreverent, "rum and strumpet history." Historians have been writing social history for some time. Even today, a frequently cited example of brilliant social history is the famous third chapter of Thomas Babington Macaulay's *History of England* (5 vols., 1849–61), in which he draws a fascinating portrait of English society during the 1680s.

Although social history has long been with us, it was only in the 1960s and 1970s that it became a thriving cottage industry in the historical profession. In Macaulay's day social history was strictly subordinated to what historians considered the more important priority of writing about political, constitutional, and military affairs. Social history was used to "set the scene" or provide a pleasant interlude in the narrative. Today, however, social history is taught and studied as a field of inherent interest and importance. Only to this extent is social history "new."

Social history is new in another sense—it is much more "scientific" and less anecdotal than had previously been the case. Social history is one area in which the application of statistical methods and computer analysis has been especially productive. Much social history today is, in effect, historical demography (demography is the statistical study of populations), by which historians systematically analyze large-scale population trends and calculate such things as average family sizes, death and birth rates, marriage ages, and average incomes. The more literary tradition of social history has by no means been abandoned, but statistical methods have given the social historian a potent analytical weapon.

The most fruitful contribution of the social historians has been to focus the spotlight on groups that have typically been ignored in traditional history—women, African Americans and other ethnic minorities, blue-collar and migrant workers, farmers, peasants, children, the aged, criminals, outcasts, and groups otherwise marginalized by society.[6] The popularity and vitality of social history is in part a reflection of the increasing sense of identity among various ethnic subcultures. It is also a product of the democratization of the history profession as women, members of minority groups, and the sons and daughters of recent immigrants increasingly have entered the field. Witness the proliferation of books on women's history, African-American history, Chicano history, American-Indian history, and the history of various immigrant groups. In sum, the "new" social history has brought to life the experiences of countless groups previously bypassed in the historical studies that had traditionally focused on the experiences of political and economic elites.

---

[6]In the area of Renaissance studies alone we find the following recent titles: Samuel Cohn, Jr., *The Laboring Classes in Renaissance Florence* (1980); Judith Brown, *Immodest Acts: The Life of a Lesbian Nun in Renaissance Italy* (1986); Edward Muir, *Mad Blood Stirring: Vendetta and Factions in Fruili during the Renaissance* (1993); Michael Rocke, *Forbidden Friendships: Homosexuality and Male Culture in Renaissance Florence* (1996); Carlo Ginzburg, *The Night Battles: Witchcraft and Agrarian Cults in the Sixteenth and Seventeenth Centuries* (1992).

Women's History

One category of social history, women's history, deserves special comment. In light of the fact that women constitute more than half of the human race it is sobering to discover that only after World War II did historians begin to pay systematic attention to the role of women in history. Of course, larger-than-life figures such as Queen Elizabeth I of England or Catherine the Great of Russia always had their fair share of attention from historians. But women as a group? For decades the male-dominated history profession systematically ignored them.

Today the situation has changed dramatically. Modern feminists and a growing number of historians have generated interest in both women's history and, more broadly, gender studies (the study of the roles played in society by gender relations and concepts of gender). The result has been an avalanche of new scholarship not only on the history of women, but also on the history of gender relationships, histories of children and families, and gay and lesbian history.

In writing the history of women, many practitioners not only have wanted to recover an overlooked past, but to use their scholarship to advance the cause of women's equality. An underlying assumption was that women everywhere, past and present, were more alike than different, and that writing the history of women would advance their quest for equal political and economic equality. [7] But what women's historians discovered was that there might be no such thing as a singular "women's history" relevant to all women everywhere. Research revealed that there was often a great gulf separating the experiences of middle-class women and working-class women, black women and white women, Western women and non-Western women, sixteenth-century women and twentieth-century women, etc. And, to make matters even more complex, there were many differences *within* each category. "[N]ot all black women or Islamic women or Jewish women share the same conceptions of femininity, or social role or politics."[8]

In sum, the same fragmentation and diversity that characterize history writing in general at the turn of the century characterizes women's history as well as many of the other subdisciplines we have mentioned. The result has been both the immense enrichment of the discipline and the frustration inherent in knowing that a single individual will never become familiar with even a small portion of the fascinating histories being written about the myriad aspects of the past. [9]

---

[7] See Joan Wallach Scott, ed., *Feminism and History* (Oxford: Oxford University Press, 1996), "Introduction," 1–13.

[8] Scott, *Feminism,* 7.

[9] A sampling of titles on only the American experience dramatizes the point. On the subject of women in America we find such works as: Susan K. Cahn, *Coming on Strong: Gender and Sexuality in Twentieth-Century Women's Sport* (1994); Angela Davis, *Blues Legacies and Black Feminism: Gertrude "Ma" Rainey, Bessie Smith, and Billie Holiday* (1998); Susan J. Douglas, *Where the Girls Are: Growing Up Female with the Mass Media* (1994); Susan Faludi, *Backlash: The Undeclared War Against American Women* (1991); Sharon Thompson, *Going All the Way: Teenage Girls' Tales of Sex, Romance, and Pregnancy* (1995); and Susan Ware, *Still Missing: Amelia Earhart and the Search for Modern Feminism* (1993).

In African-American history we find the following recent works, focusing either on a distinctive theme or locality: John Dittmer, *Local People: The Struggle for Civil Rights in Mississippi* (1994); Michael Eric Dyson, *Making Malcolm: The Myth and Meaning of Malcolm X* (1995); John Egerton, *Speak Now Against the Day: The Generation before the Civil Rights Movement in the South* (1994); Charles M. Payne, *I've Got the Light of Freedom: The Organization Tradition and the Mississippi Freedom Struggle* (1995); Brenda Gayle Plummer, *Rising Wind: Black Americans and U.S. Foreign Policy, 1935–1960* (1996); and Patricia A. Turner, *I Heard It Through the Grapevine: Rumor in African-American Culture* (1993). Our thanks to colleague John Chappell for suggesting these titles.

Computers and Quantification

Another distinctly twentieth-century phenomenon is the growing use of computers and statistical methods in history. Quantitative techniques have been especially productive (as we saw in Chapter 10) in the realms of economic and social history. Historical studies of voting behavior have also benefited from the application of well-thought-out computer programs to historical evidence. There are, of course, problems with this type of history. The most obvious is that most historical questions cannot be answered with computers, however sophisticated the machines or their programs. Quantification, therefore, has an important place in historical studies, but the limitations of "mere numeration" must be kept firmly in mind. For a fuller discussion of this topic see Chapter 10.

Psychohistory

Psychohistory is another twentieth-century innovation in historical scholarship. Although psychohistory has never been fully accepted or widely practiced by most historians, you should be aware of some of its central characteristics and claims. Psychohistory is essentially an outgrowth of the work of Sigmund Freud (1856–1939), who drew attention to the importance of the unconscious mind and irrational impulses in human behavior. Just as Marx had emphasized the importance of economics in human affairs, Freud underscored the role played by hidden psychological drives that originated in the traumas and experiences of infancy and early childhood. It was Freud and his followers who pioneered the practice of psychoanalysis as a method for discovering the "unconscious" roots of human behavior by probing for the suppressed and repressed experiences of childhood. Psychoanalysis, Freud argued, could help those whose early, and unremembered, childhood traumas had made them dysfunctional as adults. Freud also claimed—and here we get to the crux of psychohistory—that psychoanalysis could also be applied to historical figures long dead.

Freud's message was reinforced in his lifetime by the senseless slaughter of World War I (1914–18), which dramatized for a complacent Europe how easily irrationality and animal brutality could triumph over intellect and reason. In the years after that war psychiatry and psychoanalysis came into their own; in the years after World War II (1939–45), psychohistory itself made its debut. One of the pioneers in the field was Erik Erikson, whose masterful study *Young Man Luther* (1958) seemed to put psychohistory on a firm intellectual footing.

Though many psychohistorical studies have been written, in recent years the enthusiasm over the approach has dimmed. Since the publication of Erikson's book, many historians have challenged the legitimacy of psychohistory on methodological grounds. Psychoanalysis involves the recovery of repressed childhood memories, but direct evidence for the early experiences of most historical figures is sketchy or non-existent. More significant, even if we can find out something about the earliest experiences of an individual, the explanatory value of that information is questionable. Martin Luther, for example, had some rough experiences when he was growing up, but those experiences were not atypical of his time and place. Yet it was only Luther who ended up as the standard-bearer of the Reformation. Factors other than Luther's childhood development must have been more important.

Even though psychohistory is not in history's mainstream, it has made its mark. Whatever the merits or defects of Freud's theory of personality, his work opened historians' eyes to the importance of psychological dimensions of the individuals they study. Today the writing of historical biography is still a thriving enterprise, and it is the rare biographer who would totally ignore questions of psychological motivation and the psychological roots of character. To that extent psychohistory has permanently changed the way historians do business.[10]

History in the Information Age

A glaring modern paradox is that even as many critics vocally lament America's increasing historical illiteracy, history has never clamored so insistently for our attention—perhaps a sign that these pundits are not altogether correct in this matter. In the last fifty years there has been tremendous growth in the amount of history targeted for mass audiences. Originally cheap paperback books and then television and film (see chapter 8) brought popularized history into the marketplace. And more recently cable and satellite television networks (e.g. the History Channel, the Learning Channel) and the Internet have greatly increased the options for those interested in some aspect of the past.

Ultimately this is a good thing, for unless historians communicate their findings to a larger audience, they are serving no useful function in a society. On the other hand, popular history (whether presented in books, on television, in movie theaters, or on the Internet) can also be a dangerous thing. All too frequently good entertainment is bad history, for to emphasize the dramatic and sensational is often to distort the truth. Moreover, whatever the advantages of historical essays and sources on the Internet (and there are many advantages—see Chapter 6), literally anyone with an ax to grind or an overactive fantasy life can create a web page accessible by computers around the world. As a result, there is a staggering amount of nonsense and misinformation on the Internet, making it increasingly difficult for the average citizen to discriminate between accurate and inaccurate information, between good and bad history.

Moreover, so insatiable is the public appetite for the inside story of recent dramatic events that "instant" histories have become commonplace. Whether the subject is world conflict (the Gulf War, the crisis in the Balkans), a sensational murder case (O. J. Simpson), the death of a rock star or popular idol (Princess Diana), or the latest terrorist outrage, hastily written paperback "histories" and TV documentaries and miniseries are sometimes published and aired only days, or weeks, after the event. The limitations of such productions should be apparent. They are put together in haste, their evidence is even more incomplete than normally would be the case, and public passions may still be fully aroused. The authors, in many cases, are not trained historians or even trained journalists. Obviously, such instant histories should be read and viewed with a very critical eye.

Conclusion

If one can perceive a trend over time, it is this: historical writing in the West has become broader in geographic scope, casting its attention on civilizations and cultures hitherto ignored; it has become more eclectic and diverse, with few as-

---

[10]For a much more detailed overview of the diverse insights and models that constitute psychohistory see Part 3, "Psychosocial History," in Richard E. Beringer, *Historical Analysis: Contemporary Approaches to Clio's Craft* (New York: John Wiley and Sons, 1978), 69-191.

pects of life escaping critical attention; it has discovered (at last) the histories of groups hitherto ignored in traditional narratives; and it has become ever more rigorous and imaginative in its use of evidence, our comments on "instant history" notwithstanding. History as a discipline is alive and growing, telling its story of change, but telling also of how tenaciously the past survives in the present. Yet, we cannot end without a note of caution.

As positive as all these trends are, the writing of history from many and diverse perspectives is not without its costs. As one historian noted recently, "History no longer sets forth common stories that presumably speak for the identity and experience of all readers. . . . We no longer possess a past commonly agreed upon."[11] To the extent that shining history's lamp on all peoples, and not just on male elites, has helped Americans find a history that is personally relevant and meaningful, we say bravo! To the extent that groups of Americans no longer think they share either a common past or a common destiny, this trend is unhealthy.

Another indirect consequence of the recent proliferation of historical subcategories and subdisciplines has been an unsettling relativism. It is a small step from saying that it is important to study the history of African Americans, or women, or American Indians to saying that history is simply what each of the myriad groups says it is from their own perspective. And, from there, it is but a short step to argue that there is no objective truth at all, only what different groups perceive it to be. This sort of relativism has been reinforced by an array of trendy theories coming out of literary criticism and the social sciences, including postmodernism, deconstruction, semiotics, and structuralism and poststructuralism. The complexity of these various "isms" precludes a detailed discussion here, but one historian who laments their impact summarizes the situation:

> In the 1990s, the newly dominant theorists within the humanities and social sciences assert that it is impossible to tell the truth about the past or to use history to produce knowledge in any objective sense at all. They claim we can only see the past through the perspective of our own culture and, hence, what we see in history are our own interests and concerns reflected back at us. The central point upon which history was founded no longer holds: there is no fundamental distinction any more between history and myth. [12]

Personally, we would argue against the most extreme forms of relativism implicit in many of the fashionable "isms" mentioned above. But we would also acknowledge, as much of this book has argued, that history of necessity reflects the values and interests of the historians and societies that produce it. And the multiplication of perspectives that has characterized our century is much more a cause for celebration than a sign of despair. As three representatives of the "new" history have so pointedly argued, "truths about the past are possible, even if they are not absolute."[13] What the future will bring no one can say, but if the last century is any guide, the intellectual journey should be an exciting one.

---

[11]Mark T. Gilderhus, *History and Historians,* 3rd ed. (Englewood Cliffs, N. J.: Prentice Hall, 1996), 134.
[12]Keith Windschuttle, *The Killing of History: How Literary Critics and Social Theorists are Murdering Our Past* (New York: The Free Press, 1996), 2. This book provides an excellent, understandable overview of the various theories mentioned in this paragraph, as well as a detailed critique of those theories.
[13]Joyce Appleby, Lynn Hunt, and Margaret Jacob, *Telling the Truth About History* (New York: W. W. Norton & Co., 1994), 7.

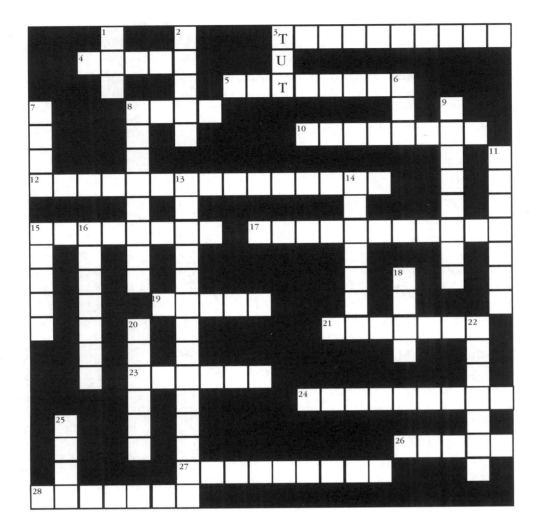

EXERCISE

The answers to the crossword puzzle above are, with a couple of minor exceptions, based on the information in this chapter. Remember, when authors or titles are mentioned, a footnote can be your friend. One word, not in the chapter, has been completed for you. Enjoy.

Across

3. Wrote history of the Peloponnesian War.
4. Proponent of critical history based on primary sources.
5. 19th-century history tended to have a _____ focus.
8. Believed economic forces were key to historical change.
10. Period of God-centered history.
12. Types of studies (pl.) with politics left out.
15. Susan Faludi's _____.
17. Renaissance historian.
19. Created psychoanalysis.
21. Macaulay's History of _____.
23. Partner of Marx.
24. Contemporary history writing is characterized by fragmentation and _____.
26. Increased attention paid to this group in new social history.

27. The "Father" of history.
28. English word derived from Greek word for "research."

Down

1. Erikson's Young _____ Luther.
2. Units of time commonly used to date events.
3. Egyptian pharaoh with famous tomb.
6. Historians should tell the truth; they should never _____.
7. Wrote history as story of the relationship with Yahweh.
8. Wrote early example of social history.
9. Subject of M. E. Dyson's book.
11. Historians usually divide the past into large blocks of time called _____.
13. The history of history.
14. Psychohistorian.
15. Wrote economic history of the Constitution.
16. Thinking historically means considering _____ over time.
18. Many people now get much of their history from _____.
20. First to write history in human terms.
22. Author of a local study of the Civil Rights Movement.
25. Psychohistory came into its own after _____. (Abbr.)

CHAPTER 14 HISTORY AND THE DISCIPLINES

"[H]istory offers living proof of the complementary nature of art and of science."
H. Stuart Hughes[1]

There is an old joke about two historians who meet at one of the annual history conventions. One historian asks the other if she knows what happened to their mutual friend, Smedley, who seems not to be in attendance. "Haven't you heard the sad news," responds the first historian. "Smedley has abandoned history to become a political scientist." "My goodness," exclaims the first, "next thing you know we'll hear that Smedley's become a sociologist!"

We didn't say it was a good joke. But the intellectual snobbery implicit in the story reveals an important truth: Even if the general public is indifferent to the labels that intellectuals give themselves, the professors themselves take the labels quite seriously. Academics derive a good part of their identity from the disciplines they study and teach. Further, since colleges and universities are usually divided into departments and schools based on those disciplinary labels, students should be minimally aware of what the labels represent.

History, clearly, is something of an intellectual chameleon. In its attempt to establish solid "truths" (or at least viable hypotheses) about humans and their world, history shares a good deal with the sciences; as a discipline concerned primarily with women and men as social beings, it shares much with the social sciences; and as a discipline that so often emphasizes telling a story about the past in a literate and engaging fashion, it aspires to the status of an art. Yet the differences between history and her sister disciplines are equally striking.

History and Science

In the nineteenth century some of the pioneers of modern historical studies were convinced that history could attain the status of an experimental science like chemistry or physics. N. D. Fustel de Coulanges, a nineteenth-century French historian, was typical when he claimed: "History is and should be a science." A moment's reflection will show that such optimism was misplaced.

The aim of many sciences is to discover regularities in nature—"laws" that can be used to generalize (i.e., predict) future occurrences. Precise measurement, careful observation, and laboratory experiments are the basic methods used for establishing such scientific "laws." For instance, repeated experiments at sea level will show that water boils at 100 degrees Celsius (212 degrees Fahrenheit). On the basis of such experiments the scientist (and the rest of us) can be reasonably sure that under similar circumstances water will always boil at that temperature.

Historians, obviously, can never discuss the past with such precision, since past events are unique and unrepeatable. The historians cannot "experiment" on

---

[1]H. Stuart Hughes, *History As Art and As Science* (New York: Harper and Row, 1964), 3.

the past. They can't, for instance, run the French Revolution over and over again to discover which variables were the critical ones, nor can they, except in the case of relatively recent events, interview the participants. Historians can never establish the revolutionary boiling point of a human community with anything like the precision with which the scientist can establish the boiling point of a liquid. The historian, then, does not aim (at least does not primarily aim) to establish universally convincing generalizations on the scientific model. Given the nature of the subject matter (unique, concrete, unrepeatable events) the historian is more interested in reconstructing *specific episodes* in all their diversity and particularity. The historian aims at truth, but not universal, timeless truth.

In spite of these differences, history shares more with science than first meets the eye. Originally "science" simply meant "knowledge," and if we think of a science as any search for knowledge based on a rigorous and objective examination of the evidence (whether the evidence is a beaker of boiling water or a diplomatic dispatch), then clearly history has some claim to being "scientific," if not a science per se. Second, not all sciences are totally experimental in approach. Such fields as astronomy, geology, ecology, climatology, evolutionary biology, and paleontology are much akin to history in their methodology, and may even be labeled "historical sciences."[2] All, like history, rely heavily on systematic *observation* and *classification* of data and must make their claims by studying the "records" of past events, whether the fossils that record the existence of past species, the rock formations that betoken upheavals thousands of years ago, or the light and radio waves of stars that originated eons in the past.

The elusive line between "history" and "science" is well illustrated by a spate of recent books. In *Guns, Germs, and Steel: The Fates of Human Societies,* biologist Jared Diamond writes: "The book's subject matter is history, but the approach is that of science—in particular, that of historical sciences such as evolutionary biology and geology."[3] Another scientist, geologist Richard Fortey, has written a "history" of life on planet earth. He tells a story that covers a period of over four billion years, the overwhelming majority of which predated human life.[4] Finally, consider British writer and photojournalist John Reader's *Africa: A Biography of the Continent,* which devotes more than half its chapters to the millions of years of geology and prehistory that most traditional histories would pass over with scarcely a mention.[5]

Even though history can never hope to achieve the level of certainty that is possible in the pure experimental sciences, it can still, through the application of rigorous canons of research, strive to attain closer and closer approximations of the past it seeks to recover. Remember, as difficult as it is to reconstruct the

---

[2]Physiologist and evolutionary biologist Jared Diamond writes: "Thus the difficulties historians face in establishing cause-and-effect relations in the history of human societies are broadly similar to the difficulties facing astronomers, climatologists, ecologists, evolutionary biologists, geologists and paleontologists. To varying degrees, each of these fields is plagued by the impossibility of performing replicated, controlled experimental interventions, the complexity arising from enormous numbers of variables, the resulting uniqueness of each system, the consequent impossibility of formulating universal laws, and the difficulties of predicting emergent properties and future behavior." *Guns, Germs, and Steel: The Fates of Human Societies* (New York: W. W. Norton & Co., 1997), 424.

[3]Diamond, *Guns, Germs, and Steel,* 26.

[4]Richard Fortey, *Life: A Natural History of the First Four Billion Years of Life on Earth* (New York: Alfred A. Knopf, 1998).

[5]John Reader, *Africa: Biography of the Continent* (New York: Alfred A. Knopf, 1998).

events of the past, those events did happen, and historical study can be used to understand and illuminate those events.

History and the Social Sciences

History is related even more closely to the social and behavioral sciences (e. g. , anthropology, sociology, political science, economics, and psychology). Indeed, many would include history among the social sciences. Whether history is a bedfellow or simply a close relative of the social sciences need not, for the moment, concern us. What is clear is that historians and social scientists share much in common. On the simplest level it is fair to claim that history provides much raw material for the social sciences. It would even be arguable (rightly we think) that history is in many ways the mother of the social sciences. Historians Jacques Barzun and Henry Graff have noted that the social sciences "are in fact daughter disciplines [to history], for they arose, each of them, out of historical investigation, having long formed part of avowed historical writing."[6]

Both history and the social sciences are bodies of knowledge that deal with women and men in society. Indeed it is often difficult to tell where one discipline leaves off and another begins. In recent years more and more works of "history" have incorporated theories and methods of various of the social sciences, for example the works of psychohistory discussed in the previous chapter. It is best, therefore, to think of history and the social sciences not as distinct categories, but as colors in an intellectual spectrum where one hue shades imperceptibly into another. The degree of overlap notwithstanding, each discipline approaches the study of the individual and society in a slightly different way.

- *Anthropology* literally means the "study of humanity." *Physical* anthropologists study the centuries-long physical evolution of human beings, whereas *cultural* anthropologists attempt to describe similarities and differences among peoples and cultures around the world (often concentrating on primitive cultures) and to explain the evolution of human social patterns. Anthropologists are historians of a sort, and history has been defined as "retrospective cultural anthropology. " In general, though, anthropologists have traditionally concentrated on preliterate peoples, both past and present, whereas historians have concentrated on the study of societies for which we have written records. Practically speaking, this limits historians to the last five or six thousand years of the human experience, and to the study of those societies that could write.

- *Sociology,* a close relative of anthropology, studies the characteristics and behavior of social aggregates and groups, especially their institutions and modes of social organization. Whereas anthropologists have focused attention on primitive societies, sociologists have concentrated on more advanced, technologically sophisticated societies. To the extent that anthropology and sociology might study the same cultural groups and institutions, they are almost indistinguishable as disciplines. Again, the overlaps with history are many. Much sociology is based on historical evidence, and many historians (for instance, social historians) have adopted a sociological approach in their historical studies of social classes, occupational groups, and institutions.

- *Political Science,* like sociology, attempts to unlock the secrets of institutional and group behavior but, as the name implies, concentrates especially on politi-

---

[6]Barzun and Graff, *Modern Researcher,* 218.

cal behavior and governmental and legal institutions. The evolution and nature of political and legal ideas (political theory) has also been a longtime interest of the political scientist. The shared interests of the political scientist and historian are many, since law, politics, war, and diplomacy are among the most traditional objects of historical study. Many scholarly works on government, international relations, and politics are impossible to categorize as history or political science with any degree of certainty.

- *Economics* is the discipline that attempts to lay bare the mechanisms through which a society produces, trades, and distributes material goods. That the historian too is vitally interested in the economic side of human affairs goes without saying (recall our comments on the influence of Marx). Economic history is a thriving sub-specialty within the discipline of history.

- Finally, *Psychology* is the study of "mental, emotional, and behavioral processes." The psychologist is interested in the unseen forces within the individual and within the social environment that make people behave the way they do. More than the other social and behavioral sciences, *psychology emphasizes the mental processes and behavior patterns of the individual,* although some branches of psychology (e.g., social psychology) do deal with group behavior. Recently, as we have seen, historians have shown a growing interest in the psychological dimension of human behavior, and a growing number of studies have attempted to apply the insights of psychology to historical individuals and groups.

Clearly, there are many parallels between history and the various social sciences. But how do they differ? First, and this verges on massive oversimplification, a major preoccupation of the social sciences is to explain how societies, economies, governments, and other groups behave today. History, on the other hand, is more interested in explaining how societies functioned and developed in the past—that is, how they changed through time. Of course, the political scientist or economist does not ignore history (i.e., the past); nor does the historian ignore the lessons of the present. But generally the social sciences are much more "present oriented" than is history. The social scientist (often using historical evidence) tries to account for present behavior; the historian (often using current insights) tries to account for past behavior.

History and the social sciences diverge in yet another way. The social sciences, like the physical sciences, often emphasize the precise quantification (measurement) of data, experimentation (when appropriate), and the development of generalizations that permit prediction (and even control) of future behavior. While the historian attempts to reconstruct individual events in all their uniqueness, social scientists attempt to discover general principles that can be used to understand many events. To oversimplify, the historian examines the uniqueness of past events; the social scientist searches for the commonalities. For instance, a historian may desire to know all there is to know about the presidential election of 1980 in order to write a thorough history of that event. A political scientist, however, might want to compare voter behavior in 1980 with that in other presidential elections in order to discover voting patterns that might help predict the outcomes of future elections.

Of course, the historian will be more than happy to utilize whatever information the political scientist discovers (intellectual parasitism has a long and noble history), but it is not the historian's primary purpose to establish such regularities. Nor is the historian especially interested in prediction, as it is difficult enough to find out what has already happened. "It is the historian's aim," claims one writer, "to portray the bewildering, unsystematic variety of historical forms—people, nations, cultures, customs, institutions, songs, myths, and thoughts—in their unique, living expressions and in the process of continuous growth and transformation."[7]

Whether history is a bona fide social science or just a close relative is a matter best left unresolved at this time. Whatever your view of the matter, it is clear that the lines separating history from the various social sciences discussed in this section will never be easy to draw with absolute clarity.

History and Art

If, at times, history seems to "belong" to the social sciences, at other times it seems more reasonable to count it among the literary arts. After all, in its most basic form, written history is, as the name suggests, a "story." To tell a story well, as we have seen, the good historian must utilize the literary skills and conventions of the novelist or poet. Arnold Toynbee, the famous British historian, said "no historian can be 'great' if he is not also a great artist," and it is true that some of the "greatest" (at least most widely read) historians have been superb literary stylists. The war histories of Winston Churchill, Edward Gibbon's *Decline and Fall of the Roman Empire,* Macaulay's *History of England,* Bruce Catton's Civil War histories, and, the works of American historian Barbara Tuchman are as much worth reading for their literary qualities as for what they say about the past. And what they say about the past, we might add, is very much worth our attention.

The historian must be an "artist" in another sense. To make the past come alive for current readers, a historian must be able to re-create on paper the passions, beliefs, and feelings of people long dead. This requires more than literary grace. The historian, as we have noted more than once in this book, must be able to empathize and sympathize with individuals, institutions, customs, and ideas that may seem foreign or strange. Like poets or novelists, historians must be able to "feel" themselves into the periods and cultures they are studying. Dispassionate objectivity is, of course, essential to good history; but so too is the imaginative insight and vision of the creative artist.[8] The basic difference between a great historian and a great novelist is that the historian's story must conform to known facts. The plausibility of the historian's narrative is determined by its adherence to the evidence. Good fiction, on the other hand, must be internally consistent and it must correspond to commonsense notions of how human beings behave, but it need not conform to any external body of source materials.

A Summary: The Main Features of History

If you are still somewhat confused about exactly where history fits into the jigsaw puzzle of intellectual life, don't despair. The lines that separate one branch of

---

[7]Hans Meyerhoff (ed.), *The Philosophy of History in Our Time* (New York: Doubleday, 1959), 10.
[8]John Clive, until his recent death a Professor of History and Literature at Harvard University, made a career of studying the works and ideas of the great historians. What makes these historians (Macaulay, Jules Michelet, Alexis de Tocqueville, etc.) worth reading, Clive argues, is that their writing is a product of "the encounter between personal commitment and scholarly curiosity which lies at the heart of all great history." Clive says: "the quality of their writing, which turns out to exert the greatest power over us . . . is intimately related to each historian's chief intellectual and personal concerns." Quoted in Windschuttle, *Killing of History,* 244.

knowledge from another have never been precise. In simplest terms, the basic characteristics of history are three:

1. *History is concerned with human beings operating in society.* The historian is not primarily concerned with the origins of the earth (the task of the geologist), or with the organic processes of life (the task of the chemist and biologist), or with when and how humanoid creatures emerged on the land (the task of the anthropologist and paleontologist). The historian's work only begins in the presence of reliable records—especially written records—that indicate that a specific human group shared a specific set of experiences in a specific time and place.

2. *History is concerned with change through time.* Quite obviously, human society is also a central concern of many disciplines other than history. As distinct from these other disciplines, however, history traces and explains a society's experiences through time. It is important to note that history—good history—does not merely list events like a chronicle or a diary; history attempts to explain how and why things happened as they did.

3. *History is concerned with the concrete and the particular.* This is not always true, of course, because many historians do try to make generalizations that apply beyond a single situation. But, in the final analysis, a basic defining characteristic of history is its continuing preoccupation with the unique circumstance, and with the particulars that give substance to generalizations and distinctiveness to a given point in time. In other words, broad generalizations, however important, are secondary to those insights that provide knowledge of a particular, unique past.

EXERCISES

We acknowledge that the distinctions we are asking you to make in the exercises below are, to some extent, artificial and overly simplistic. In reality the line separating one discipline or approach from another is quite ambiguous; each discipline tends to shade imperceptibly into the next. However, there are differences between history and the other disciplines, and even an overly simplified set of contrasts can help you more effectively perceive those differences.

Exercise 1

This chapter is devoted to outlining some of the major similarities and differences between the study of history and the other disciplines. In the selections below, see if you can distinguish the examples of historical writing from those drawn from a variety of other disciplines. Before doing so, however, recall the central characteristics of history: (1) a concern with humans in society, (2) a preoccupation with change through time, and (3) a preference for explaining the interrelationship of concrete, particular events rather than elaborating comprehensive generalizations or hypotheses. Also, historians generally limit themselves to the study of societies for which there are written records.

Mark the passages drawn from history with an "H." Mark the passages drawn from other disciplines with an "O." You need not identify the other disciplines specifically. But do show your reasons for choosing as you do by indicating the absence or presence of the characteristics of history (1, 2, and 3) listed in "The Main Features of History" on pages 247–248. See the example below.

Example:

___O___ A. We have now got so close to our present that we have to count in tens of thousands of years rather than in millions. Beginning at some undefined point in time, perhaps 70,000 years ago, Neanderthal Man appeared on the scene. As we shall see in Chapter IX, he represents the beginning of civilized man in the sense that he went in for religious observances, which suggests an intellectual capacity for abstract concepts. It also suggests that he must have had the kind of spoken language we have, if less refined and subtle. Indeed, his brain was as large as ours, although presumably rather different, for his skull was low-browed and bun-shaped rather than domed. . . . They inhabited Europe, the Middle East, and central Asia until roughly 35,000 b.p. [before the present], when they disappeared, perhaps because they were unable to compete with or defend themselves against men of our own kind, who were replacing them.

Comment: *This passage is challenging to categorize. If you labeled it history, we would not object too strenuously. The passage does deal with humans in society (note the reference to religious observances), and it attempts to describe and explain change through time. Yet we would label this passage with an "O" because the author is describing a period long before the invention of writing and hence written records—a period often referred to as "prehistoric." The subject matter belongs more properly in the domain of the anthropologist.*

_____ B. Naturally, the larger and more massive a star, the more tremendous a red giant it will balloon into. The red giant into which our Sun will someday bloat will not be a particularly impressive specimen of the class. Red giants such as Betelgeuse and Antares developed out of main sequence stars considerably more massive than the Sun.

Reasons:_____

_____

_____ C. Leadership of Europe moved north to France, England, and Holland in the seventeenth century. In France, Henry IV (1589–1610) restored the monarchy to authority after a long bout of civil and religious wars. The state remained officially Catholic; but French national interests were kept carefully distinct from the cause of the papacy or of international Catholicism. Effective royal control of the Church in France dated back to the fourteenth century and was vigorously and successfully maintained against the revivified papacy in the sixteenth and seventeenth centuries.

Reasons:_____

_____

_____ D. The day after his landslide defeat in 1984, Walter Mondale observed, "Modern politics requires a mastery of television. . . . The thing that scares me about that," he added, "is American politics is losing its substance. It's losing the depth." Since the presidential campaign season of 1980, candidates of both parties have tended to treat voters less like citizens of the polity than like consumers considering the purchase of a major product. High-tech mass marketing of particular candidates does not always work, but all candidates must have copious access to the media, and for this access to be used effectively, they must surround themselves with media advisers who can package the candidate effectively.

Reasons:_____

_____

_____ E. The Administration that came to power in January 1961 under President John F. Kennedy presented an attitude towards American responsibilities for "leadership" of the free world that one could call either "vigorous" or "frenzied," depending on how one felt about it. Our NATO allies were quickly apprised of the fact that the Americans had many new ideas for the defense of Europe, and that the Europeans would have to make some endeavor to understand and implement them. These ideas were themselves significant for what was to happen in the Far East, because they involved a complete dismantling of the "massive retaliation" concept in favor of a whole new complex of ideas stressing the use of conventional forces in limited wars. The man who as a true believer presided intimately over this change was the new Secretary of Defense, Robert S. McNamara.

Reasons:_____

_____

_____ F. Seventeenth-century America had none of the speculative vigor of English Puritanism. For Massachusetts Bay possessed an orthodoxy. During the classic age of the first generation, at least, it was a community of self-selected conformists. In 1637 the General Court passed an order prohibiting anyone from settling within the colony without first having his orthodoxy approved by the magistrates. . . . Here was a community formed by free consent of its members. Why should they not exclude dangerous men, or men with dangerous thoughts? What right had supporters of a subversive Mr. Wheelwright to claim entrance to the colony?

Reasons:_____

_____

_____ G. **410** In this year Rome was destroyed by the Goths, eleven hundred and ten years after it was built. Then after that the kings of the Romans no longer reigned in Britain. Altogether they had reigned there **470** years since Gaius Julius first came to the land.
596 In this year Pope Gregory sent Augustine to Britain with a good number of monks, who preached God's word to the English people.
671 In this year there was the great mortality of birds.
715 In this year Ine and Ceolred fought at "Woden's barrow."
733 In this year Aethelbald occupied Somerton, and there was an eclipse of the sun.

Reasons:_____

_____

_____ H. We have already seen the two major models of economic organization: the market mechanism and the command economy. . . . Today, neither of these polar extremes represents the reality of the American economic system. Rather ours is a "mixed economy," in which both private and public institutions exercise economic control: the private system through the invisible direction of the market mechanism, the public institutions through regulatory commands and fiscal incentives.

Reasons:_____

_____

Sources
A. Louis J. Halle, *Out of Chaos* (Boston: Houghton Mifflin, 1977), 241.
B. Isaac Asimov, *The Universe* (New York: Avon, 1966), 162–63.
C. William H. McNeill, *The Rise of the West* (New York: Mentor, 1965), 635.
D. Daniel Hellinger and Dennis Judd, *The Democratic Facade,* 2nd ed. (Belmont, Calif.: Wadsworth Publishing Co., 1994), 87.
E. Bernard Brodie, *War and Politics* (New York: Macmillan, 1963), 124–25.
F. Daniel Boorstin, *The Americans: The Colonial Experience* (New York: Random House, 1958), 7.
G. "The Anglo-Saxon Chronicle" from B. L. Blakeley and J. Collins (eds.), *Documents in English History* (New York: John Wiley & Sons, 1975), 18.
H. Paul Samuelson and William Nordhaus, *Economics,* 12th ed. (New York: McGraw-Hill, 1985), 41–42.

Exercise 2

We have noted that recently many historians have applied some of the categories, insights, and methods of the various social sciences to historical problems. In the history passages below—these dealing with witch beliefs and witchcraft persecutions—see if you can determine which of the social-science approaches (i. e. , anthropology, sociology, political science, economics, psychology) the historians have tried to utilize. If more than one answer seems appropriate, please so indicate. Also, identify those passages that simply narrate "what happened" in a more traditional manner. Use the word "traditional" for such passages. You might want to review the brief definitions of the various social sciences on pages 245–246.

A. Among the Navaho, witches are active primarily at night. This is also so among the Tale, the Azande and the Amba, but there is little trace of night meetings in Essex, [England]. Navaho witches are believed to meet most frequently in a cave, and there is general agreement that all types of witch activity must be carried on away from home. Likewise, witches among the Kaguru meet in unfrequented places. . . .

Answer:_____

B. Early in the year 1692 several girls of Salem Village (now Danvers), Massachusetts, began to sicken and display alarming symptoms [interpreted later as manifestations of witchcraft]. . . . These symptoms are readily recognizable. The most cursory examination of the classic studies of hysteria—of Charcot, of Janet, of Breuer, and Freud—will demonstrate that the afflicted girls in Salem were hysterical in the scientific sense of that term.

Answer: _____

C. The preliminary hearings began on Tuesday, March 1 [1692]. The magistrates arrived via the road from Salem town, gathering into formation around them the local constabulary and other prominent personages in a solemn yet impressive entourage. With 'pennants flying and drums athrob,' as one writer has described it, they arrived at Ingersoll's ordinary, where the court was to meet. Finding the space too small to accommodate the crowd that had gathered, the magistrates moved the hearing to the nearby meetinghouse.

Answer: _____

D. [In Salem, Massachusetts] almost every indicator by which the two Village factions may be distinguished, in fact, also neatly separates the supporters and opponents of the witchcraft trials. . . . The connection is clear: that part of Salem Village which was an anti-Parris stronghold in 1695 (the nearest part of Salem Town) had also been a center of resistance to the witchcraft trials, while the more distant western part of the Village, where pro-Parris sentiment was dominant, contained an extremely high concentration of accusers in 1692. . . . Similarly with wealth: . . . the average 1695–96 tax of the Villagers who publicly opposed the trials was 67 percent higher than that of those who pushed the trials forward. . . .

Answer: _____

E. The association of witchcraft with "weak points in the social structure" suggests two research questions of large importance. First, what was the predominant pattern of relationship between the parties chiefly involved? Second, what situations most frequently yielded witchcraft suspicions—and accusations?

Answer: _____

F. The fifteenth century witnessed a vast expansion of witch literature and witch trials. In part this geometric progression of the witch phenomenon can be attributed to the decay of those ideas and institutions that had held medieval society together. Deprived of the old securities, people responded in panic that at that particular time found vent in terror of witchcraft.

Answer: _____

G. As Lyndal Roper states, 'witchcraft confessions and accusations are not products of realism, and they cannot be analysed with the methods of historical realism.' She draws out how individuals borrowed the language and stereotypical images of witchcraft to express their own psychic conflicts, which centered on the earliest stages of the mother-child relationship. Although this approach is particularly effective for the Augsburg material, with its exceptional focus on the care of infants in the strictly feminine space, it can be extended more widely.

Answer:_____

Sources
A. A. D. J. Macfarlane, *Witchcraft in Tudor and Stuart England* (New York: Harper & Row, 1970), 211.
B. Chadwick Hansen, *Witchcraft at Salem* (New York: Mentor, 1970), 21–22.
C. Bryan F. Le Beau, *The Story of the Salem Witch Trials* (Upper Saddle River, N.J.: Prentice Hall, 1998), 68.
D. Paul Coyer and Stephen Nissenbaum, *Salem Possessed* (Cambridge, Mass. : Harvard University Press, 1974), 185.
E. John Putnam Demos, *Entertaining Satan: Witchcraft and the Culture of Early New England* (New York: Oxford University Press, 1982), 278.
F. J. B. Russell, *Witchcraft in the Middle Ages* (Ithaca, N.Y. : Cornell University Press, 1972), 227.
G. Robin Briggs, *Witches and Neighbors: The Social and Cultural Context of European Witchcraft* (New York: Viking, 1996), 282.

Exercise 3

Among historians there is disagreement whether history is more a social science (like political science or sociology) or a humanity (like literature). As we have seen, history shares characteristics with both camps. Usually historians do not state explicitly where they stand on this issue, but often their attitudes are implicit in the books and articles they write. In the passages below indicate whether you think the historian in question seems to view history more as a social science or a humanity.

One clue to look for is the emphasis given to literary evidence (written records) versus statistical and quantifiable evidence. A preference for the latter would indicate a more social-scientific approach. Another clue would be the relative weight given to description and analysis of *particular* events versus analysis and generalization about a range of similar events or situations. Again, the latter emphasis may indicate a more social-scientific approach to the study of the past.

On a scale of 1 to 3, mark the most social-science-oriented passages with a "1" and the most traditional or "literary" passages with a "3." Those that you feel are in the middle, or for which you are unsure, mark with a "2."

_____ A. [In the Middle Ages] one sound rose ceaselessly above the noises of busy life and lifted all things unto a sphere of order and serenity: the sound of bells. The bells were in daily life like good spirits, which by their familiar voices, now called upon the citizens to mourn and now to rejoice, now warned them of danger, now exhorted them to piety. They were known by their names: big Jacqueline, or the bell Roland. Every one knew the difference in meaning of the various ways of ringing. However continuous the ringing of the bells, people would seem not to have become blunted to the effect of their sound.

_____ B. At whatever level one conducts research, roll-call votes offer versatile data that can be used to explore a variety of questions. Along with collections of session-laws and statutes, they comprise the most systematic body of data extant on the legislative process in the states. Roll calls offer data with which to discriminate systematically between contested and consensus issues and to compare the levels of voting conflict evoked by particular policy areas among various states.

_____ C. The extravagant conversations recorded by Hermann Rauschning for the period 1932–34, and by Dr. Henry Picker at the Fuehrer's H. Q. for the period 1941–42, reveal Hitler in another favourite role, that of visionary and prophet. . . . The fabulous dreams of a vast empire embracing all Europe and half Asia; the geopolitical fantasies of inter-continental wars and alliances; the plans for breeding an elite, biologically pre-selected, and founding a new Order to guard the Holy Grail of pure blood; the designs for reducing whole nations to slavery-all these are fruits of a crude, disordered, but fertile imagination soaked in the German romanticism of the late nineteenth century. . . .

_____ D. To be more precise, only one of the manifestations of sexual change will occupy us here: a rapid increase in the incidence of illegitimate births between the mid-eighteenth and mid-nineteenth centuries. . . . We may bring to bear other kinds of evidence as well upon sexual history, such as the observations of contemporaries, various 'medical' surveys of the population conducted by the cameralist governments of western and central Europe, court records on sexual crimes and aberrancies, or the study of pornography. . . . Yet in this paper, I wish to present the evidence of illegitimacy alone.

First we examine potential objections to illegitimacy data as a measure of real sexual attitudes and practices; second, we briefly discuss the dimensions of the increase in illegitimacy between mid-eighteenth and mid-nineteenth centuries; third, a review of some current theories about sexual behavior and illegitimacy is in order; fourth, a general model linking modernizing forces to sexual change and illegitimacy will be proposed; finally I shall present empirical data confirming some of the linkages in this model from a region of central Europe which participated in the illegitimacy explosion—the Kingdom of Bavaria.

_____ E. In 1941 Frederick Williams introduced Frederick Mosteller to the problem which we shall consider in detail in this paper, namely the problem of the authorship of the disputed Federalist papers. Williams and Mosteller, influenced by the work of Yule and of C. B. Williams (1939), studied the undisputed Federalist works of Hamilton and Madison but found that sentence length did not discriminate between the two authors. They then computed for each known paper the percentages of nouns, of adjectives, of one- and two-letter words, and of the's. On the basis of these data they constructed a statistic that was intended to separate Hamilton's writings from Madison's. This statistic, however, was not sensitive enough to assign the disputed papers with any degree of confidence, although it pointed to Madison for most of them.

_____ F. Joan [of Arc (1412–31)] was born in that atmosphere of legend, of folklike dreamings. But the countryside offered another and very different kind of poetry, fierce, atrocious, and, alas! all too real: the poetry of war . . . War! That single word sums up all the emotions; not every day was marked by assault and pillage; but rather by the anguished expectancy, the tolling of the alarm bell, the sudden awakening, and, far in the plain, the sullen glare of fire. . . . A horrible condition: yet with an aura of poetry: even the most down-to-earth of men, the Lowland Scots, turned into poets amid the perils of the Border; from that blasted heath, which still seems under a curse, the ballads blossomed forth like wild and vigorous flowers.

_____ G. John Stuart Mill [1806-73] is thought of today as the archetype of the liberal, the author of that classic of liberalism, *On Liberty*. But there was another John Stuart Mill, who was anything but the perfect liberal and whose writings were of a quite different character. . . . Mill's responsibility for the creation of his own stereotype is only now becoming apparent. The publication of his correspondence with Harriet Taylor, for twenty years his intimate companion and later his wife, and the more recent publication of the original draft of his Autobiography, are enormously revealing. It remains for scholars to collate these materials, as well as to reexamine his early writings in their original versions.

_____ H. It all seems clear and consistent enough. The women in Shakespeare's plays, and so presumably the Englishwomen of Shakespeare's day, might marry in their early teens, or even before, and very often did.

Yet this is not true. We have examined every record we can find to test it and they all declare that, in Elizabethan and Jacobean England, marriage was rare at these early ages and not as common in the late teens as it is now. At twelve marriage as we understand it was virtually unknown. . . .

It is indeed hazardous to infer an institution or a habit characteristic of a whole society or a whole era from the central character of a literary work and its story. . . . The outcome may be to make people believe that what was the entirely exceptional, was in fact the perfectly normal. . . . This is a cogent argument in favour of statistical awareness, and of the sociological imagination, in studies of this sort.

_____ I. For Churchill it [the Japanese attack on Pearl Harbor and U. S. entry into World War II] was a moment of pure joy. So he had won, after all, he exulted. Yes, after Dunkirk, the fall of France, the threat of invasion, the U-boat struggle—after seventeen months of lonely fighting and nineteen months of his own hard responsibility—the war was won. England would live; the Commonwealth and the Empire would live. The war would be long, but all the rest would be merely the proper application of overwhelming force. People had said the Americans were soft, divided, talkative, affluent, distant, averse to bloodshed. But he knew better; he had studied the Civil War, fought out to the last desperate inch; American blood flowed in his veins. . . . Churchill set his office to work calling Speaker and whips to summon Parliament to meet next day. Then saturated with emotion, he turned in and slept the sleep of the saved and thankful.

For Discussion

In what ways might the books/articles represented by the passages you labeled "1" (social-science approach) be superior as history to those books and articles represented by passages labeled "3"? Is one approach better than the other or do both approaches have potential benefits and liabilities?

Sources
A. J. Huizinga, *The Waning of the Middle Ages* (New York: Anchor. 1954), 10.
B. Ballard Campbell, "The State Legislature in American History: A Review Essay," *Historical Meth ods Newsletter,* September 1976, 193.
C. Alan Bullock, *Hitler,* rev. ed. (New York: Bantam, 1969), 325-26.
D. Edward Shorter, "Sexual Change and Illegitimacy: The European Experience," *Modern European Social History,* ed. Robert Bezucha (Lexington, Mass.: D. C. Heath, 1972), 231-32.
E. Ivor S. Francis, "An Exposition of a Statistical Approach to the Federalist Dispute," Quantification in *American History,* ed. Robert P. Swierenga (New York: Atheneum, 1970), 98.
F. Jules Michelet, *Joan of Arc* (Ann Arbor, Michigan: University of Michigan Press, 1967), 10.

APPENDIX A FUR TRADE ON THE UPPER MISSOURI RIVER: DOCUMENTS

The six documents that follow regard the beginnings of American fur trade on the upper Missouri River. This trade had great potential economic value, since animal furs and hides were regarded as the major resource of the developing West. The events described in the documents took place within what was legally American territory (as part of the Louisiana Purchase in 1803). One must remember, however, that for more than a hundred years British fur traders had operated successfully throughout the forest and mountain areas of North America, with little regard to who owned them.

There are many possible themes you might choose to develop, e. g., the role of the British in the failure of the Ashley expedition, leadership deficiencies of Gen. Ashley, blunders of the federal government, justification for Rickaree Indian attacks, or the attitudes and outlooks of the men on the expedition. There are, of course, many other possibilities.

Documents

These documents are taken from *The West of William H. Ashley,* edited by Dale L. Morgan (Denver: Old West Publishing Co., 1964), pp. 17, 22, 29–31, 33, 36–37. Published with permission. The original spelling has been retained.

> *John C. Calhoun, Secretary of War, to William Clark, Superintendent of Indian Affairs at St. Louis, Washington, July 1, 1822*
>
> Sir,
> . . . I have received a letter from Major O'Fallon, in which he states that he understands a licence has been granted to Gen. Ashley and Major Henry, to trade, trap, & hunt, on the upper Missouri, and expresses a hope that limits have been prescribed to their trapping and hunting on Indian lands, as, he says, nothing is better calculated to alarm and disturb the harmony so happily existing between us and the Indians in the vicinity of the Council Bluffs.
>
> The license which has been granted by this Department by order of the President to Gen. Ashley & Major Henry confers the privilege of trading with the Indians only, as the laws regulating trade and intercourse with the Indian tribes do not contain any authority to issue licenses for any other purpose. The privilege thus granted to them they are to exercise conformably to the laws and regulations that are or shall be made for the government of trade and intercourse with the Indians, for the true and faithfull observance of which they have given bonds with sufficient security; consequently, it is presumed, they will do no act not authorized by such laws and regulations, which would disturb the peace and harmony existing between the government

and the Indians on the Missouri, but rather endeavor, by their regular and conciliatory conduct, to strengthen and confirm them.

Missouri Republican, *St. Louis, March 12, 1823*

Two keel-boats belonging to general Ashley, left this place on Monday [March 10] for the Yellow Stone [River], having on board about 100 men. They have started to join the establishment commenced by that gentleman last year, above the mouth of the Yellow Stone, for the purposes of hunting and trapping. If enterprise could command success, it would certainly await upon the exertions of the head of these expeditions.

We understand a man fell overboard from one of the boats, on Monday morning, and was drowned.

William H. Ashley to a Gentleman in Franklin, Missouri

On board the keel boat Rocky Mountains, opposite the mouth of the Shegan River [a tributary of the Missouri River], June 7, 1823.

As I ascended the river I was informed by some gentlemen of the Missouri Fur Company, that in a reccent affray which they had had with a war party of the Rickaree Indians, two of the Indians were killed, and that their conduct during the last winter, had shewn a hostile disposition towards the Americans. I therefore used all the precaution in my power for some days before I reached their towns; not one of them, however, did I see until my arrival there on the 30th of May, when my boats were anchored about the middle of the river. I took with me two men & went on shore, where I was met by some of the principal chiefs, who professed to be very friendly disposed, and requested me to land some goods for the purpose of trading with them. I had just received an express from Maj. Henry, desiring me to purchase all the horses I could get; consequently I proposed to exchange goods for horses, intending to send a party of forty men by land to the Yellow Stone River. I requested that the principal chiefs of the two towns would first meet me on the sand beach, where there should be a perfect understanding relative to the principles of our barter. After some consultation, the chiefs made their appearance at the place proposed. I then stated to them what I had heard below relative to their conduct, and the impropriety of repeating it. They said they much regretted the affray between some of their nation and the Americans, and confessed that they had been much displeased with us, but that all those angry feelings had left them; that then they considered the Americans their friends, and intended to treat them as such.

The next morning I commenced the purchase of horses, and on the evening of the 1st inst [of the present month, hence June] was ready to proceed on my voyage, intending to set out early the next morning. Late in the afternoon an Indian came down with a message to me from the principal chief (the Bear) of one of the towns, requesting that I would come and see him. After some hesitation (as I did not wish to let them know that I apprehended the least danger from them) I went to the lodge of the chief, where I was treated with every appearance of friendship.—The next morning, about half past 3 o'clock, I was informed that Aaron Stephens, one of my men, had been killed by the Indians, and that in all probability the boats would be attacked in a few minutes. The boats were anchored in the stream, about 90 feet from the shore. My party consisted of ninety men, forty of whom had been selected to go by land, and were encamped on the sand beach, to whose charge the horses were entrusted. The men on the beach were placed as near as possible between the two boats.

At sunrise the Indians commenced a heavy and well directed fire from a line extending along the picketing of one of their towns, and some broken land adjoining, about six hundred yards in length. Their aim was principally at the men on shore. The fire was returned by us, but, from their advantageous situation, I presume we did but little execution. Discovering the fire to be destructive to the men on shore, the steersmen of both boats were ordered to weigh their anchors and lay their boats to shore; but, notwithstanding every exertion on my part to enforce the execution of the order, I could not effect it—the principal part of the boatmen were so panic struck, that they would not expose themselves in the least. Two skiffs, one sufficient to carry twenty men, were taken ashore for the embarcation of the men, but, from a predetermination on their part not to give way to the Indians as long as it was possible to do otherwise, the most of them refused to make use of that opportunity of embarking, the large skiff returned with four, two of them wounded, and was immediately started back, but unfortunately one of the oarsmen was shot down, and by some means the skiff set adrift. The other was taken to the opposite side of the river by two men, one mortally wounded; some swam to the boats, others were shot down in the edge of the water and immediately sunk, and others who appeared to be badly wounded sunk in attempting to swim. To describe my feelings at seeing these men destroyed, is out of my power. I feel confident that if my orders had been obeyed I should not have lost five men.

If our government do not send troops on this river, as high as the mouth of the Yellow Stone, or above that place, the Americans must abandon the trade in this country—The Indians are becoming more formidable every year. The Rickarees are about six hundred warriors, three fourths of whom, I think, are armed with London fusils, which carry a ball with considerable accuracy and force—others have bows and arrows, war axes, &c. [etc.]. They are situated in two towns about three hundred yards apart.— Immediately in front of them is a large sand bar, nearly in the shape of a horse-shoe. On the opposite side of the river the ground is very high and commanding, and at the upper end of the bar they have a breastwork made of dry wood. The river there is narrow, and the channel near the south side.

From the situation of my men and boats, when the men had embarked, I concluded to fall back to the first timber, and place them in a better state of defence, then to proceed on my voyage; but to my great mortification and surprise, I was informed, after my men had been made acquainted with my intentions, that they positively refused to make another attempt to pass the towns, without a considerable reinforcement. I had them paraded, and made known to them the manner in which I proposed fixing the boats and passing the Indian villages. After saying all that I conceived necessary to satisfy them, and having good reason to believe that I should be, with but very few exceptions, deserted in a short time by all my men, as some of them had already formed a resolution to desert, I called on those disposed to remain with me under any circumstances, until I should hear from Maj. Henry, to whom I would send an express immediately, and request that he would descend with all the aid he could spare from his fort at the mouth of the Yellow Stone.—Thirty only have volunteered, among whom are but few boatmen; consequently I am compelled to send one boat back, having secured [some of] her cargo here [opposite the mouth of the Cheyenne]. I am determined to descend no lower until I pass the Rickarees, should it be in my power so to do.

Hugh Glass to the Parents of John S. Gardner

[June, 1823]

Dr Sir,

My painfull duty it is to tell you of the deth of yr Son wh befell at the hands of the indians 2nd June in the early morning. He lived a little while after he was shot and asked me to inform you of his sad fate We brought him to the ship where he soon died. Mr Smith a young man of our company made a powerful prayr wh moved us all greatly and I am persuaded John died in peace. His body we buried with others near this camp and marked the grave with a log. His things we will send to you. The savages are greatly treacherous. we traded with them as friends but after a great storm of rain and thunder they came at us before light and many were hurt. I myself was hit in the leg. Master Ashley is bound to stay in these parts till the traitors are rightly punished.

Yr Obt Svt
Hugh Glass

Letter by One of Ashley's Men to a Friend in the District of Columbia

Fort Kiawa, ten miles below the Big Bend of the Missouri, June 17th, 1823.

. . . We retreated down the river about 20 miles, intending to fortify ourselves until we could get assistance from the Bluffs [a military post]; the French boatmen were so panic-struck they would listen to no terms—they would return and forfeit their wages sooner than remain. Ashley paraded his men, told them his situation, and called for volunteers; one third, being twenty-five, only remained, and of these one half are boatmen, who intend returning when Henry's boat comes down. Out of one hundred men, the number he left St. Louis with, I question much whether he will arrive at the Yellow Stone with more than ten, (and of this number I hope to be one;) finding he could not obtain men enough to remain with sufficient to man both boats, he determined to fortify his own [the Rocky Mountains]—take all those on board who were willing to stay, and those goods only that might be wanted—send the balance of the goods to this place and the large boat to St. Louis. With the goods, I was left in charge, and shall remain here until I hear from him or Henry. . . .

Council Bluffs is 600 miles below this, a very injudicious place for a military post. Here, and above this, is the spot where the Indians have always been most troublesome. You will hardly believe it, but I assure you it is a fact, our Indian Agent has never been above the Bluffs. He has never made himself known to the Indians in this quarter. They have been told of troops, &c. &c. at the Bluffs, but they do not believe it; they have never seen more of the white people than the few traders that come among them; and each tribe thinks we are less numerous than they—they have reason to think so, having never been punished for the numerous robberies and murders committed by them. . . .

I have been told, though I cannot vouch for its authenticity, although I think it highly probable, from their determined hostility, that they [the British] have erected trading establishments within our territories. One thing is certain, they are not willing we should rival them in this valuable trade. All the injury they can do us they will do. The hostility of the Ricarees, Black-feet, Snake, Chiaus [Cheyennes], and Assiniboines, is entirely owing to the influence of the Northwest or Hudson Bay Company [a British Company]. The late act [of May 6, 1822] prohibiting the sale of spirituous liquors to the Indians has not that good effect which the framers of it had in view. It was passed without mature deliberation and a knowledge of the circumstances. No act that Congress could have passed could have such a tendency to aggrandize the North-West Company. In consequence of this, most of those tribes that formerly frequented the river have now left it, and more contemplate doing so, should that act not be repealed or amended. From the English they can get what liquor they want, and the distance is nothing to an Indian, when he has in view the gratification of his passions. Among the Ricarees I saw several English medals, and some of British manufacture.

The government must remedy these abuses; she must divest herself of that appalling slowness that attends all her operations. She must show more energy than she has done, if she wishes to preserve the fur trade; otherwise, our traders may as well abandon the business. The risque is too great for individual enterprise when unaided and unassisted by the government. Adieu. For myself I am determined to have revenge for the loss of two young men to whom I became very much attached, and I never will descend this river until I assist in shedding the blood of some of the Ricarees. It would give me pleasure beyond the power of language to express, could I personally extend my hand and greet you, &c.

Benjamin O'Fallon, U.S. Indian Agent, Upper Missouri Agency, to William Clark, Superintendent of Indian Affairs at St. Louis, Fort Atkinson, June 24, 1823

Dear Sir,

I arrived at this place [from St. Louis] on the 6th instant after a long and disagreeable trip of more than twenty days and have been anxiously waiting an opportunity to write you a long letter on many subjects, but more particularly on the subject of Indian affairs—But I now take up my pen to announce to you a circumstance, which not only wounds my national pride, but grieves my heart greatly—it is the defeat of Gen. Ashleys Expedition by the Aricharars [i.e., Rickarees]—One of his boats arrived here on the 18th instant with forty three men including five wounded, who are now in the Hospital, bringing me a letter from the General which I herewith enclose, giving a more detailed account of the affair, than I without reference to it would be enabled to do—From his hurried account and that of the most inteligent of his men with whom I have conversed it appears to have been the most shocking outrage to the feelings of humanity ever witnessed by Civilized men—unexampled in the annals of the world—

As those inhuman monsters will most probably be made to atone for what they have done by a great effusion of their blood, I shall (however painful it may be) endeavour to restrain my feelings, and defer (untill a later period) giving you a gloomy picture of a scene, which if justly portrayed would from a man of your sensibility extract tears of blood—Although young in years, and without a polished or even a common education, I have for a long time been endeavouring to Arouse the better feelings, and excite the Sympathy of my Country in favour of the most daring, the most energetic, and enterprising portion of the community. I mean those of our fellow Citizens, who from our forbearance are dayly exposed, and falling victims to the tomihauk and sculping knife of the Indians

On being apprised of this unfortunate circumstance, which has not only put in Jeopardy upwards of two hundred of our Citizens, who are legally engaged in the fur trade above this, but threatens to arrest for a long time the individual enterprise of the fairest portion of the western country Co. Levenworth and myself consulted, and considering the best interests of our Country, was not slow to determine what steps should be taken, consequently, he lost no time in organizing and fitting out an Expedition of upwards of two hundred regular troops, exclusive of Officers, which set out on the 22ⁿᵈ insᵗ. accompan[i]ed by Mr. Pilcher, several other Partners of the Missouri fur Company and about fifty of their men . . . This expedition, when it reaches the A'richarar Village, will including trading [traders?] and trading men, consist of upwards of three hundred effective white men, and about five hundred Souix Indians I expect will join them at or near the grand Bend—enough to look down all opposition-no Indian force can posibly resist them—

This unprovoked and dreadful massacre of white men, by the A'rickarar nation of Indians (men, women and Children Concerned) has awakened the peaceful natives of the land It has directed the attention of all the neighboring tribes, who are suspending their opinion of us untill they hear the result of this expedition—Now, say the Indians "all will see what the white people intend to do—We will see the extent of their forbearance—We will also see (if they have any) the extent of their spirit of resentment—" For a long time we have been presuming upon the forbearance of the whites, slowly bleeding their veins, and they have born it patiently, for we have heard but the murmer of a single man—"But now the A'richarars have by sticking and sticking made a deep incision—They have made a dreadful wound, in which even their men, women, and children have stained their hands with blood—"

This expedition (as your experience of the Indian character will tell you) is big with great events The peace, and tranquility of this Country depends upon its success, which, with great anxiety I calculate on surely—The Indian nations about here continue as friendly as usual—The Ottoes & Missouris are here and now assembling to council with me.

APPENDIX B ORAL HISTORY: STANDARDS AND PRACTICES

Sample Release Form

Tri-County Historical Society

For and in consideration of the participation by *Tri-County Historical Society* in any programs involving the dissemination of tape-recorded memoirs and oral history material for publication, copyright, and other uses, I hereby release all right, title, or interest in and to all of my tape-recorded memoirs to *Tri-County Historical Society* and declare that they may be used without any restriction whatsoever and may be copyrighted and published by the said *Society* which may also assign said copyright and publication rights to serious research scholars.

In addition to the rights and authority given to you under the preceding paragraph, I hereby authorize you to edit, publish, sell and/or license the use of my oral history memoir in any other manner which the *Society* considers to be desirable and I waive any claim to any payments which may be received as a consequence thereof by the *Society*.

PLACE *Indianapolis, Indiana*

DATE *July 14, 1975*

Harold S. Johnson
(Interviewee)
Jane Rogers
for *Tri-County Historical Society*

Source: From Collum Davis, Kathryn Back, and Kay MacLean, *Oral History: From Tape to Type* (Chicago: American Library Assn., © 1977, p. 14.) Reprinted by permission of the American Library Association.

Principles and Standards of The Oral History Association
(Published by permission of The Oral History Associaton)

The Oral History Association promotes oral history as a method of gathering and preserving historical information through recorded interviews with participants in past events and ways of life. It encourages those who produce and use oral history to recognize certain principles, rights, and obligations for the creation of source material that is authentic, useful, and reliable. These include obligations to the interviewee, to the profession, and to the public, as well as mutual obligations between sponsoring organizations and interviewers.

Oral history interviews are conducted by people with a range of affiliations and sponsorship for a variety of purposes: to create archival records, for individual research, for community and institutional projects, and for publications and other media productions. While these principles and standards provide a general framework for guiding professional conduct, their application may vary according to the nature of specific oral history projects. Regardless of the purpose of the interviews, oral history should be conducted in the spirit of critical inquiry and social responsibility, and with a recognition of the interactive and subjective nature of the enterprise.

Responsibility to Interviewees:

1. Interviewees should be informed of the purposes and procedures of oral history in general and of the aims and anticipated uses of the particular projects to which they are making their contribution.
2. Interviewees should be informed of the mutual rights in the oral history process, such as editing, access restrictions, copyrights, prior use, royalties, and the expected disposition and dissemination of all forms of the record.
3. Interviewees should be informed that they will be asked to sign a legal release. Interviews should remain confidential until interviewees have given permission for their use.
4. Interviewers should guard against making promises to interviewees that they may not be able to fulfill, such as guarantees of publication and control over future uses of interviews after they have been made public.
5. Interviews should be conducted in accord with any prior agreements made with the interviewee, and such preferences and agreements should be documented for the record.
6. Interviewers should work to achieve a balance between the objectives of the project and the perspectives of the interviewees. They should be sensitive to the diversity of social and cultural experiences, and to the implications of race, gender, class, ethnicity, age, religion, and sexual orientation. They should encourage interviewees to respond in their own style and language, and to address issues that reflect their concerns. Interviewers should fully explore all appropriate areas of inquiry with the interviewee and not be satisfied with superficial responses.
7. Interviewers should guard against possible exploitation of interviewees and be sensitive to the ways in which their interviews might be used. Interviewers must respect the right of the interviewee to refuse to discuss certain subjects, to restrict access to the interview, or under extreme circumstances even to choose anonymity. Interviewers should clearly explain these options to all interviewees.

Responsibility to the Public and to the Profession:

1. Oral historians have a responsibility to maintain the highest professional standards in the conduct of their work and to uphold the standards of the various disciplines and professions with which they are affiliated.

2. In recognition of the importance of oral history to an understanding of the past and of the cost and effort involved, interviewers and interviewees should mutually strive to record candid information of lasting value and to make that information accessible.

3. Interviewees should be selected on the basis of the relevance of their experiences to the subject at hand.

4. Interviewers should possess interviewing skills as well as professional competence or experience with the subject at hand.

5. Regardless of the specific interests of the project, interviewers should attempt to extend the inquiry beyond the specific focus of the project to create as complete a record as possible for the benefit of others.

6. Interviewers should strive to prompt informative dialogue through challenging and perceptive inquiry. They should be grounded in the background of the persons being interviewed and, when possible, should carefully research appropriate documents and secondary sources related to subjects about which the interviewees can speak.

7. Interviewers should make every effort to record their interviews. They should provide complete documentation of their preparation and methods, including the circumstances of the interviews. Interviewers, and when possible interviewees, should review and evaluate their interviews and any transcriptions made from them.

8. With the permission of the interviewees, interviewers should arrange to deposit their interviews in an archival repository that is capable of both preserving the interviews and eventually making them available for general use. Interviewers should provide basic information about the interviews, including project goals, sponsorship, and funding. Preferably, interviewers should work with repositories prior to the project to determine necessary legal arrangements. If interviewers arrange to retain first use of the interviews, it should be only for a reasonable time prior to public use.

9. Interviewers should be sensitive to the communities from which they have collected their oral histories, taking care not to reinforce thoughtless stereotypes or to bring undue notoriety to the communities. They should take every effort to make the interviews accessible to the communities.

10. Oral history interviews should be used and cited with the same care and standards applied to other historical sources. Users have a responsibility to retain the integrity of the interviewee's voice, neither misrepresenting the interviewee's words nor taking them out of context.

11. Sources of funding or sponsorship of oral history projects should be made public in all exhibits, media presentations, or publications that result from the projects.

12. Interviewers and oral history programs should conscientiously consider how they might share with interviewees and their communities the rewards and recognition that might result from their work.

Responsibility for Sponsoring and Archival Institutions:

1. Institutions sponsoring and maintaining oral history archives have a responsibility to interviewees, interviewers, the profession, and the public to maintain the highest professional and ethical standards in the creation and archival preservation of oral history interviews.

2. Subject to conditions that interviewees set, sponsoring institutions (or individual collectors) have an obligation to prepare and preserve easily usable records; to keep accurate records of the creation and processing of each interview; to identify, index, and catalog interviews; and to make known the existence of the interviews when they are open for research.

3. Within the parameters of their missions and resources, archival institutions should collect interviews generated by independent researchers and assist interviewers with the necessary legal agreements.

4. Sponsoring institutions should train interviewers, explaining the objectives of the program to them, informing them of all ethical and legal considerations governing an interview, and making clear to interviewers what their obligations are to the program and to the interviewees.

5. Interviewers and interviewees should receive appropriate acknowledgement for their work in all forms of citation or usage.

SUGGESTIONS FOR FURTHER READING

The Nature of History—The Philosophy of History

Ankersmit, Frank, and Hans Kellner, eds. *A New Philosophy of History*. Chicago: The University of Chicago Press, 1995.

Becker, Carl. *Everyman His Own Historian*. New York: Appleton-Century-Crofts, 1935.

Beringer, Richard E. *Historical Analysis: Contemporary Approaches to Clio's Craft*. New York: John Wiley and Sons, 1978.

Bloch, Marc. *The Historian's Craft*. New York: McGraw-Hill, 1964.

Braudel, Fernand. *On History*. Chicago: University of Chicago Press, 1980.

Butterfield, Herbert. *Man on His Past*. Cambridge: Cambridge University Press, 1955.

———. *The Whig Interpretation of History*. London: G. Bell, 1931.

Carr, E. H. *What is History?* New York: Random, 1967.

Collingwood, R.G. *The Idea of History*. Oxford: Clarendon Press, 1946.

Commager, Henry Steele. *The Nature and Study of History*. New York: Garland, 1984.

Conkin, Paul K., and Roland N. Stromberg. *Heritage and Challenge: The History and Theory of History*. Wheeling, Ill.: Harlan Davidson, 1989.

Dray, William H. *Philosophy of History*. Englewood Cliffs, N.J.: Prentice-Hall, 1964.

Fischer, David Hackett. *Historians' Fallacies: Toward a Logic of Historical Thought*. New York: Harper and Row, 1970.

Gardiner, Patrick L. *The Nature of Historical Explanation*. New York: Oxford University Press, 1952.

Gottschalk, Louis. *Understanding History*. New York: Knopf, 1969.

Gustavson, Carl G. *The Mansion of History*. New York: McGraw-Hill, 1976.

———. *A Preface to History*. New York: McGraw-Hill, 1955.

Hexter, J. H. *The History Primer*. New York: Basic Books, 1971.

Hughes, H. Stuart. *History as Art and as Science*. New York: Garland, 1985.

Kitson Clark, George. *The Critical Historian*. London: Heinemann, 1967.

Marwick, Arthur. *The Nature of History*. London: Macmillan, 1970.

Meyerhoff, Hans, ed. *The Philosophy of History in Our Time*. New York: Doubleday, 1959.

Nash, Ronald H., ed. *Ideas of History*. 2 vols. New York: E. P. Dutton, 1969.

Nevins, Allan. *The Gateway to History*. Chicago: Quadrangle Books, 1963.

Norling, Bernard. *Timeless Problems in History*. Notre Dame, Ind.: University of Notre Dame Press, 1970.

Smith, Page. *The Historian and History*. New York: Knopf, 1964.

Tholfsen, Trygve R. *Historical Thinking*. New York: Harper and Row, 1967.

Trevelyan, G. M. *Clio, A Muse and Other Essays*. New ed. London: Longmans, Green, 1930.

Vaughn, Stephen, ed. *The Vital Past: Writings on the Uses of History*. Athens, Ga.: University of Georgia Press, 1985.

Walsh, W. H. *An Introduction to Philosophy of History*. 3rd ed. rev. London: Hutchinson University Library, 1967.

Historical Methodology

Altick, Richard D. *The Scholar Adventurers.* Columbus: Ohio State University Press, 1987.

Aydelotte, William O. *Quantification in History.* Reading, Mass.: Addison-Wesley, 1971.

Barzun, Jacques. *Clio and the Doctors: Psycho-History, Quanto-History and History.* Chicago: University of Chicago Press, 1974.

———, and Henry F. Graff. *The Modern Researcher.* Rev. ed. New York: Harcourt, Brace, 1985.

Benjamin, Jules R. *A Student's Guide to History.* 7th ed. New York: St. Martin's Press, 1998.

Brundage, Anthony. *Going to the Sources: A Guide to Historical Research and Writing.* 2nd ed. Wheeling, Ill,: Harlan Davidson, 1997.

Cantor, Norman F., and Richard I. Schneider. *How to Study History.* Wheeling, Ill.: Harlan Davidson, 1967.

Daniels, Robert V. *Studying History: How and Why.* 3rd ed. Englewood Cliffs, N.J.: Prentice-Hall, 1981.

Davis, Cullom, Kathryn Back, and Kay MacLean. *Oral History: From Tape to Type.* Chicago: American Library Association, 1977.

Davidson, James W., and Mark Lytle. *After the Fact: The Art of Historical Detection.* 2nd ed. New York: McGraw, 1985. 3rd ed., 1992.

Dunaway, David K. and Willa K. Baum, eds. *Oral History: An Interdisciplinary Anthology.* Nashville: American Association for State and Local History, 1984.

Elton, G. R. *The Practice of History.* London: Sydney University Press, 1967.

Gray, Wood, et al. *Historian's Handbook: A Key to the Study and Writing of History.* 2nd ed. Boston: Houghton Mifflin, 1964.

Greenstein, Daniel I. *A Historian's Guide to Computing.* New York: Oxford University Press, 1994.

Handlin, Oscar. *Truth in History.* Cambridge, Mass.: Harvard University Press, 1979.

The History Teacher. Long Beach, Calif.: The Society for History Education. Published Quarterly.

Kyvig, David E. and Myron A. Marty. *Your Family History: A Handbook for Research and Writing.* Wheeling, Ill,: Harlan Davidson, 1978.

Lichtman, Allan J. and Valerie French. *Historians and the Living Past.* Wheeling, Ill,: Harlan Davidson, 1978.

Lowenthal, David. *The Past is a Foreign Country.* Cambridge: Cambridge University Press, 1985.

Marwick, Arthur. *What History Is and Why It Is Important; Primary Sources; Basic Problems of Writing History; Common Pitfalls in Historial Writing.* Bletchley, England: The Open University Press, 1970.

Reiff, Janice L. *Structuring the Past: The Use of Computers in History.* American Historical Association, 1991.

Renier, G. J. *History: Its Purpose and Method.* Macon, Ga.: Mercer University Press, 1982.

Shafer, Robert Jones, ed. *A Guide to Historical Method.* 3rd ed. Belmont, Calif.: Wadsworth Publishing, 1980.

Shorter, Edward. *The Historian and the Computer.* Englewood Cliffs, N.J.: Prentice-Hall, 1971.

Sitton, Thad, George L. Mehaffy, and G. L. Davis, Jr. *Oral History: A Guide for Teachers (and Others).* Austin: University of Texas Press, 1983.

Stanford, Michael. *A Companion to the Study of History.* Oxford: Blackwell, 1994.

Stephens, Lester D. *Probing the Past: A Guide to the Study and Teaching of History.* Boston: Allyn and Bacon, 1974.

Teaching History, A Journal of Methods. Emporia, Ka. Division of Social Sciences and the College of Liberal Arts and Sciences, Emporia State University. Published semi-annually.

Thompson, Paul. *The Voice of the Past: Oral History.* 2nd. ed. Oxford: Oxford University Press, 1988.

Tosh, John. *The Pursuit of History: Aims, Methods and New Directions in the Study of Modern History.* London: Longman, 1984.

Trinkle, Dennis A., Dorothy Auchter, Scott A. Merriman and Todd E. Larson, *The History Highway: A Guide to Internet Resources.* Armonk, N.Y.: M. E. Sharpe, 1997.

Tuchman, Barbara W. *Practicing History.* New York: Knopf, 1981.

Winks, Robin W., ed. *The Historian as Detective.* New York: Harper Colophon, 1970.

Historiography

Appleby, Joyce, Lynn Hunt, and Margaret Jacob. *Telling the Truth About History.* New York: W. W. Norton, 1994.

Barnes, Harry E. *A History of Historical Writing.* 2nd rev. ed. New York: Dover, 1963.

Benson, Susan P., Stephen Brier, and Roy Rosenzweig. *Presenting the Past: Essays on History and the Public.* Philadelphia: Temple University Press, 1986.

Breisach, Ernst. *Historiography: Ancient, Medieval, and Modern.* Chicago: The University of Chicago Press, 1983.

Gay, Peter, and Gerald J. Cavanaugh, eds. *Historians at Work.* 4 Vols. New York: Irvington, 1975.

Geyl, Pieter. *Debates with Historians.* New York: Meridian Books, 1958.

Gilbert, Felix, and Stephen R. Graubard, eds. *Historical Studies Today.* New York: Norton, 1972.

Gilderhus, Mark T. *History and Historians.* Englewood Cliffs, N.J.: Prentice-Hall, Inc., 1987.

Gooch, George Peabody. *History and Historians in the Nineteenth Century.* Rev. ed. London: Longmans, Green, 1952.

Halperin, S. William, ed. *Some Twentieth-Century Historians.* Chicago: University of Chicago Press, 1961.

Higham, John, Leonard Krieger, and Felix Gilbert. *History: The Development of Historical Studies in the United States.* Englewood Cliffs, N.J.: Prentice-Hall, 1964.

Himmelfarb, Gertrude. *The New History and the Old.* Cambridge: The Belknap Press of Harvard University Press, 1987.

Kren, George M., and Leon H. Rappoport, eds. *Varieties of Psychohistory.* New York: Springer, 1976.

Noble, David W. *The End of American History.* Minneapolis: University of Minnesota Press, 1985.

Novick, Peter. *That Noble Dream.* Cambridge: Cambridge University Press, 1988.

Stannard, David E. *Shrinking History.* New York: Oxford University Press, 1980.

Stephens, Lester D. *Historiography: A Bibiliography.* Metuchen, N.J.: Scarecrow Press, 1975.

Stern, Fritz, ed. *The Varieties of History from Voltaire to the Present.* New York: Random, 1956.

Sternsher, Bernard. *Consensus, Conflict, and American Historians.* Bloomington: Indiana University Press, 1975.

Thompson, James Westfall. *A History of Historical Writing.* 2 Vols. New York: Irvington, 1942.

Windschuttle, Keith. *The Killing of History: How Literary Critics and Social Theorists Are Murdering Our Past.* New York: The Free Press, 1997.

Wise, Gene. *American Historical Explanations.* Minneapolis: University of Minnesota Press, 1980.

Wolman, Benjamin B., ed. *The Psychoanalytic Interpretation of History.* New York: Harper and Row, 1971.

Writing Skills

Anderson, Richard. *Writing That Works.* New York: McGraw-Hill Publishing Company, 1989.

Barnes, Gregory A. *Write for Success.* Philadelphia: ISI Press, 1986.

Bennett, James D. and Lowell H. Harrison. *Writing History Papers.* Wheeling, Ill.: Harlan Davidson, 1979.

Cuba, Lee. *A Short Guide to Writing about Social Science.* 2nd ed. New York: Harper-Collins College Publishers, 1993.

Hacker, Diane. *A Writer's Reference.* 4th ed. Boston: Bedford/St. Martins Press, 1999.

Hashimoto, Irvin Y. *Thirteen Weeks: A Guide to Teaching College Writing.* Portsmouth: Boynton/Cook Publishers, 1991.

Meyer, Herbert E., and Jill M. Meyer. *How to Write.* Washington, D.C.: Storm King Press, 1987.

Ponsot, Marie, and Rosemary Deen. *Beat Not the Poor Desk.* Portsmouth, N.H.: Boynton/Cook Publishers, 1982.

Rathbone, Robert R. *Communicating Technical Information.* Reading, Mass.: Addison-Wesley Publishing Company, Inc., 1966.

Strunk, William, Jr., and E. B. White. *The Elements of Style.* 3rd ed. New York: The Macmillan Company, 1979.

Film and History

Carnes, Mark C. *Past Imperfect: History According to the Movies.* New York: Henry Holt and Co., 1995.

Ferro, Mark. *Cinema and History.* Detroit: Wayne State University Press, 1988.

Mintz, Steven, and Randy Roberts. *Hollywood's America: United States History through Its Films.* St. James, N.Y.: Brandywine Press, 1993.

Monaco, James. *How to Read a Film.* Rev. ed. New York: Oxford University Press, 1981.

O'Connor, John, ed. *Image as Artifact: The Historical Analysis of Film and Television.* Malabar, Fl.: Robert E. Krieger Publishing Co., 1990.

———, and Martin A. Jackson. *Teaching History with Film.* Washington, D.C.: American Historical Association, 1974.

Rollins, Peter, ed. *Hollywood as Historian: American Film in a Cultural Context.* Lexington: University Press of Kentucky, 1983.

Short, K. R. M., ed. *Feature Films as History.* Knoxville: University of Tennessee Press, 1981.

Smith, Paul, ed. *The Historian and Film.* Cambridge: Cambridge University Press, 1976.

INDEX

The Methods and Skills of History: A Practical Guide, Second Edition
Development editor and copy editor: Andrew J. Davidson
Production editor: Lucy Herz
Proofreader: Claudia Siler
Printer: Versa Press, Inc.